I dedicate this book to my mom,
Virginia Elaine Hammond Wills,
who chose to give me life.

*Her legacy is our family: People of faith,
compassion and good humor, world travelers
and animal lovers. Mom prayed boldly and spoke
directly, I think she would be proud of us.*

SEARCHING FOR MY
TWODADS

———

Copyright ©2023 / Mary Wills Perry
All Rights Reserved

———

ISBN: 979-8-9888993-0-3 - *softcover*
ISBN: 979-8-9888993-1-0 - *ebook*

———

Book Design & Production
timmyroland.com

SEARCHING FOR MY TWO DADS

MARY WILLS PERRY

THE SERVANT OF THE LORD

"Listen to me, you islands (distant nations): you people who live far away. Before I was born the Lord called me; from my mother's womb he has spoken my name.

He made my mouth like a sharpened sword; in the shadow of his hand, he hid me; he made me into a polished arrow and concealed me in his quiver.

He said to me, "You are my servant, Israel, in whom I will display my splendor."

Isaiah 49:1-3

FOREWORD

My Mom used to quote two nursery sayings to me when I was naughty. One was . . .

"Mary, Mary quite contrary how does your garden grow? With silver bells and cockle shells and pretty maids all in a row."

Little did she know the origin of this gentle rhyme. "Mary, Mary Quite Contrary may be about Bloody Mary, daughter of King Henry VIII and concerns the torture and murder of Protestants. Queen Mary was a staunch Catholic and her "garden" here is an allusion to the graveyards which were filling with Protestant martyrs."

The second she recited often was by Henry Wadsworth Longfellow:

"There once was a little girl, and she had a little curl, right in the middle of her forehead. When she was good she was indeed very good, but when she was bad she was horrid."

I had the curl and the contrary temperament. I think few who knew me at all well would have predicted that my life could have turned out as it did. I believe that the prayers of my Grandpa and Grandma Robbie, Mom and my godly ancestors intervened to change the course of my life.

i

SEARCHING FOR MY TWO DADS

TABLE OF CONTENTS

TABLE OF CONTENTS

TABLE OF CONTENTS

TABLE OF CONTENTS

SEARCHING FOR MY
TWO DADS

PART ONE

SEARCHING FOR MY
TWODADS

DANCING IN MY DREAM

I was dancing the polka with a one-legged fat man. We were breathless as we whirled around the room. Though I could not see his face, I knew he was my father. How could I know he was my father? I had never met him.

I jolted awake from my dream, heart throbbing as I told my husband, Jon, "I think God wants me to search for my father." My life changed forever from that moment as I began in earnest my search for clues to my southern father's disappearance.

I'm writing this detailed account for our family in the future and for anyone who is interested to know what happened in my life. I am not claiming to be a fabulous example of a Christian. I would have liked to be, but you'll understand better when you read this.

I have changed some of the names in this book because the people are still living and I didn't want to or know how to contact them. These names are in italics.

Mary

Virginia

THE STRANGER

That morning after my dream I began making phone calls, first to townhalls and then to prisons in Georgia. Why? My mom told me once that I should not look for my father because he was not a good man. Because of a story her friend told me, I concluded he might be in prison.

When I say I never met my father, it's not entirely accurate. Mom told me that he held me in his arms when I was a tiny baby. He told her he didn't want a child, but that he would come back when I grew up! He then left for his hometown.

My mom's response must have been clear and to the point because he never returned. She soon filed divorce papers for *"irreconcilable differences."*[1] This came after years of a marriage when she seldom knew where he was. Neither of us heard from my father again until I searched for him and found him forty-five years later. At least I never knew if he contacted Mom. Because of her gutsy choice, her life was difficult and often lonely. She didn't believe she could marry again after divorce because of her religious belief, even though her spouse had been unfaithful.

I invite you to join me as I tell the next part of our story.

1- A reason given for divorce. Representing findings or points of view that are so different from each other that they cannot be made compatible.

Mom & Me in 1948

FROM HOSPITAL TO GAS STATION

TEN MOVES IN FIVE YEARS

Mom and I spent twenty-six days in the Corry, Pennsylvania Hospital during her prolonged post-partum hospitalization. She told me she had a tipped kidney. I will never know if that is the real reason, or if Mom may have been depressed. One interesting clue is that Mom bragged about how the nurses enjoyed carrying me around and one or two offered to adopt me. After I had children of my own I couldn't imagine why they would offer to do that unless a mother was considering giving up her baby.

Mom's father was working in his Quaker State gas station and neither Mom nor he may have known how to communicate regarding the shame of a failed marriage and an inconvenient baby.

I consider my life on earth a miracle for three reasons. On one of his infrequent visits, my father told my mother that he did never wanted nor planned to have children. He wanted her to abort me.

She refused, saving my life, which is one of the reasons she decided to divorce him. This is the first miracle. My mother's friend, Harriott, later added details to this story suggesting how strongly he felt about this.

When Mom was pregnant with me he took her out skeet shooting and speculated aloud on what would happen if the shotgun went off killing her and the baby she carried. My mom never told me that story but it terrified her.

She told me another story about my survival on the day my Grandpa Hammond died. I think of this one as a second miracle.

Grandpa enjoyed taking me with him when he drove into the neighboring town of Spartansburg to the grocery store. He'd put me into the flimsy baby carrier on the front seat. One day, after spending several hours in town chatting with friends he drove back home, brought me inside and told Mom that he wasn't feeling well. He went into his bedroom to lie down and in a matter of minutes, died of a coronary.

I doubt I would have survived if he had the heart attack on the drive home. Mom was devastated at her father's death. He was the only family member remaining in her life on whom she could depend.

I can imagine Mom's feelings at that moment, utterly alone and without anyone to depend on. Her father had advised against marrying my father. Given the strict fundamentalist background she grew up in, I wonder if she might have felt guilty going against her father's wishes.

From every story Mom told me about her youth, she was an exuberant and happy young person. Her life as a young mother was tinged with sorrow and trauma. This was reflected in the way she raised me.

A third possible miracle in my life on earth was my O-negative blood type. This is my speculation but I like to think of it as God's intervention.

In 1948, babies were dying from incompatibility between their mother's blood protein with that of their baby's. It resulted in a condition called isoimmunization. This causes the mother's immune system to react and destroy the baby's blood cells.

During a pregnancy, Rh positive antibodies made in a woman's body can cross the placenta and attack fetal blood cells. This can cause a serious type of anemia in the fetus in which red blood cells are destroyed faster than the body can replace them.

My mother was Rh positive. This is usually not a problem with the first pregnancy; however, it would have been if my mother had been pregnant before and had an earlier miscarriage. How much had Doc Earnest, her rural country physician, known in 1948 about the latest developments in the study of hemolytic disease? It was only recently, since 1939, when Immuno-hematologists published their first findings about Rh Disease.

Mom had a shock when she was seven months pregnant with me. A British woman showed up at her door in search of my father. She also appeared to be around seven months pregnant. Mom wasn't too surprised because letters addressed to my father had been arriving at the house from this woman for months. I'm sure she didn't know my father was married. Mom invited her in and fixed lunch for her then sent her on her way, probably to Georgia where my father's family lived. For that reason, I suspect I have a half-sibling in England, the same age as me. I would like to meet that person someday.

My Grandfather Hammond had worked for the Pennsylvania Railroad as a telegrapher and then as a station manager for years until the stock market crashed in 1929. He lost his small fortune and moved to Riceville, in northwestern Pennsylvania where he had extended family. He set up a competing filling station directly across the highway from his younger brother Ken.

Grandpa Hammond & Me

Mom told me that I was an exceptionally good baby. She needed a good baby to stay in the playpen, day after day, with occasional interaction from her. She told me that she could vacuum the whole house and I never bothered her. She kept house for my grandfather Harry and helped him run their gas station on a busy highway intersection. Mom pumped gas and served ham sandwiches and coffee to travelers in her free time.

I know Grandpa and my Mom loved me. She sewed homemade nightshirts and flannel gowns for me. There are photos of me with stuffed animals that Mom thoughtfully saved for my own children. Grandpa called me "Coonie" because he said I reminded him of a racoon with my big brown eyes.

RICEVILLE, SPARTANSBURG & CORRY
COMMUTING

I don't remember a great deal of laughter in our home when I was young. My mom was, after all, living a life she never intended. She told me once that she, like every other young girl, had hopes and dreams of having a nice husband and family. Our pets provided distraction and reasons to laugh.

When my grandfather Hammond died, she sold the filling station and the Riceville house that went with it to move to Spartansburg into an upstairs apartment in the home of Geraldine and Harry Brown. They became my mother's lifelong friends and their daughters, my built-in babysitters while Mom taught school.

I'm a bit confused as to the timing but when I was little more than a toddler, every Sunday afternoon, Mom put me on board the Pennsylvania Railroad train that ran through our town. I traveled by myself an hour to Oil City. Mom's Aunt Bessie and her Scottish husband whom everyone called, Robbie, pastored the Free Methodist Holiness[2] church there. The train conductor, Mr. McCoy, watched over me

---

2 - Begun in 1835, A branch of the Methodist Church, It has its roots in the teachings of John Wesley. The Holiness Movement involves a set of beliefs and practices that emerged within Methodism. It is defined by its emphasis on a second work of grace leading to Christian perfection. *Wikipedia*.

and often sat beside me to make sure that I got off the train at the right stop.

Two things that I remember about Mr. McCoy were his conductor's cap with a shiny Pennsylvania Railroad badge pinned on the front, and his broad smile. The Robbies usually brought me back home on Friday for a weekend visit in their blue 1953 Chevrolet.

My life during those years was a study in contrast. Mom was a schoolteacher, open-minded in her beliefs for that time. She allowed me the freedom to wear shorts and have my hair cut short. On Saturday mornings, we listened to radio programs together. Aunt Bessie, by contrast, was a strict religious fundamentalist and we seldom listened to the radio at her house. Aunt Bessie thought that worldly activities such as bowling, dancing, drinking and playing cards were sinful. Mom was from that same background and but her father had often debated with Robbie. He was a strong Conservative Christian but held his views much more loosely.

Doc Earnest & Me

I loved visiting my mother on weekends, wearing shorts, sitting with her at the kitchen table eating Wonder Bread toast and listening to *Hopalong Cassidy* on the radio, first in Titusville then in Corry, Pennsylvania.

Doctor Earnest often visited my mom in Titusville. He was courting her at this time.

At Robbies, I wore braids and long dresses but I also felt cheerful and happy. I fed and played with Robbies' "chooks," red chickens that lived underneath the parsonage, and I attended all the weekly church services, which for a gregarious little girl was a treat.

I had the run of the empty church building most days. Often I stood on or behind the altar (or stage as I called it) as I sang church hymns such as *Dare to be a Daniel*. Sometimes I laid over the altar in the mode of a torch singer draped over a piano. I'll never know how it occurred to me to do this.

I called my Uncle Robbie, Grandpa Robbie because my third cousins did. He still spoke with affection about "blessed Queen Mary," as he called her, the head of the British Monarchy when he was a little boy.

In 1953, we must have had a special dispensation from Aunt Bessie because we spent days listening to a British radio station in the build-up to the Coronation of the young Queen Elizabeth. Grandpa's sister Alice sent me a little red knitted sweater and tam from Scotland. Either my mother or Aunt Bessie created a scrapbook for me with pictures of the coronation, golden carriage, and all. I updated it throughout my childhood with pictures of Prince Charles and Princess Anne from magazines. It was a few years before I became aware that our nation had a president. I was much more familiar with the House of Windsor than I was with the families of President Truman or Eisenhower who were the Presidents when I was a child.

I loved going on errands with Grandpa Robbie to visit his diverse group of friends. As we strode down the streets of Oil City, he greeted people he met along the way in his hearty Scottish brogue, "Hello Brother!"

He was "Brother Robbie" to each person who responded with a broad smile. I liked to hold on to his big strong arm with both hands as he'd sweep me up to carry me with a hearty laugh. I took such pleasure in being with Grandpa Robbie, whom everyone in town seemed to know and respect. I especially remember the owner of a clothing store whom Grandpa referred to as, "Old Abe the Jew Man." Grandpa Robbie and I would stop in to visit him at least once a week. At the end of our visit, Grandpa Robbie would pull out his pocket watch and announce that it was time to leave.

Grandpa & Grandma Robbie & Me

It seemed to me that Oil City must have been under constant threat of attack because air raid sirens sounded frequently throughout the day and night. This was the period of the Cold War. I wonder if this was happening in other cities or if ours was special because of the huge stinky petroleum refineries located nearby in the suburb of Rouseville.

On hearing the sirens, the Robbies and I would "duck and cover," sheltering underneath their big, round, oak, kitchen table.

I never knew where the threats came from or why we were hiding under the table. But it was an adventure! Far from a fearful experience, I thought it was great fun to have the adults in my life hiding with me underneath the table. I remember giggling with them wishing my mom could join us. It was a time of warmth and comradery when my dour Aunt Bessie was willing to get down on her knees and sit on the floor.

This was something Grandpa Robbie did often! He was full of fun always calling me "wee Mary," sometimes running through the apartment with a pair of my underpants on his head and laughing. Often in the evenings he brought out his black concertina to play and sing songs from the coal mines of Scotland.

I remember that I liked the odor of the small portable gas heaters situated around the apartment so much that I once locked myself in the bathroom to better inhale the fumes. Their anxious voices rose in panic as Grandpa Robbie and Bessie began loudly coaxing me to unlock the door. I tried, but the lock was too tight. Eventually, Grandpa Robbie had to take the door off its hinges to free me. Another day I assembled a little campfire in the center of their living room.

Though I did not light the fire, Robbie and Bessie seemed alarmed and told Mom about it. These were the times I was reminded that I was a guest in their home but not their child. It was never expressed but even at that early age, I felt a difference.

ROCKY GROVE & TITUSVILLE

LIFE ON THE MOVE

We lived for two years in the upstairs apartment in the Brown's large home in Spartansburg. Then Mom found a new substitute teaching position in Titusville, PA so we moved to a duplex there. This is the first time I remember having a yard to play in. I continued to commute to and from Oil City. Grandma Robbie helped me write little letters to my mom each week.

The next school year, Mom moved to Rocky Grove near Oil City where we rented a small house. We lived on Mom's savings from her single days when she taught in a one room schoolhouse at Britton Run[3] and what remained of the inheritance from her father.

Around that time, our finances were running low from her teaching job. It was in Rocky Grove, where a con woman named Mrs. Mae Moore worked her way into our lives. She offered us a deal in an investment plan and cultivated my friendship by giving me a tiny pink pearl necklace and a large, lifelike doll that I named, Mae. To our shock Mrs. Moore turned around and swindled Mom out of all that remained of her life's savings.

---

3 - Britton Run School, Spartansburg, Pennsylvania
spartansburgcommunity.site

Letters to Virgina

Mom never recovered the money though she tried to prosecute Mrs. Moore but failed.

I must have been about four years old, but I remember Mrs. Moore and Mom and the Robbies talking about her.

I had been looking forward to playing in the little yard and taking walks in the neighborhood in Rocky Grove, but before we unpacked many of our boxes or hung curtains we moved again.

CORRY

A PERFECT LITTLE HOUSE

Next we moved to a cute little house in Corry, Pennsylvania close to an elementary school where Mom got a job. The house seemed perfect in every way; it had a fireplace and a backyard with a hill that I could roll down. It was a short walk to the grocery store and I got my first puppy, whom I adored. Unfortunately, he must have been too much for Mom to care for because he did not stay long.

I remember the house in Corry, because of an incident that happened to me there. A married couple with no children were babysitting me. I was four years old.

Their names were Tom and Shirley Schiewe. I had never met Tom. He had very dark hair and a mustache and I remember Mom didn't really seem to like or trust him. Referring to him she would say, "**That** Tom Schiewe . . . " but she knew his wife Shirley's family, the Henton's who were from one of Grandpa Robbie's churches at Fink's Ridge. So possibly, because she was desperate, she left me in their care.

I sensed immediately that they had little idea what to do with a child. I begged them to let me go over to the school playground, next door. They let me swing on the tall swing set. I remember standing to pump up high in the air, and them standing underneath me telling me to be careful. I was feeling very bold and defiant as I stood up on that swing. I pumped as hard as I could when suddenly, with no warning, I flew forward out of the swing landing face down on the dirt with all my breath knocked out of me. Tom and Shirley ran to pick me up, carrying me to a day bed in our front room.

I remember them yelling loudly, "You're all right!" I must have been partially unconscious because I feel like I woke up to their yelling. I didn't say anything, but I felt deeply angry and offended, shouting at them in my mind, "I am not all right, you don't know anything!" They busied themselves applying wet, cold washcloths to my head, and worrying aloud what my mother would say and whether they should call her.

Mom & Me

I don't remember what happened when my mother returned, I'm sure she was gracious, but I never saw Tom and Shirley again. We moved again after I turned five.

MEADVILLE

Our next move was to an upstairs apartment in the city of Meadville, Pennsylvania. Mom enrolled me in the first grade and began teaching full time. I made a friend for the first time, our next-door neighbor, Bobbie Petersen, a rosy-cheeked little boy who was my age. He was a sweet, sunny playmate with whom I remember playing bikes, and cowboys, and Indians. I got my first small bike with training wheels in Meadville.

I was five years old and found attending school all day long was exhausting. I remember walking home each afternoon and sprawling at the foot of the stairs, unable to drag myself up them. To Mom this was a sign that I was not ready for school, so she took me out. Mom said that I told my teacher and friends that I was leaving school because I had a new two-wheeled bicycle at home.

I don't remember who took care of me while Mom was teaching, though it may have been Bobby's mother, Mrs. Petersen. Mom and I walked everywhere because she never got her driver's license and did not own a car.

Occasionally, we hired a taxi, but it was too expensive to do this regularly. We walked to school, which was one block from our apartment, walked to the grocery store and back and forth to church.

One Christmas Eve we walked back and forth about three miles together from our apartment at one end of the city of Meadville to the other to buy a Christmas tree. We dragged it home through the snowy streets up the hill to our apartment which was near Alleghany College. That was an exhausting walk for both of us, but I remember it as magical because the long walk was punctuated with dazzling Christmas lights, and softly falling snow. On that memorable walk, my mother bought me a little boy Johnny doll with a yellow shirt and red jeans. I had been begging her for this dolly and I looked forward to reaching home so I could play with him.

Meadville was the place where I first became aware of my mother as a person. She entered recipes in cooking and baking contests and won prizes, which gave her satisfaction. Her prizes were often cookbooks, but occasionally, she won flatware and once, a set of Revere Ware pots and pans, which became her pride and joy. My memories of her entering these contests are the excitement of her dressing up and putting on her lipstick, walking up the stairs into a building with a swing in her step and the feeling of exhilaration she had afterwards. She wore her beautiful hats which were the style in the fifties.

Mom first began to seem happy in Meadville, she smiled more. I wonder if it were there when she began to feel confident that she could succeed as a single mother and teacher. Or if she began to forgive herself for past mistakes.

My final memory from Meadville is when I was very ill with a high fever. Mom had repeatedly taken me downtown to see a specialist. The doctor suspected I had either Rheumatic Fever or another mysterious illness. On our final visit we had to get into an elevator to go up to his office. I laid down on the floor in the lobby of the office building and began to scream, refusing to get on the elevator. A crowd gathered around us. Mom said, even though she felt embarrassed, she could hardly blame me for being upset. The doctor had been poking and prodding me for days but he never helped me. That day, at last, I broke out in spots and the doctor finally diagnosed me with Measles. I wonder if my temper tantrum brought out the rash.

Our houses and apartments were always nicely furnished with a mix of family antiques and modern fifties furniture. In those early days, Mom kept our homes neat and clean and did not let things pile up.

Our apartment kitchens were small and cheery with colorful curtains. We always had a radio and together we sat at the kitchen table or on Mom's bed listening to programs like *Fibber Magee and Mollie, Hoppy (Hopalong Cassidy) Gene Autry, and Roy Rogers.*

In our living room we had a console record player which I later learned my father had bought for Mom. Before I owned a small portable player of my own, Mom bought me a collection of colorful plastic 45 rpm children's records which I played on her big record player. I often put on shows with my baton, where I marched around to the music and begged Mom to watch me. She was often half asleep, exhausted after a busy day of teaching.

Our House in Spartansburg

SPARTANSBURG

A REAL HOME AT LAST

Meadville became a distant memory in the summer of 1954 when I was six. A huge Mayflower moving van moved us back to Spartansburg, Pennsylvania in time for me to enter first grade and for Mom to begin teaching elementary school.

Spartansburg, Pennsylvania is the place I will always consider my hometown.

Mom bought our neglected eight-room Salt Box-style house situated on one acre of land. It was a real buy for $4000, with a broken toilet, a broken furnace, a leaking roof, a broken sump pump and fourteen broken windows. The water tasted strongly of iron and minerals colored the sinks and toilet red.

It was what she could afford. The house was located on Main Street directly across the highway from Geraldine and Harry Brown's house, our first apartment after Grandpa Hammond died in 1949. It was on a dangerous curve going out of town where speeding cars sometimes took flight off the road and directly into our front yard, or worse, into our front living room.

I loved the fragrant yellow rose bush growing wild beside our driveway. Two old maple trees in our front yard shaded our home on the hottest of days. Mom tapped them one year, boiling down the sap in a large metal tub over an open fire in the backyard until we got a bit of maple syrup. We stirred and stirred that syrup finally getting a small amount of maple sugar candy which we loved. There were fragrant Lilies of the Valley in our shady front yard, and beautiful red Peonies in the back. Grandpa Robbie hung a swing for me from a large walnut tree in the back.

An old one-seater outhouse on our property fascinated me and I was determined to make it into my clubhouse. It had one hole and tilted precariously to one side. I painted, Clubhouse. Stay Out! on it. Mom was never keen on me playing in there, and eventually it disappeared, either it collapsed, or Mom had it taken down.

Mom felt proud of our home and often told me that our house had once belonged to the Superintendent of Schools, Mr. Rice. It had been a beauty. The interior woodwork and Bullseye moldings around the doorways were in the classic style of the architect Stanford White. It had two beautiful bay windows, the one in front with stained glass and a window seat. Layers of old wallpaper hung in strips off the walls in every room and the ceilings in most rooms showed brown watermarks with signs either of roof leakage or damage to the chimney.

It was the original money pit. Mom's solution was to apply paint over the wallpaper and to leave some of the least damaged spots. She hoped for the best with the electric wiring, and purchased a new furnace so we wouldn't freeze. Each winter morning when I got up, I stood on one of the hot air registers to warm up until my feet and bottom felt burning hot. We turned the heat down before we went to bed. The drafty house didn't retain warmth. Mom lined the downstairs windows with heavy plastic until we couldn't see out of them. I assumed it was for insulation. As I grew older, I began to wonder if she lined the windows so no one could peek into them.

Huge icicles hung from the eaves, a few reaching from the roof to the ground. Each winter Mom worried that one would kill me.

Mom's option for art at that time was to hang calendar pictures wherever there was a nail. However, one lasting memory of art that meant a lot to me was a copy of a painting of Jesus as a young child that hung in our living room.

She told me that she gave the picture of Jesus that I loved to our next-door neighbor, a young pastor. I felt puzzled, wondering if I had never told her how much I liked that painting. I tried for years to find it on the internet and recently found out that it is a painting called *The Light of the World* by Charles Bosseron Chambers.[4]

Mom must have studied art in college because she had several large books with important works of art from many famous artists. Our calendar art was mostly pictures of animals but if there was a pretty girl in a low-cut dress, Aunt Bessie filled in her bare chest with crayon to make it "modest." Mom and I giggled about that.

I spent hours looking over Mom's art books as I also poured over the *World Book Encyclopedia* that

---

4 - Born in St. Louis, Missouri, he was called the
"Norman Rockwell of Catholic art." *Wikipedia*

she bought around this time.

She must have felt gratified that she had chosen this set of encyclopedias well because I used them constantly. All through high school as I drafted my essays, I piled the encyclopedias beside my blue portable Smith-Corona Typewriter and wrote, often the night before papers were due.

I especially loved looking at the sections about horses and dogs! Horses were an early obsession of mine. I marked up the pages with a pen detailing my favorite horse breeds, which were the Kentucky Walkers and Appaloosas. After a vacation trip to Assateague, Virginia, I was hopeful that we could rescue a wild pony like *Misty*[5] from Chincoteague or failing that, a Quarter Horse from out west. Mom told me I could get a horse when I was willing to wake up early enough in the mornings during the winter, go out into the barn, feed it, brush it down and clean out its stall. I was a realist even then, to the extent that I knew I could never promise to do those things

Mom was a wonderful cook and baker, but she had little time and paid little attention to housekeeping in the Spartansburg years. I think she felt overwhelmed by the immensity of all the repairs and maintenance required by our eight-room house. As I grew older, I sometimes asked Mom if I could clean our house. She responded as if it was a personal criticism, which it was. She told me that she was tired of cleaning because she had cleaned houses for people when she was younger. She told me that she worked hard all day and wanted to relax in her own home. She

---

5 - Misty of Chincoteague, a book.

didn't want me to clean, because she said, "You will have plenty of time to clean and wash dishes when you're married." Consequently, I never learned how to do any routine household chores such as how to wash dishes, do laundry, iron, or scrub a floor until I lived with other people. Much of it I had to learn when I was a married woman. Fortunately, when we moved to Indonesia, I had house helpers.

Mom did the best she could to have the house fixed up on her limited teacher's pay, and we were fortunate to have several dependable handymen and repairmen. One man, John Barr, was our furnace maintenance person, who brought his wife and one or two of his eight children on his calls. We became well acquainted with them, and I, predictably, had a crush on his two sons who were near my age, John Jr., and Homer.

Another of our faithful helpers, Jim Caldwell, was a man with a kind heart but little education. He had twelve children all of whom Mom taught. He was our *go-to* man who could fix or patch anything or knew somebody who could. Our two closest neighbors, Chuck Shreve and Reverend McNeely were also very helpful and their wives more than gracious in lending them to us.

To conserve heat in winter, Mom closed off all but the kitchen, living room and bedroom and the bathroom making it quite cozy. Mom and I slept together in her double bed in the winter. I continued to sleep with her even when I came home from college if it was winter.

I remember as I grew older, sleeping far over on my side of the bed so as not to cuddle or touch my mom. It felt creepy. We often had a dog sleeping at the bottom. We never discussed my feelings about this. I think this was an old-fashioned custom that she felt was practical. There were no options.

Our bedroom had three layers of boxes, chests of drawers and dressers along the walls and in front of the windows making it as dark as night even during the daytime. No one could peer into our house even if they had wanted to.

In the summer, our upstairs was comfortable enough so that I could sleep in the front bedroom which was the nicest room in our house. Mom bought frilly, blue curtains which went nicely with the vintage wallpaper. I slept in an old metal bed where Mom had been born. Sleeping alone upstairs was a thrill for me, though I was frightened that something might be lurking in the darkness. I had seen mice running along the walls of the upstairs hallway and into my room and I had an irrational fear of tiny little mice. As a little girl, every night I gave a quick peek under my bed and in the closet before I jumped into bed, to ease my fears that someone or something might be hiding in my bedroom.

THE EDGES OF LIFE

My mom taught me that I had to look out for myself because nobody else would. She taught me that we were in constant danger from that "unforeseen moment" as she called it. This referred to the moment when we forgot a purse in a store or would be a victim of a robbery in a lavatory, or when our puppy or cat ran into the road and was killed by a car. We lived life on the edge.

I feel like Mom catastrophized our lives. She seems to have felt anxious all the time. We depended on God in our own way. Before we left for school each day she prayed for protection. Looking back, I felt reassured by my mom's prayers, "To lead, guide, keep, and protect us."

Even though Mom never admitted this or probably was unaware of it, I wonder if she felt these prayers were like a talisman to keep us safe. Nothing bad would happen to us if we prayed before we began our day. I understand now how vulnerable and scared my mother might have felt to be raising me all on her own with no one in her family she could confide in or trust. She came from a large extended family of cousins and all of them had either drifted away or had died.[6]

---

6 - Refer to my first book, *The Grandmothers of Force*

I realized as I grew older and compared my childhood with other children's that many mothers taught them to be kind to others, to say a good word or say nothing, things we taught our own children. As I hear my older adult friends speak of their mothers' wise, calming words of positive input into their lives, I consider the ragged edges of life where Mom and I lived one step away from disaster. Lightening might strike her (it did), the house might catch fire, or someone might swindle us (they did).

Mom was capable and wise in many ways, but her anxiety was constant. Whether checking and rechecking to make sure the stove was turned off at night or going back to recheck whether she had locked the doors, I understand as an adult that my lovely mom was tormented by OCD.[7] In the summertime when her friend, Harriott Beckwith visited, I remember laughter in our kitchen but seldom any other times unless we were watching TV or playing with the pets.

---

7 - Obsessive Compulsive Disorder

SCHOOL DAYS

In our town, all twelve grades attended school in one large brick building. Mom and I walked to the school together in the mornings. This was a little more than a two-mile hike, along a major highway, across railroad tracks, over a bridge, up through town, across another street, and into the school. I walked home alone every night because Mom had to stay longer to finish her schoolwork.

After school, sometimes I went to my former babysitter's house. *Julie* was Harry and Geraldine Brown's daughter and my babysitter when I was a toddler. *Julie* had married *Joe* and lived up the street from us. They had a little boy named *Michael*. Julie spoke to me like a small friend, seldom like a child. She often had the latest gadget, and once she bought a bright red Italian microcar, a BMW Izetta[8]. It resembled a huge bubble with two seats and a door on the front that opened like a spaceship hatch. I felt like a celebrity when she let me ride around with her in that car.

Michael's dad, *Joe*, was so much fun. He let *Mike* and me sit in the front seat of his car as he sped down the highway purposely hitting all the potholes

---

8 - Called 'The Bubble Car', The BMW Izetta was a microcar produced in Germany between 1955 and 1962.

yelling "Judas Priest!" We would scream with laughter each time we hit a pothole, as if by mistake. I remember our little heads practically bumping the dashboard as we bounced around the front seat! He was handsome and charming like a movie star and would apologize each time he swore. I loved that family and sometimes felt I was actually related to them! One year, around the time of the Spartansburg Centennial, Mom made yellow colonial sunbonnets for us. I marched in the parade pushing *Michael* in his baby carriage.

Michael is the baby whose life I saved one summer. We were sitting in a baby pool in his grandmother Geraldine's side yard when he tipped face first into the water. I was little, about four, and I immediately set him upright. It was a simple thing, but I knew that I had saved his life. I yelled for *Julie* and she and her mother came running, *Michael* grew up to be a lawyer.

Shortly after we moved to Spartansburg Mom had to go out of town to an all-day teacher's meeting and left me with an elderly woman who was a total stranger to me. It was the first and last time this happened. To this day I remember it as a day of heart throbbing terror. I can still point out the house on the back street in Spartansburg where the elderly woman lived. I remember standing on her gray couch in the living room all day long, looking out her window towards the street, crying and screaming in fear that my mother would die in a car accident.

From that time on, Mom found another person to take care of me. A pastor's wife from Harbor Ridge, Mrs. Finnicum, lived in an apartment down the street from our house. I began staying with her in first grade when Mom had late meetings after school. We watched soap operas together. TV commercials were so effective that I learned about *LUX* soap and asked my mom to buy us some. Mom never watched *Soaps*, and neither did I as I grew older, until the summer before my senior year. I was working as a mother's helper for *Roger and Irene Lenhart*. As I watched their kids, *Dale*, and *Roy*, I ironed clothes and watched *The Edge of Night*.

I was rarely naughty in school, though my first-grade teacher, Miss Halfast, punished me once by making me stand in the hallway outside our classroom. She accused me of showing my test paper to a classmate, Frankie Nichols. I knew that had not been my intent; I had been showing him the place on a page where we were supposed to be writing. I knew it was useless to try to explain. However, as I stood outside the classroom, all the upperclassmen (middle and high schoolers) went by and gave me high fives, knowing that I was a teacher's kid. This made me feel like a school hero. The punishment did nothing except to give me a feeling that Miss Halfast was unjust.

Around age seven, I had a difficult chore when I arrived home from school. I had to clean up the dog poop and pee that was on newspapers we had laid out on the kitchen linoleum before school. I had continually begged Mom for a dog, and she allowed me to have one or two. That meant I did the cleanup when I got home. I also let them out on their chains or took them for a walk. I don't remember Mom insisting that I do chores, but I felt that this should be my responsibility and Mom shouldn't have to face it when she came home.

After school, in mild weather, I often rode my bike up the hill to a beautiful forest behind our house called, The Glen. My friends and I explored up there pretending to be on the lookout for bad guys. Though we never saw anybody bad, we continued to search for clues.

However, once when I was sitting all alone beside a stream, two black bear cubs ambled down to the stream. I was both excited and scared because I knew that a mother bear was somewhere nearby watching her cubs. I got up and ran out through the path my friends and I had made, got my bike, and rode home with the exciting news.

Mom always listened to my adventures with interest, but one time I didn't tell her about something that we found.

▲   ▲   ▲

My friend *Kelly* and I often explored the glen after school. Once we discovered a shoebox hidden in a thicket of bushes and fir trees. We opened the lid to discover a skeleton of a baby. We knew right away that this was serious, so we went to tell *Kelly's* mom. I'm not sure why we/I chose to tell her and not my mom. Maybe I thought she would know what to do, plus she had a car.

Even as an elementary-aged child, I may have instinctively known that some families were better equipped to network than Mom was. She kept herself distant from many of the townspeople. I may have thought that she would be too tired to deal with such a stressful situation. I don't remember if I told her, and I never learned what happened.

▲   ▲   ▲

Each winter, we had to walk to and from school on the side of the highway during heavy snowfalls because people seldom shoveled their sidewalks. Sometimes cars slowed down and followed behind me in the dusky fog of early evening, and I felt that twinge of fear one does when our instinct tells us something is wrong. In retrospect, I wonder if those drivers were simply driving slowly, taking precautions to not hit a little girl walking alone along the slushy, icy highway.

I assumed the drivers were planning to kidnap me, so I evaded them by walking up onto a neighbor's porch until the car passed by. I didn't want those dangerous kidnappers in the car to follow me home and discover where I lived. Those were again times when terror struck my heart.

My favorite part of walking home from school those long winter days in the snow was to drop into a grocery store in town where we had great friends! Mr. Albert Hahn, a rotund Jewish man, and his red-headed Irish wife owned and operated that grocery store. It was located on our route home, just before the small hill going down to the railroad tracks. The next part of the walk home was the coldest because we had to cross a bridge over a creek where the wind was very strong.

The Hahns were a large family with four rowdy teenagers. Many a late winter afternoon, Mom and I stopped in at the store to pick up meat for dinner, warm up around their potbellied stove, and talk and laugh before we crossed the railroad tracks and that bitterly cold part of our trek home.

The teenagers were very clever, much like standup comics, playing off one another's jokes. They liked to tell stories about the Spartansburg school faculty with Mom joining in. She enjoyed hearing the latest gossip from them and hearing the nicknames they gave the teachers! Their knack for storytelling was captivating and their comedic timing perfect. Mom giggled like a teenager herself. Even as a small child, I suspected that our unreserved laughter urged the kids to dig deeper into their absurd humor. As we sat around that old woodstove in the back of the store, I felt so accepted and loved. What an example of unconditional love they showed us. I was also learning how to hone my sense of humor.

My best friend during these early years was a little girl named Cookie. Those teenagers were Cookie's, aunts, and uncles.

When I grew older, I walked home before my mom and sometimes I stopped into their store get a little snack. When I got home, I'd turn on the heat and to be honest, after spending time with the Hahn family, our home felt a bit cold and hollow.

Mom after teaching, with Elsa

I remember pacing back and forth anxiously looking out the window waiting for my mom. I felt relief when I saw her climbing up the hill from town just before dusk. I felt worried that Mom would fall, or for some reason not get home safely. This insecurity lasted for many years and remained with me into my marriage. I wonder if it is the insecurity of the rejected child.

During the winters, Mom arrived home from school utterly exhausted after her long walk in the snow. She preferred that I not cook, so after she arrived home, she made herself a strong cup of tea, settled into her rocker in the front room and fell asleep.

In the meantime, I played on the sofa with my dolls, pretending they were my family. When she woke up, she made something for us to eat as we watched the news on TV and then she graded papers. As a special treat we'd have Swanson TV Dinners. Turkey and mashed potatoes were my favorite and continue to be a treat today.

Mom bought an electric frying pan and forbade me to use it by myself. It was too tempting for me, though, so some days after school, I made date pudding or fried up slabs of bacon. She scolded me but I don't remember her punishing me for using it. She seemed mostly relieved that I had not burned down our house. My obedience was not her greatest value, in fact, she seldom punished me for anything other than sassing her.

▲ ▲ ▲

Looking back, I always considered my childhood happy, but I wonder if I was a lonely little girl, longing for a family with siblings and a father. I used to make believe that I had siblings. At Christmas, I spread Christmas wrappings all over the floor pretending I had a large family. I played house on our couch after school naming all my children in pretend family time. I don't remember talking on the phone to my friends more than once or twice. It felt really special to call someone on our one black rotary phone that sat in the living room.

While going through photos from my childhood recently, our daughter, Juliana pointed out that I wrote other children's names on the backs of some of my own photos. I remember doing this so that it would seem like I had siblings or friends by various names such as, Judy or Patty. I used a pseudonym, Amy Kirk, for stories I wrote. Another nickname I gave myself was Scout.

Once when I was little, Mom invited another teacher who had a little girl my age, over for tea, so I could have a play date. She was usually exhausted so this was a really special treat. In those early elementary school days, children from school seldom had play dates except during summer. At least, I didn't. I just played with kids in our side of town. Our rural school district was spread out and Mom didn't have a car to drive me around. Most of my friends' parents had one car and their fathers used it for work. On the rare occasion when I visited my girlfriend's homes, I had fun and loved their nice rooms. However, when their fathers arrived home after work, I remember feeling so terribly awkward and uncomfortable that I disappeared into another room, or I asked to go home.

When I was in elementary school, the few men I felt very comfortable around were Grandpa Robbie, and our next-door neighbors Chuck Shreve, and Reverend Meneely. As I grew older, I grew more composed around adult men but it took a long time.

Harriott

HARRIOTT LOUISA BECKWITH

Other than handymen and the Robbies, few people and even fewer men visited our home in Spartansburg. Our one regular visitor was Mom's lifelong friend, Harriott Beckwith. Harriott, or Becky, had frizzy, permed auburn hair, wore bright red rouge, red lipstick, and colorful dangling earrings. She taught music and art in Oil City, PA public schools all of her adult years.

Her exuberant style was such a contrast to my mom who dressed primly and appropriately like a schoolteacher, seldom raising her voice. Harriott liked to tell us about her heritage, that she was "seven generations from a Russian Princess." Her home was decorated with souvenirs from her sailing trip around the world.

In the summers, when she visited, she stayed for three or four weeks at a time, bringing three dogs, adding to our one or two. When she walked her dogs down our main street sidewalk, she twisted and turned, laughing aloud and talking with her little pets, the clothes lines she used as leashes wrapping around her legs. It is a wonder she never fell. She was friendly with all our neighbors and by the end of summer they too, were her friends.

Harriott was a great ally. Often, the three of us sat around the kitchen table laughing hysterically late into the evening. I remember Mom laughing so hard she had tears running down her cheeks. It was a nice feeling to see her like that. I recall the sounds of the night, with the screen door open, the crickets singing, and a cool evening breeze blowing through our kitchen. When we were alone, we usually closed the house up by that time of night. There was a feeling of safety in numbers when Harriott was with us.

Summers were wonderful at our house in Spartansburg. Mom had flowers on the kitchen table, usually Sweet Peas. She grew every kind of flower imaginable in her yard. She, Harriott and I took daily car trips into the surrounding countryside to dig up native flowers and trees. Mom considered that she was saving these plants from future development.

Sometimes we went with Harriott to rescue a dog that was ill or uncared for. She had heard about these dogs on some mysterious dog lovers grapevine. Mom went reluctantly, fearing that the owner might show up and catch us trespassing, but Harriott was intrepid and oblivious to such things when a dog's welfare was at stake. Sometimes, Harriott brought the dog home with us. Swampy was the first dog I ever met from Harriott's rescue operations. She found the little dog abandoned beside a swamp alongside a road.

We took other trips with Harriott, on picnics, to county fairs in the area and to drive-in theaters. The films Mom and Harriott watched were sophisticated stories, not children's movies. The first drive-in movie I remember was Lana Turner's *Imitation of Life*. When I was small, I often fell asleep before the movie ended.

Sometimes we took one of my little girlfriends with us. Sonja was the friend who came most often. Harriott was up for anything fun. She always had a fancy car in her favorite color, turquoise. Her favorite car was her turquoise Packard. To me, her most memorable car was a turquoise and white Dodge with huge fins.

Harriott, Me & Swampy

Harriott & Me

In the summertime, Harriott and I slept upstairs. I was in the front bedroom; she and her dogs were in the back. When I closed my bedroom door the fun began. I would hear a dull thud hit my door. It was playtime! Opening my door, I would find a cottage cheese container lid that Harriott had rolled down the hall from her room! The game was on!

We rolled that lid back and forth, laughing hysterically. She must have been in her sixties or older, but she was so much fun! She called children, *"Scalawags,"* and liked nothing better than when we included her in our fun.

Once, I had been sitting on our porch swing banging it loudly and repeatedly against the wall of the house because I was angry for some reason. I overheard Harriott comment to my mom that she had better "Do something about that child's temper." I felt proud when I heard her say that, like I was powerful and beyond Mom's control. My temper became fully developed after we moved into our home in Spartansburg. Mom was working full-time, and I seemed to have felt secure enough to let my temper loose.

I have only recently learned a term, "Complex Trauma[9]," which I believe may have occurred during my time in the womb due to my father's threats, our frequent moves, my mom's anxiety and other factors. Sometimes when my temper erupted, Mom teased me and told me that I was related to Peter Stuyvesant, the Governor of New York, whose bad temper was renowned. This always made me feel good.

---

9 - Complex Trauma is defined as the response to an ongoing environment of danger where one never feels safe. The response constantly signals a stress response such as fight, flight or freeze. It affects every aspect of a person, their bodies, relationships, brains and ability to have a spiritual connection. *my.clevelandclinic.org*

The story goes that he took off his wooden leg and threw it at people in fits of anger. We often laughed together about this. Thinking back, I wonder if I displayed my temper in part to get attention from my busy Mom.

Harriott was a part of my life as long as she lived. Our last visit with her was in her nursing home with our kids when they were pre-teens. As we were coaxing her to eat her dinner, she was giggling insisting that each of us eat a spoonful of her food. The last words I heard her say were, "I love children in their natural state."

SEARCHING FOR MY
TWO DADS

HAPPY TIMES WITH MY MOM

When the weather was comfortable, Mom and I sat out on our front sun porch every night talking, sometimes until my voice went hoarse. We would sit out there until it got so dark, we could barely see each other, or in the fall, until it got too cold. I treasured these evenings.

I sat in the rocking chair we bought from our neighbor Gordon Brown, now owned by our son in law, Scott. Mom sat in the porch swing. I wish I could remember all that we talked about. I know I shared my hopes and dreams, my fears, and my dilemmas with her. Often, I sought assurance that I would marry a good man someday and have a happy life. She was always good at assuring me that I would have a happy future.

This eased my anxiety. These were the days before I knew about her own heartbreak. I look back on these times and I know that Mom loved and spent good quality time with me. I regret that I had times when I was such a mean daughter.

Mom enjoyed spinning stories and making up songs. When I was little she would ask me to name something so she could make up a story or song about it. She had a vivid imagination and was very curious. When we traveled, she would talk about the indigenous people who had lived on the land before colonization.

As I write, I realize that elementary school didn't occupy a huge part of my thoughts as a child. Mom had a surprisingly casual opinion about school attendance. One year I missed over fifty days, another over forty, all because I was ill. She told me once that my teachers didn't know very much. She was faculty, so I figured she knew what she was talking about. Once when I was in elementary school, Mom told me that the earth was rotating so fast that we weren't aware of the speed. I went to school and told my sixth-grade science teacher who made fun of me and my Mom for saying that. For years, I thought that Mom didn't know her science, until I found out that she actually was right. That teacher didn't know as much as he thought he did.

Sometimes Mom brought home her disadvantaged pupils for a nice meal. She gave them clothing or helped them with homework. I thought about how nice it would be to have siblings sitting around our table for an evening dinner. Because she had taught school in Spartansburg for over thirty years, quite a few of these students were the children of Mom's former pupils.

She had often repeated a saying about hardened criminals when she heard a frightening report on the news, "They were somebody's innocent little baby once." This was her attitude towards anybody who had fallen on challenging times. She said the same thing about old, abandoned houses, "That house was somebody's dream." This often set me to thinking. She was always an advocate for the "underdog."

I had a lot of fun in school and loved recess, which appeared to be, but probably was not, completely unsupervised. We could swing high on the huge swings, standing to pump ourselves up even with the top of the bars. We wandered all over the school yard and even across the road to Clear Lake. One of my favorite games was to play "Red Light, Green Light" and another was one where we made up colors. I made up a few, "Sky Blue Pink," and "Candy Apple Red." One time a friend whom I admired complimented me on my invention of color names, and I felt so proud. The few times I didn't like to be outside at recess was when we divided up into teams to play ball. I was always the last person or next to the last person chosen to be on anybody's team. I had no skill at playing ball and I put this down to not having had anyone to teach me how to do it. These were the few times I remember feeling rejection and shame in my life. Several times I asked Mom to toss me a ball in our yard, but neither of us was really interested in it.

In the fifth grade I went through a phase when I was extremely shy in school. I began to wear eyeglasses and was so self-conscious that whenever I walked up to write on the chalkboard, I removed them.

Around this time I became a bit wild and formed a little gang of tough children on my street in a group I named, The Brave's Club. I invented the initiation which required each child to allow an earthworm to crawl across our head until it fell off.

My classmate, *Sadie*, and a neighbor, Billy Perry were among the Braves Club members. I'm sure my best friend, Cookie, was involved too, and a boy who was one of my constant companions through my youth, Troy Murdoch. We were quite obnoxious. On a dirt street, called Blakeslee Street, we hid in the bushes and jumped out making noises to scare drivers as they drove by. We got a lot of amusement out of alarming them.

I imagine I got my period when I was around the age of thirteen like most every other girl, but I don't remember. Mom had given me a little pamphlet about it, and I vaguely remember we were taught about it in school. I suppose I felt a certain pride about it, a feeling that I was growing up. I remember asking Mom if I could use tampons and she seemed pretty shocked. She stood outside the bathroom door checking in with me every few seconds, to see if I'd got it in. All in all, it was no big deal.

In high school I loved to write papers and give reports and I would most often wait to prepare them until several nights before or even the night before they were due. I would type them up on my beautiful blue Smith Corona typewriter. I got good enough grades, at least B+.

My mother always told me to do the "best I could" which signaled to me that I didn't have to try very hard because she would never know. I never felt challenged to live up to my potential during my teenage years.

Mom was always inordinately prouder of me than I thought I deserved. Whenever I would mention one of my friends accomplishing something, she would say that I was "smarter" or "prettier." I knew this had no basis in fact, and I felt a little sorry for her. I took it in stride as her need for me to excel and be better than other people's children. I didn't feel any pressure to be better, in fact, I learned that her opinions weren't based on substance. It did make me feel that I could just coast, and not strive to become good or accomplished at anything. I began to develop a feeling that I was not very accomplished or talented except in relationships. Fortunately, I had learned the art of how to read people's emotions and reactions through observing my mother. This helped me relate well with people outside our home. I learned how to be gracious and charming to prevent offense. I learned how to be tough and bold towards bullies and sweet and humorous towards friends and elderly people, but I failed to learn kindness towards the sensitive person in my home.

When I was thirteen, one of my teachers assigned us to write down our parents' information. We were to write their names, careers, education and so forth. This assignment was very difficult for me because my mother and I had never spoken one word about my father, other than her assurance that I had one. I felt hesitant and embarrassed to ask my mom about this.

I shyly brought up the assignment and she took it in with her lips pursed. She made no comment at all. The next morning, I came out to breakfast to find a three-by-five card waiting for me at my place on the table.

On it was written:

Lynton Azelle Wills
Alpharetta, Georgia
Emory University, elementary teacher

Mom never spoke another word to me about my father until I was eighteen, but I carried that three-by-five card with my father's information on it for the rest of the year. It was my only link with him.

TAKING A BREAK

During my elementary years, Mom got a break from me during the summers when the Robbies took me down to stay with their son George Robbie's family. They lived in Aliquippa, which was a suburb outside of Pittsburgh, PA. Sometimes I spent three weeks with my third cousins, Billy, Gayle, and later, Lloyd who were all around my age. Occasionally, their redhaired cousin, Curly, made an appearance which added to the fun.

Gayle, Me & Billy

I adored Billy who was two years older than I and who thought up all sorts of adventures, often having to do with going to the dump.

George and Margaret sometimes took us to the Pittsburgh airport to watch the airplanes arrive and take off. It was thrilling to us but I never imagined that I would someday travel around the world multiple times. It never even occurred to me or interested me.

At home we helped Margaret shuck peas and tip and tail green beans. The kids had a long rope swing hanging from a tall tree in their yard where we could swing right out over a busy highway. Sometimes I sat up in their big bedroom whistling a perfect imitation of a bob white quail bird. It was gratifying to watch the boys searching for that bird.

The younger Robbies did not conform to the rigid dress standards of the senior Robbies. We all wore shorts on sweltering summer days. However, I remember times when we heard Grandpa Robbie's Chevrolet coming up the driveway. Margaret, Gayle, and I would run into the house to change into skirts so Grandpa and Grandma Robbie wouldn't see us wearing offensive pants. We took this in stride, never questioning the elder Robbie's expectations.

In those days, parents did little to supervise kids. We were free to make poor choices but survived them. Once when the cousins visited us in Spartansburg, we four went out on Clear Lake in a leaky rowboat. We were chasing ducks on the pond while bailing the water from the bottom of the slowly sinking boat. No one had a life preserver, and I could not swim. However, I always felt completely safe because Billy was an Eagle Scout.

I looked up to him and felt he could do anything. I loved those times together, but I remember it was always a relief to return home to be with my mom.

Sometimes we went down to Sandy Lake, Pennsylvania to stay with the elder Robbies when they had the pastorate there. A river ran behind their property, and one summer I discovered clams there. I collected them and brought them home to Spartansburg in a bucket as pets. I put them in the creek behind our home and was crushed one day when I discovered that a neighbor boy had pried them open and killed them all.

Sandy Lake was a small town to explore, and it was the first place where I realized that Robbie and Bessie were aging. They looked and smelled old. I remember Aunt Bessie's long hair which she always kept up in a bun, was beginning to look yellow and greasy.

They also had Bessie's brother, Elmer, a veteran of the Spanish American War living with them. He sat in Robbie's wicker rocking chair, bundled up in a woolen sweater peering down at me with a stern face a bit like the statue of Abraham Lincoln in the Memorial in D.C. He seldom spoke or smiled.

It was during this time when I met Grandpa Robbie's Scottish relatives, his sister, Aunt Alice, her husband and a young niece, Renee, who had traveled from either Canada or Scotland. They had visited Uncle Robbie's brother John who was in a mental institution in Canada. He had been gassed in World War I and never recovered. These days we call his condition, PTSD or Complex Trauma. I never saw the family again. I spent at least one summer vacation with Robbies when they had their church in Fairmont, West Virginia. This was my first experience with poverty in the south and with people who were difficult to understand because of their accents. One woman told Grandma Robbie that she couldn't make it to church on Sunday because she had been up on the roof all day Saturday and she was "all tarred." Grandma Robbie imagined her covered with black tar! She had a laugh when she realized what the lady meant was that she was too *tired* after working on the roof all day.

The Robbies spent part of every summer at a rustic cabin that Grandpa had built years before at a Wesleyan Methodist Campground called Stoneboro. During the time we went it was ultra conservative, just as the Robbies were. I felt ambivalent about our visits there, but whenever Mom and Harriott went I realized they stood out like beautifully feathered birds among the other women in their plain long dresses, oxfords and hair up in buns. I felt embarrassed for them, and also proud of them. I remember asking my mom to not wear lipstick and she seemed perplexed about what to do. Harriott, of course, would have never considered changing her customs so I didn't ask her to.

My own noncompliant nature served me well during one of the children's meetings at Stoneboro camp. I don't remember that I ever made friends with any of the other children at the camp, I think our friends the Parkers (next chapter) came occasionally and I'm sure I played with their daughter there. In one of the children's meeting I was sitting by myself when the speaker stood up front and said he was sending an offering basket around for children to put our gold rings and other jewelry into.

I happened to be wearing my little Garnet birthstone ring and I remember thinking immediately, "That man up front is wearing gold rimmed glasses. I will not put my ring into the basket if he's not going to put his glasses into it."

I didn't feel any pressure or shame in not doing it, though at the moment I may have felt a little bit of guilt. However, because of my frequent temper outbursts, I was accustomed to feelings of guilt and I knew they would soon pass. Later, I told my mom and Harriott who were predictably indignant about the "offering," as I knew they would be.

SEARCHING FOR MY
TWODADS

A LIFE OF CONTRAST

I often traveled with the Robbies, and sometimes we visited their friends, the *Parkers*, who lived in a mansion on a hill in Oil City. Mom sometimes came along and Harriott, who lived in Oil City, joined us there for lunch.

Mrs. *Parker* and her mother were supporters of Robbie's Holiness ministry. *Angela*, their daughter was my age. Her father, *Will*, did not seem to be interested in the holiness aspect of faith and when we visited them, my mom, Harriott, and when I grew older, I, often sat separately with *Will* to talk about world events while the others sat in the kitchen to talk about religion.

Their home had more rooms than I had ever seen in a house, and I was free to explore them all. I mostly remember the sinks and bathtubs with gold fixtures! At least, they looked like gold. None of the rooms were shut off to preserve heat like ours were and each one had thick, colorful carpeting. *Angela* had a playroom plus a bedroom! There was always an abundance of delicious homemade food in their large kitchen.

In contrast, some of our rooms and even the refrigerator in our home were off limits to me. I learned to ask permission before I opened the refrigerator.

Mom always got the food out, seldom did she let me search around in it. I realized as I got older that it was because she didn't want me to criticize her for the mess in there. We had loads of food that often went bad. Mom rarely had the time or the inclination to check what she had before buying something else to eat.

Most of the rooms in our house, by contrast, were filled with garbage bags and cardboard boxes containing mysterious treasures from Mom's past. Mom called these rooms that only had a single pathway through them, "storage rooms."

I considered the bags and boxes sources of information and history. One room, Mom called the playroom, had things tossed into it like a city dump and no pathway in, but at the far end I could see an easel, doll bed and other things that interested me. These rooms provided my curiosity with unending resources. Each time Mom left the house I would go exploring despite her warning me most times to not "get into things." This was always a source of frustration for me; however, two things limited my adventures. The rooms were unheated and had mice.

RAGE

The times I remember Mom spanking me as a child were when I "sassed" her, which was often. I never remember those spankings hurting, and they didn't affect me in the least. This happened after we moved to Spartansburg, so I was in first grade and older, around 8,9 and 10 years old.

We would argue because she said she did not want me to have the "last word" which of course, I would say I did not want, but by simply telling her that aloud I added a word which made her angry. I have no memory of why we argued.

Sometimes, I ran away from her, laughing while she chased after me to spank me, and once, I bumped into my nice childhood desk breaking off its leg. I remember hopping on and off the bed, as she swung at me with a yardstick. Most often though, she spanked me on the bottom using her hands. I always felt bad after I had led her on such a chase, and I would ask her for forgiveness. She was quick to forgive and said she knew I did not mean it when I was rude and sassy. Nevertheless, despite feeling true remorse, I soon went on to repeat my sassiness.

I could not explain my temper and I'm only beginning to understand it now. Occasionally, I became so angry as a teenager that I banged my head against the bathroom door. I realize we can't self-diagnose, but in my reading about Oppositional Defiance Disorder,[10] it certainly describes me. I wonder if it helps to explain my seething rages. Back then, there were no doctors to diagnose these things, or we didn't know about them. I wonder if I might have inherited this temperament from my father or my "Piss Ant" Grandfather Hammond (as a man who knew him once described him to me).[11] The fact that I began to act out as I grew into my mid elementary and teenage years seems to fit. When my mother was not able to give up controlling me as I grew into independence, I began to rebel.

I'm ashamed to write this but once, as a young teenager, I slapped my mom and told her that I hated her. I wish that I had known how to use my words to better express my rage filled feelings. I also realize now that teenage girls normally have rebellion and anger issues. No one ever talked about this when I was young, but my rages were extreme. After each angry rage, I felt terrible remorse.

On the other hand, Mom felt she was always right. As I grew older, I felt that she baited me, wanting to start an argument. Things she said triggered me. I wish I had been able to resist. As I look back, I understand that Mom was operating out of her brokenness, but I was not mature enough to realize this. I wish my mom had a partner to help her parent me. It might have helped to take the stings if she had someone other than me to talk

---

10 - A disorder in a child marked by defiant and disobedient behavior to authority figures. The cause is unknown but likely involves a combination of genetic and environmental factors. This condition cannot be cured and can last for years.

11 - See my book, *The Grandmothers of Force*

to. I see our family now and thank God that my husband, Jon's constant presence was a buffer to all of us in our present-day family.

I also realize that I might have been angry that I didn't have a father and didn't know what had happened to him because Mom never said a word about him. Also, in many ways, I felt confused because I was given almost total freedom to do things outside our home, but at home Mom was upset if I got into the refrigerator or certain rooms of our house without her permission.

Mom's response when I sassed her was often to say, "Mary, Mary, Mary, if I had ever treated my mother like this..." Or, she would say, "When I'm dead you'll know I'm right," and, "When you've taught school as long as I have, you'll know I'm right." Once she told me, "I hope you have a child just like you."

Her words were intended to shame me but had negligible effect on me.

Mom used to place excessive emphasis on my minor accomplishments and didn't hold me to excellence. I knew in my heart that I was not living up to my capabilities because I never felt challenged to do it.

Though Mom assumed she knew me, I don't think she knew me at all. I wonder if my anger was because I felt a need for mom to pay more attention to me. She worked hard and was exhausted much of the time. I was a generally happy person outside my home but inside, chaos seemed to prevail and I felt comfortable creating it, but not happy.

I had read somewhere that it's a mistake to vow to be different from our mothers because then our focus is on the past.

My greatest regret is that I was too strict with our children when they were little. We read certain books about strong-willed children[12] and since I related so well to that concept, I assumed our children were defiant like me when they were simply behaving like toddlers. They needed loving direction and instruction. I, instead, repeated my mom's mistake by not learning to understand my children.

Instead of rebelling, their tender hearts were wounded by my actions whenever I felt I was losing control. I was very concerned that my children would become oppositional like I had been. I wanted to forestall the disaster that I had felt in myself. However, I failed to realize that our children were gentle and merciful souls like Jon. Unfortunately, many child rearing books of the seventies fed into my "black and white" thinking. Due to my strong personality, I sometimes behaved like a Marine Corp sergeant commanding troops of two-year-olds. "Do this, don't do that," was my mantra, instead of instructing them as a Biblical mother.

Fortunately, Jon was what I considered a "push-over" and was considerate with the children. It turned out he was simply a merciful person. We both believed in loosening up on discipline as they grew older, which helped to lessen the tension around control, for me.

I remember Jon asking me once, "Don't you want the children to love you?" I said, "That's not my

---

12 - James Dobson wrote a book call *The Strong-Willed Child*

job." I honestly thought my "job" was to make the children good.

In other ways we focused on the positive in childrearing. I made an effort to encourage our daughters and listen to their ideas. But I responded angrily to the slightest stress, and Jon and my differences in stamina along with our inability to communicate well in our marriage, was one continual stress over the years.

Our daughters took my anger personally, and though they didn't react to my rage outwardly, it wounded them causing scars that has affected our adult relationships.

The idea that relationships with Mom, Jon or the kids should be above our differences never once occurred to me. I overreacted to forgetfulness, broken dishes, messes.

Sadly, despite my great remorse and repentance, my unpredictable temper was not helped except by medication which I continue taking to this day.

▲   ▲   ▲

Mom often resorted to humor to disarm our conflicts and so do I. She reminded me to smile. In fact, throughout my young life, she never gave suggestions about how I should dress, or wear my hair, or even who to date, but she often told me to smile.

I recently found a journal entry that reminded me, Mom told me that I looked so much prettier when I smiled. This created in me the idea that I wasn't good looking unless I smiled. I made an effort to smile throughout my life, and looking back through my photographs, I see to my amazement that I was attractive. Despite having an underbite which I thought made me look like a bulldog, I had boyfriends all throughout my young years. I marked that down to my sense of humor and personality, assuming that they ignored my looks. Of course, having acne only deepened my assumptions, though to be honest, once I was out and away from a mirror I rarely thought about how I looked.

My assumption for years was that Mom wanted me to smile so that people outside our family would conclude that I was happy, and that she was a successful mother. At times, though, I had a tough time thinking of anything I liked about her. I sometimes wished she was as nice to me as she was to her students. One time I wrote in my diary that the only good thing about my mom was her kindness to animals. However, my viewpoint depended on our current state of relationship. Mom was very charming, but at home, she needed control. As I grew older, I didn't like to be controlled. I became more like her, I wanted control.

▲ ▲ ▲

Mom and I did have many special times together usually away from home. Once a month she hired a taxi to shop at the larger grocery store in Corry, which was seven miles away. She collected *S & H Green Stamps*,[13] and I had the job of counting and

---

13 - A line of trading stamps popular in the United States from 1896 until the late 1980's. The S & H stood for Sperry and Hutchinson Co. The stamps were distributed by retailers as rewards for shoppers. They were collected and pasted into booklets which were redeemed for "rewards" from S&H Catalogs. *Wikipedia*

pasting them into the little booklets so we could earn prizes.

Our trips to town were a treat. We always had dinner at the Ritz restaurant owned by a Greek family. There was an expensive chocolate candy shop and soda fountain in the front part of the restaurant. In the back, the restaurant had carved art deco booths with dusty pink and blue colored leather cushions where we ate delicious dinners. Even when I was very young, the colors always seemed a little off putting to me. Each month, the owner, Mr. Zafiropoulos, greeted us like old friends and gave me a piece of chocolate cream candy before we left. My favorite dishes were his turkey dinner and the Greek salad. When I grew up, I asked for his secret Greek salad dressing which he shared with me.

SEARCHING FOR MY TWO DADS

SEX? & FRIENDSHIPS

I remember sitting out in the school yard on the teeter totters with girls in my fifth-grade class making a vow that we would *never* wear bras until we were fifteen! We laughed about growing breasts and I laugh now, at the thought that we would be grown up by the age of fifteen! Maybe this came up because we were secretly envious of girls who were developing early.

In sixth grade I grew tired of my neighborhood gang activities and began experimenting with sex. It was not as we look at it these days, but it was shocking to me because it was with a girl.

Looking back from my perspective today, it wasn't a huge thing, but I felt guilty for decades. *Sadie* developed earlier than the rest of the girls I knew. One time she wanted me to get into bed with her to look at her breasts. I was fascinated and did just that. I don't remember touching them, but because of that incident, I worried for years that I was a lesbian after I learned what the word meant. Yes, it was a worry. I clearly liked boys very much. Breasts fascinated me since I developed late. I never had any romantic interest in girls besides that incident. I've concluded that this was a normal phase of curiosity and affection that children often pass through.

Childhood friendships among the girls changed frequently. However, my best friend Cookie, who was several years younger than I, remained a constant friend for years. I went to her house most Saturday mornings while her parents were sleeping in from Friday. She and her sister would sample the beer left over in cups from the night before. This didn't appeal to me at all.

I was best friends with Pam for a few months, then with Sonja or Marlene then overnight our friendship pairs switched. Alice became my best friend and for a while, the other girls didn't speak to us. By the time graduation came around, we had sorted ourselves out and we were all friends, several of us for our lifetime.

I don't remember being mean and spiteful to other little girls, except one time, when I was a bully. In fifth grade a little red-haired girl who was one year younger than me came into the girls' bathroom. We were alone and I said to her out of the blue, "I don't like you and I never will." She looked at me in horror and ran out. I avoided her for the rest of the year.

This was entirely out of character for me, and the only way I can explain it is that her mother was a teacher at our school and for some reason my mother had a grudge against her which she passed onto me.

Our classes were small, around twenty-five to thirty students, and some of our teachers were young, so we got to know them well and liked to tease them.

As I remember, our Social Studies focused entirely on South and Central America in fifth and sixth grades. I wonder why? A memory from fifth grade is our teacher, Mrs. Litzinger, who paced back and forth while teaching. Whenever the kids acted up, she would point to the wall of windows in our second-floor classroom and said, "I'm going to jump right out those windows if you don't behave."

Only one friend ever mentioned the absence of my father, and I wonder now if my friends talked about it among themselves? While playing at my house one day, she told me that she didn't believe I ever had a father. I remember she said it in the front room of our house, and how it stung. I also remember believing her and running to hide in our kitchen. My mom found me hiding in the kitchen beside our large green dish cupboard and asked me what was wrong.

When I told her what my friend said, she told me in a most comforting voice, "Well of course you had a father." I don't remember how I entered back into play, but Mom's assurance was all it took. Being me, I'm sure that I corrected my friend and told her that I certainly did have a father, my mother said so! I never remember again feeling any shame or awkward feelings over being different from the other kids because I had no father.

In fact, I felt kind of special because Mom was more like a friend than a parent and not restrictive in my activities outside our home.

At this time, I had thick frizzy dark hair because of an accident at the beauty parlor. Mom told me, but I think she speculated, that the beautician had been drinking the day she gave me a permanent and permed my hair using chemicals at twice the strength she should have.

My cute little Poodle cut which was all the rage at the time, turned into a child's Afro years ahead of its time.

The perm changed the texture of my hair for several years. Once in Seventh grade our class clown, Timmie, who sat behind me commented when I got my hair cut, "You look so different, I just thought you had a big head!"

This is the same Tim who disappeared years later only to be arrested and jailed for fraud. He was passing himself off as an Oxford University History Professor and author with no credentials.

During my fiftieth high school class reunion, Jon and I visited him, and he showed no regret or shame, but instead a sense of adventure and fun as always. He was sorting out of his parent's home in preparation for selling it and showed us around. Antiques filled the downstairs rooms. He offered to send us one of several books he said he had authored as a historian. However, he didn't follow through on his offer to send the books. I googled his name and couldn't find any references to books authored by him.

LORNA

Our Polish neighbors, Jenny and John Sawchyn who had sold us our house, lived directly across a small field beside us. They had a granddaughter named Lorna Daszynick. Her name reminds me of one of the happiest times in my childhood as well as the first time I experienced anguish.

Cookie, Me & Lorna

Lorna came to stay one summer when we were in fifth grade. We soon became friends. She was a golden girl, with lovely blond hair, rosy cheeks, and a smile that lit up my day. We played with dolls, explored the glen, and spent every free minute together. She was my ideal playmate. We never fought, our interests coincided, and I genuinely loved her. The first thing I did every morning that summer after I woke up was to run over to Sawchyn's house to wake up Lorna. I ran through Jenny Sawchyn's kitchen where she stood at the stove welcoming me with a big smile. Vaulting up the stairs two steps at a time to Lorna's bedroom I would wake Lorna up and wait while she got dressed. We would be off for a day of fun. It was the first time that I had ever felt such freedom in a friend's home. She was like a sister to me.

Then one day, I ran past Grandma Jenny and up the stairs to find Lorna's bedroom empty. All her things were cleared out! There was not even one trace of her left in the room. Her grandma looked with sympathy at my teary face but couldn't speak a word of English to comfort me. I never found out what happened to Lorna.

Looking back, I suppose it was time for her to go back to wherever she lived because it was the end of summer, but no one prepared me. I ran home and upstairs to my own bedroom sinking to the floor beside my window crying as I looked across the field at Sawchyn's big green house. I was devastated, I sat beside that window crying and grieving for days for my friend whom I never saw again.

▲   ▲   ▲

One summer John Sawchyn tied a little brown Jersey calf in the field beside our house. I named her Strawberry and went out to visit her every day and took a lick from her salt block. In the beginning there were white salt blocks and then they changed to blue ones. I wondered whether the blue ones were safe to lick or not. It didn't bother me that cows were licking them!

We thought the Sawchyns spoke Polish and very few words of English. I have recently discovered through Ancestry.com that John was originally from Ukraine, and Jenny, his second wife, was Polish but by way of Germany before WWI. Between them, their blended family consisted of more than ten children.

Jenny had a chubby, suntanned face and always had a brilliant smile. She fascinated me because she was the first woman I had ever seen wearing large, golden hoop earrings. Every day we would see her outdoors tending to her huge gardens of flowers and vegetables. During the winter, she did hand sewing, decorating linen dresser scarves and dishtowels with fancy embroidery. I now have these, which were holiday gifts from Jenny to Mom.

John was an old farmer who wore dark clothing and the type of farmer's cap you typically see Eastern European migrant workers wearing. He worked the fields around our house with last-century farm tools, plowing with a horse-drawn plow, cutting hay by hand with a huge scythe taller than him with a blade half his size. The hay lay in piles until he and his wife heaved it by pitchfork onto the hay wagon pulled by their huge black draft horse named Prince.

I was in love with Prince and since he was right next door, I took every opportunity to catch a ride on his back. Once, my mom looked out our front window and saw me riding bareback on old Prince down Main Street, which was also Route 77, a busy and dangerous highway. John was holding the reins riding behind on his ancient hayrack. I was in my element. I caught ringworm on the top of my head from Prince, and still have a hairless place on my scalp to prove it!

John and Jenny had two other grandkids that I knew besides Lorna. Dickie and Carla Spiesman lived with them for a while so they could go to school in Spartansburg. They were darkly exotic and while Carla was quiet and shy, Dickie was always getting into trouble. I used to ride on the hay wagon with them.

One time Mom and I looked across the field and saw that John Sawchyn's haymow was on fire right beside their barn full of cattle. What we saw next clued us into what had happened. Dickie came running around the corner of the haymow with his grandma Jenny chasing him with a pitchfork! Shortly afterwards, the local fire department arrived to put out the smoldering fire that Dickie had set! We didn't see much of Dickie after that.

LIFE IN THE TOWN

We didn't have a television for the first few years after I started school. In winter, I played outside in the deep snow for hours, making snow forts and getting very cold. Snow piled up so high around our mailbox that naturally it was where I chose to build a snow fort. Mom worried that the snowplow might come along and hit the huge pile with me in it. She worried too about me playing in the summertime with my little cars in the front yard because my favorite place to play was right under the big maple trees by the highway. She had good reason to worry because there had been several serious accidents when drunk drivers had come around the curve and gone out of control plowing right into our front yard hitting those trees. Drivers had died in our yard. Mom suffered a nervous reaction for months each time a car hit our home or our trees.

One evening, she was sitting in our front room, watching television when a car came speeding around the corner, missed the curve, hit our trees throwing a person out onto our front lawn. He died. Another time, an accident brought a car into our front room in the middle of the night as Mom slept in the next room. We would both cringe and hold our breath when we heard the squeal of breaks as speeding cars unexpectedly approached the curve in front of our house, sometimes on two wheels as if they were on a speedway.

Mom told me she never learned to drive because she had seen too many tragic car accidents at Riceville Corners when she was younger. She said she was afraid she would kill someone.

Her parents were Red Cross workers and always went to the scene of accidents to help the victims. Mom said she felt haunted by the screams of the injured men and women she could hear from her home on the corners. She told me about a bride whose husband had died in a car accident on their honeymoon. Much of my life I thought this had occurred when Mom was a child, but I understand now that mom wasn't a little girl but a young adult when they lived at Riceville Corners. Her trauma occurred when she was much older than I had realized.

I feel sad that the consequences of Mom's fear of driving which prevented her from getting her license as a young woman, eerily returned to haunt her as an older adult when the accidents came right into our front yard, and even into our house. I sometimes wondered if she would have avoided much of the trauma if she had overcome her fears and learned to drive earlier.

Mom often told maudlin stories of what might have been, or near misses. Her tendency to pathos cautioned me to avoid it. In fact, I believe I taught myself to respond to life as a thinker rather than a feeler due to my mom's melancholic tendency to evoke emotions of nostalgia, pity and sorrow. She often reminisced about her family and how wonderful they had been. I know she felt lonely and missed them. However, I think I was largely impatient or inattentive to her reminiscences. She was a sensitive soul.

▲   ▲   ▲

Chuck, our neighbor took his boys and me swimming in summer over to Canadotha Lake for our weekly hair washing with Dial Soap. I loved it when Chuck dunked me and the boys underwater to wash our hair. Nobody cared about pollution. Chuck washed our hair in the same area where we swam. Back then, old houses didn't have showers, but instead, big claw foot bathtubs, so filling them up and taking a bath in the house was at most a weekly event. Houses were cold and drafty much of the year. I remember the dreaded sensation of getting out of the bathtub and breaking out in goosebumps while I toweled off.

I usually took sponge baths, which Mom never supervised when I was in grade school. I remember the little gray porcelain basin in the bathroom sink where I used to give myself these sponge baths. I was shocked once to notice that I had streaks of black dirt going down my forearms where my washcloth had not completely washed away the week's soil. I am sure my neck was dirty too, and I wonder if I even smelled bad.

▲   ▲   ▲

During my elementary years, I was physically fragile, catching multiple colds and sore throats during the winter. Since she didn't drive, Mom had me stay home from school when I was sick rather than walk the two miles through the high drifts and slush. I remember the care she gave me when

I had Bronchitis. She heated up Vicks Vapo Rub or Camphorated Oil and rubbed it on my chest and then after heating odd bits of flannel over the furnace ducts, she laid them on my chest and pinned them to my pajamas. It was such a comforting feeling to go to sleep inhaling the Vicks, a remedy from her own childhood.

Every fall, Mom and her friend Mrs. Byler drove out to McCray's family farm to tramp through their boggy pasture to pick large baskets of Boneset flowers. She dried these and later brewed the white flowers into a terribly bitter tea, which she strained and forced me to drink during the winters.

NINE MEN IN OUR UPSTAIRS

In the winter of 1957 when I was in the third grade, Mom learned that the hotel downtown was at full capacity and there were linemen from West Virginia who needed a place to board. She offered our house as a place for them! This was a juicy tidbit for our elderly next-door neighbor who was a renowned gossip. Nine men moved into our home in the middle of winter! They took up the entire upstairs and the other side of the first floor of the house where we had an antique wood stove. Mom had somehow cleared out all of the bags of treasures. I have no idea where she put it all. I truly did wonder. On cold nights, they fired up that old woodstove until it was so hot, they all went out on the front sun porch in their sleeveless undershirts to cool off.

Mom cooked breakfast for them before she went to school and dinner when she came home. One evening Mom came home to a shock! The linemen had killed and skinned our cat and left it in the kitchen sink! That is what she thought when she saw it! They laughed and assured her that it was roadkill possum which they "et all the time in West Virginia." They showed her how to dress it for dinner. It was tasty, but very greasy.

The men established a no smoking or swearing rule inside our house and set up a special swearing jar so whenever they forgot and used bad language, especially in front of me, they had to put money in. I got quite a bit of money in that swearing jar. I loved hanging out with those men, soaking up their fathering, but Mom limited my time over there in the stove room.

ENTERTAINMENT

I had been begging Mom for a TV for years and we finally could afford one the year the linemen came, in 1957. It had a metal cabinet painted olive green. We received three local channels. The linemen joined us for a couple of programs each night. I had such snug and cozy feelings when I came home from school to watch TV.

Before this, the first few years after we moved to Spartansburg, our neighbors, Chuck and Edna Shreve, invited us to their house across the driveway to watch *"Gunsmoke"* every Friday night. Now we had a TV of our own, but I missed going to their home and sitting with the Shreve's and their high school sons, Glenn, and Marty.

Each night after dishes were done, Mom would invite the linemen over to our side of the house to watch a TV show. One of our favorites was about submarines during WWII. I remember my thrill of hearing "up periscope," of spotting an enemy ship, and then the thrill of taking it out! We all cheered. It never occurred to me that some of these men may have been in WWII even on submarines themselves.

Before our linemen arrived, I stayed alone when I was sick from the ages of seven and eight. After they began boarding with us, very occasionally, if one of them happened to be sick, he stayed home with me. My favorite was Eugene. He had curly dark hair and a deep southern drawl. We watched TV all day, and he fixed me noodle soup for lunch. He also vacuumed the whole downstairs.

I vaguely remember watching cartoons on Saturday morning. I first heard classical music on the Micky Mouse Cartoons. I did not hear it elsewhere in our home. Mom had an aversion to classical music and made me turn it off. She said it was too repetitive, but I wonder if it triggered unhappy memories for her. We seldom had any music in our home unless I played her collection of records from the Big Band Era. I watched all the game shows like Johnny Carson's early shows, *Who Do You Trust?* and *I've Got a Secret*. On Saturday nights we stayed up late to watch movies.

Mom liked to tell me about the actors she admired like Greer Garson, and especially Jimmy Stewart who had a connection to Penfield, PA, where she grew up. I vividly remember the grown-up TV programs Mom let me watch, I don't remember her telling me any shows were off limits. The first two films we watched together were *Key Largo* and *The Last of the Mohicans*. Mom often fell asleep while I of course, stayed up watching until the last note of the sign off music at 1 A.M. Then I woke up Mom and reluctantly headed for bed. One movie really frightened me and that was *The Night of the Hunter* with Robert Mitchum. This movie about a circuit riding preacher who kills a young mother and then hunts for her children still gives me the shivers!!!

As I grew older, we watched the news together. Sometimes we watched *The Dean Martin Show*, Mom said, "Just to see how bad he is." We often watched a movie or show like *Alfred Hitchcock Presents*. When things got too intense, I ran into the next room and hid around the corner. Sometimes I had nightmares about those shows. I watched *American Band Stand*[14] a show filmed in Philadelphia. Imagine my excitement when I went to Bible College in Philadelphia and I met and began to date Paul, one of the former dancers on *Band Stand*. I enjoyed hearing him talk about my favorite dancers, especially a girl named Marilyn.

I had to stay home alone at night sometimes while Mom went to a PTA meeting, and I felt scared. Two times, a strange man knocked at our front door. My panicked reaction was to turn on all the lights, turn up the volume on the TV and hide. The first time, I could see the shadow of the man cast by the streetlight. He was wearing a Fedora hat like Grandpa Robbie's. I had never seen any man around our town wearing a hat like that. His shadow loomed larger than life as I peered through the curtains. We lived on a busy highway and Mom had warned me to never open the door to anyone I didn't know. I still remember the feeling of my heart pounding in terror.

---

14 - A popular national music television program 1956-1989, with strong Philadelphia roots, which shaped the music industry and society of generations. Dick Clark was the DJ during the 1950s. *philadelphiaencyclopedia.org*

Fluffy & Me

MY ANIMALS

I had an intuitive understanding and love for animals, often finding stray dogs on my walks from school and bringing them home with me especially in harsh weather. When Mom came home to find wet dogs sprawled out on our living room couch, she was always kind. Fortunately, she kept the couch well covered in sturdy denim. She fed them and put them out on our front sun porch with the promise that we could keep them if we couldn't find their owner. By the next day, they were gone. I have no idea where or how she managed this.

Among our pets were Petey, a blue Parakeet we taught to say, "Pretty boy," Tar Baby a coal-black Bunny, Penelope/Penny my black mixed Cocker Spaniel, Tippy and Jeroboam or Jerry, two Beagles. Blacky a large black Lab didn't last long because he dragged Mom around the snowy yard on his leash. Mom had liked cats as a child, but I favored dogs. We had three cats, Tinkerbell, my pretty kitty, Bootsie a gray kitty, and Fluffy a yellow kitty whom I found in an abandoned building. Mom made him live in the woodshed attached to our house after Bootsie jumped on her and bit her leg. That attack triggered a fear of cats in Mom, so we kept poor Fluffy out there as a mouser for the rest of his life.

Fluffy peered at us through a window in the bathroom, affectionately rubbing his head up against it as if he were rubbing up against our legs. Occasionally, I begged Mom to let him in, which we did. In the summertime we put him outside in a little harness on a clothesline.

Mom and I took loving care of our pets, hiring a friend to take them with us on regular veterinarian visits until they reached old age, which in most cases was about thirteen. At this point, they all got sick with Cancer, and we took them in to be put to sleep. As I remember, Mom and I got a ride to the Vet's, we mourned and felt sad, the Vet took care of their little bodies, and we came home with me chattering about getting the next pet. Mom usually wanted to wait a while. I only remember Harriott arguing with my mother about one thing and that was putting our pets to sleep. Harriott was adamant that putting our beloved pets to sleep was just like euthanizing an elderly person which we would never do.

Previously, I mentioned my disagreeable after-school household chore, which was to clean up after the dogs. I had another chore that was very pleasant. From the time I was eight, my chore was to get raw milk from the neighbor's farm every evening. I walked across the fields and pasture behind our house to the Morris sister's farm at milking time carrying two glass quart jars for milk.

I loved walking through the fields behind our house. In the springtime, there were daffodils, and the creeks ran high. In the summer, there were dandelions, and the creeks were dry. I spent time talking to and patting the cows in the pastures. I had names for all of them. One sweet, brown Jersey was my favorite. She was a heifer when I first began to visit her and she never really got big and fat as the other cows did.

I loved the warm sweetness of the Morris' barn in winter, the heavy aroma of hay and manure, the deep drawn-out lowing of the cattle, and the steady chug-chug-chug of the milking machines. Each night when I entered their barn as the sisters milked, I handed out bits of hay to their ten cows.

The Morris sisters were wonderful mentors to me throughout my youth though I didn't realize that's what they were doing. One of the sisters, Margaret (Peggy) was my high school Latin teacher, our school librarian (my friend Pam and I were her assistants), English teacher, and the most informative Sunday school teacher I ever had. Peggy and her sister Freda made space for me even after I graduated from High School when I visited them as often as possible. Freda served us tea and cookies while we three talked about my hopes and dreams. I remember Freda, leaning against the door separating the kitchen from the dining room, responding to my news with smiles and sometimes, gasps. Peggy was more subdued, smiling with eyes downcast but always appearing to be interested in whatever I was doing.

Me Riding My Bike

CREATING ADVENTURES

When I was six years old I got a blue 26-inch bike. I spent all my elementary years riding up and down the sidewalks and the backyards of houses adjacent to our home. I made believe that it was our family car or I pretended that I was a school bus driver dropping off my children on a route.

I never considered what the neighbors thought about me making a little dirt bike path through their backyards. Sometimes they looked out their windows and waved at me. One creepy older man used to beckon me, trying to coax me off my bike and into his barn. He also tried to get me to ride on his shoulders which was the last possible thing I planned to do. I had snooped in his barn once and I knew it was dark and spooky and filled with junk and tools. I never went in when he was there. I became a daredevil on my bike. Once, I decided to strap on my roller skates and see how it would work out to ride my bike with them attached. That resulted in a bad scrape. When I was older, I liked to race my bike down the steep blacktop road behind our house as fast as I could go. I would hold my hands high in the air, screaming at the top of my lungs while the wind rushed through my hair.

The neighbors knew about my habit of sitting in a lone apple tree in a field behind the houses on Main

Street talking to my imaginary friends. One of them must have mentioned this to Mom because one day she strolled out to my tree, wearing her ever-present apron.

She had never visited my imaginary world or my tree before. I rarely could get her to take a walk with me down to Morris' pasture. She might not have liked the idea of going through the barbed wire fence. It might have felt to her like trespassing. It was trespassing. She spent several minutes talking with me as I sat up in the crook of the apple tree and then she went back home. It didn't seem to bother her; she told me that some neighbors were asking her about me. I sat in that tree for hours on end, talking but she never said any more to me about it. Until about fifth grade, my imaginary friends were my closest companions.

I used to lie down in our grassy field and look up at the cloud shapes imagining them to be horses and other animals. Once when I was lying alone in our field among some Dandelions, I heard a very loud, mournful cry echoing through our valley. It seemed to come from the Glen where my friends and I liked to play. It shocked and frightened me so much that from that moment on I feared going to the Glen. It no longer felt like the safe, innocent playground where my friends and I had always found refuge. I was convinced that I had heard a mountain lion, but I never could confirm it.

I liked excitement and sometimes created my own. I dropped a note in our Methodist Pastor's driveway claiming to be a prisoner held captive on an airplane and begging the neighbor for help to free me. Our neighbor, the pastor, appeared to take this call for help very seriously. He began to hurry around our neighborhood showing the note to my mother and other neighbors until they all seemed to become sufficiently alarmed. About that time, I must have confessed that I had written the note because he laughed aloud and congratulated me on a good prank!. Looking back, I suspect now that the pastor turned the joke on me! It wasn't until recently that I realized that he knew what I had done!

The Spartettes

GROWING UP IN APPALACHIA

In our small rural town in Western Pennsylvania teachers' salaries were inordinately low. Once a month Mom, a full-time elementary school teacher, stood in line to pick up delicious cheese and butter from the US Government sponsored supply warehouses.

However, we never considered we were on Welfare.[15] Until I moved away from Spartansburg, the only cheeses that I knew existed besides delicious government cheese were Velveeta Cheese, Kraft American Cheese slices, and the little cans of Parmesan cheese that came in the boxes of Chef Boyardee Pizza mix. It was after I became an adult that I learned our town, Spartansburg, PA, was a part of Appalachia.

As I grew older, my interests centered on school activities, and I learned that I was good at collecting funds for school projects. I had learned to relate well to adults and engage them in conversation by visiting neighbors with my mom since I was a little girl. I could walk up to a complete stranger's home to solicit money. I loved going door- to-door around my neighborhood selling magazines, school sweaters, candy, cookies, anything to raise funds for

---

15 - Social Assistance providing government benefits based on a low income.

our senior class trip to Washington D.C. and Luray Caverns

The first time I went door to door to solicit money for charity was for a friend's family. Terry Morris was the nicest boy in our class who died when a tractor rolled over on him when we were thirteen. It was the **first of many tragedies** in our town that we children were to experience.

As the years passed, there were more tragic deaths in our small town. One of my mother's closest friends shot herself with her hunting rifle and another hanged herself. Two farm kids died from lightning strikes, and another school friend was crushed when his tractor overturned on him. All the boys went out hunting, but I never heard of any hunting accidents. Boys learned how to handle guns from their fathers and older brothers. Most of the farm boys carried rifles in the back windows of their trucks that they drove to school.

Many years later, I asked Peggy Morris, who was my schoolteacher and spiritual mentor, whether she thought these deaths might be the result of a demonic influence in our area. She hesitated to label it as such but agreed that it was worth considering. Other events in our Christian and Missionary Alliance Church also made me wonder whether there was spiritual darkness over our town which was creating havoc.

I learned in later years that several of the pastors fell away spiritually. Legalism was rampant. I never joined the Spartansburg church because I could not agree to its emphasis on following rules as compared to what I saw as a need for a relationship with Jesus Christ. At least this was the way it appeared to me.

Once, a girl in our youth group told me that she "Saw me standing out in front of the movie theater in Corry." I thought her intent was to shame me, so I told her that she had indeed seen me, and that the movie had been very good. I didn't respond well to shame.

The overall effect of my time at the Christian and Missionary Alliance Church in Spartansburg though, was very positive. I felt loved and cherished by the people there. They were like my extended family. I loved the hymns we sang and learned to sing in harmony. I relished the opportunities to play the part of the Virgin Mary (who else?) in the Christmas plays. I sang in the choir and played special solo numbers on the piano. I taught elementary Sunday school and led the youth group when I was a teenager. I felt like I was their special girl. I was sensitive to spiritual things and frequently felt called to the front when there was an altar call.

I frequently worried that I might have committed the *unpardonable sin*, but I wasn't entirely sure what that was. I worried about that for years. The people I knew and the churches I attended in our area saw the world as largely black and white. I felt in my heart that there were other ways to perceive life.

My varied experience with Mom and the Robbies showed me that, but I didn't yet know what to call it. I always felt proud when my pretty Mom came to church with me, though she seldom came in the mornings. It wasn't until years later that mom revealed to me the reason she didn't go to church.

When she was a young, single schoolteacher with a child, there was a rumor around the high school that Mom had never married. In our small-town divorce was rare and few people had seen or met my wandering father. I suppose some of the teenagers may have heard their parents gossiping about my mom, the attractive new teacher. They were from Christian homes and by the time I began attending church, several of these girls had married, started families of their own and began to attend the church regularly.

Back then the church was focused on attendance, and I fit in because I loved showing up for church. It always seems easier for people to follow a set of outward rules than to live as a loving community. I get it, because I honestly thought I understood what it meant to be a Christian when I was in high school. I spoke in our youth group and lived a moral life. I read my Bible faithfully. However, my core ideas remained unchanged. God the Holy Spirit had not really transformed my life. That came years later. I followed the light that I knew at the time. My mom thought that I was a Christian from the time I was a little child. I know she felt badly when I referred to my becoming a Christian after I became an adult. I had a desire for spiritual things, and a love for serving God throughout my young life. It was the personal relationship with God which I lacked.

Fifth grade was the year I had my first crush on a little boy, Bobby Oviatt. He was very cute but came from a very tough family and used crude words that I had never heard before. Once, he followed me home after school and sat swinging his legs on the little cement bridge over our driveway. My mom asked me why he was out there, and I didn't know. Mom went out and told him, "We don't have any boys here."

My friends and I were very active in school events, though I was not athletic. I was an avid fan of basketball, attending every home game and riding the booster's bus to away games. I was not interested in becoming a cheerleader and felt that I did not stand a chance given the competition, but eventually, my friend Karen Earhardt and I established a majorette group, which we named the *Spartettes*. It continues to this day, over fifty years later. Karen and I performed at basketball games. Our goal was to develop a troop of little girls to twirl batons and march in the fair parade. We dressed up in little white Go-go boots and short red skirts. We made quite an impression.

SEARCHING FOR MY TWODADS

FIRST LOVE

Studies show that the absence of father or a significant father figure makes a difference in a child's life.[16] They will present with a need for attention from men, depression, eating disorders and self-esteem issues. Sometimes girls become promiscuous. I was fortunate to have had Grandpa Hammond and Robbie early in my life. I also had powerful moral grounding in my life that made sense to me and served me well throughout my teenage years, preventing me from going down that path.

I was, however, excessively interested in boys, in fact, I would say it was my primary interest in life until I was in my twenties. I developed charm from my mom's example and enjoyed flirting, but I seemed to sense natural boundaries. I was fortunate to have met some wonderful boys who helped me to develop high expectations for the man I would eventually marry.

The Spartansburg Fair was our town's largest community event, and it provided an opportunity for my first serious crush in 1962 when I was fourteen years old. It was there that I met John Hemminger, a country boy from a neighboring school, who was

16 - Wall Street Journal March 4, 2023, *Why Children Need Nurturing Fathers*

sixteen and drove an old navy-blue Packard. John faithfully showed up at our house on weekends. Mom did not allow me to go out on dates, so our activity was sitting on the couch, holding hands, watching TV and talking. When Harriott was in town, she gave John the keys to her big Dodge and let us race around in the field behind our house. I will always remember how we stretched the limits, worrying if she would get mad at us, but she was always sweet, no matter how reckless he was. He came along with us on our adventures. Mom and Harriott liked John who was fun to have along and made us all giggle.

Once in our backyard, he sang to me, crooning Dean Martin's song with the lyrics, "I Don't Know Why, I Love You Like I Do, I Don't Know Why, I Just Do." He was so romantic, and sweet. He was the picture of sincerity and won my heart with his dusky olive skin and watery blue eyes.

First love is sweet, and he will always be in my memory. We grew apart when we went on to high school; he graduated and went away to Viet Nam in 1965. He survived and came back to visit me once or twice.

Though music was not a big interest of mine, I loved to listen and sing along with female singers, like Shelly Fabares, and Annette Funicello. It was handy that Shelly had a song out called *Johnny Angel* at the time since I had a boyfriend named John Hemminger! Looking back on groups like the Beach Boys, I liked them but I didn't listen to music very often. I was very active doing other things outdoors.

The Beatles were becoming popular around this time, but my friends and I lived far enough out of mainstream America that we weren't very aware of popular stars in general. I had never heard of any big bands other than the Beatles. Joni Mitchel or famous hard rock stars who weren't on television were unknown to me. In fact, I had not heard of the group, Chicago, or of Billy Joel until I returned from Indonesia to the USA in the nineties.

I was, however, a fan of The Everly Brothers, Ricky Nelson, Fabian, and a few others because they had been on the Ed Sullivan Show or a TV series. My mom let me buy very few rock and roll records. She let me know that this music didn't please her. It didn't bother me very much, though I did listen to modern music at lunchtime in the school cafeteria. After lunch, all of us danced the *Stroll* which was a very mild line dance. Christian kids like me never went to school dances, even a prom, but those times after lunch were great fun. We, instead, had Prom Parties hosted by Youth for Christ in Meadville. These parties lasted all night and included bowling, good food and interaction with boys (and girls) from other schools!

I don't remember begging my mother for things we couldn't afford. I had things in my mind that I wished for, but I knew in my heart that she was doing the best she could. She told me that she and her female colleagues earned less than the male faculty members earned. Our school district was also one of the poorer in the area.

Some of my clothes came second-hand from the Salvation Army or new from the Sears Roebuck Catalogue on Christmas, unless I needed a fancy dress for chorus or graduation. Then Mom was very generous, and once or twice we splurged at a fancy-dress shop in Corry. I remember the dress we bought for my graduation; it was pastel pink with white embroidery all over it. Later, I had my engagement picture taken in it.

Thankfully, none of the twenty-seven kids in my class were from wealthy families. One or two were very poor with rags stuffed in the broken windowpanes of their homes. Others were from homes where their fathers were farmers and factory workers.

HIGH SCHOOL

I took the SATs in my junior year and got a score of eight hundred in total. It was unimportant to me or Mom; I wonder if I might not have filled in half the blanks on the math sheet.

I enjoyed school because I was curious and liked to learn about the world. Math was a mystery to me though, and it still is. I managed to skip every math course in high school except Algebra I, II and Geometry. I remember sitting down in Chemistry class and transferring out the next day. I never even entered Trigonometry. How did I manage to graduate from high school? Well, I took a lot of languages, extra credits, and Biology. Who knows, for sure?

I have recently read about a condition called, "Math Dyslexia"[17] and I wonder if it's a real thing, and if I've had that all my life. **I discovered this week that this condition is officially called "Dyscalculia."** The more I try to focus on numbers the worse I do. In nursing school, I was terrified that I would calculate the wrong dosage of medication for a patient, and I always had someone check me. For that reason alone, I didn't go on to become an

---

17 - A learning disorder that affects a person's ability to do math. Much like dyslexia disrupts areas of the brain related to reading. *Wikipedia*

RN. I wasn't confident I could do the numbers. I never volunteer to keep the tab whether in bowling or in a card game. I fear I will make a mistake. I am apt to make mistakes in measuring ingredients in cooking too. I prefer to just loosely follow a recipe but if I make something special, I will check and recheck to be sure I've read the recipe correctly. That's where my OCD appears.

It has been a pattern in my life that when I'm unsure of something, I become clumsy and self-conscious. The more effort I make, the more I stumble. Making a speech or leading a group is like that. I feel good about impromptu speaking, and if I'm impassioned about a subject, or Bible Study, I can do it. But, often, the more I practice, the more nervous I become.

I'm like that with many things. When I decide to do something, I can stick to it, but if I falter and question myself too much about that decision, I become anxious and might fail.

I loved writing term papers and essays like my mom had, but I never wrote them for other people for pay as she told me she did. One term paper I was especially proud of was my defense of American Black English as a course in high school. This was long before I had heard of the term Ebonics.[18] I theorized that Black English should be regarded as a valid form of language. I think I got a C or D on that paper.

I seldom thought deeply about what I would write, but I had a natural ability to connect thoughts

---

18- African American English, especially when regarded as a language in its own right rather than as a dialect of standard English. *Wikipedia*

and compose good papers. At least, I received good enough grades. Academics were not a high priority for me, although I received mostly A's and B's. I enjoyed taking exams because it was my way to discover what I knew. I seldom felt it was necessary to "cram" for an exam, though I may have.

Besides enjoying English and Spanish, one of my favorite classes was Mr. Frisina's Biology. He had a reputation among some of us, as a bully. He was husky and gruff and enjoyed bellowing, easily intimidating students. Our assignment in his class was to give oral reports each week on an article we found in the newspaper on a subject related to Biology.

I would give my report with the goal of making the entire class laugh and as a bonus, I aimed at making Mr. Frisina laugh aloud. I usually succeeded. I loved this class, watching Mr. Frisina sitting in the back of the class with his head down, arms folded across his chest, struggling his hardest not to laugh. It made my day.

When I wasn't up front giving my report, I sat in the back row of his class with the unruly boys. We would make jokes and giggle and Mr. Frisina would call out,

"Miss Wills, is there something you'd like to share with the rest of the class?"

My partner in crime was *Bobbie*. He was very cute and never did any homework.

I participated in all the drama presentations and chorus where I sang second soprano. I loved going to district chorus where I could meet and form hopeful friendships with boys from other schools. I always hoped these relationships would last but they never did. Of course, we all had our autograph books and later, yearbooks where we faithfully wrote of our devotion to one another.

I remember things happening in high school that seem surreal. When we were fifteen, I had a boyfriend, *Steve*, from out in the rural area of Rome Township. He walked thirteen miles into school during a blizzard one day because the buses weren't running. He told me he did this to see me. He wasn't a great fan of school, so I assumed it was true.

I was a terrible girlfriend to *Steve*. One bitter winter night, his family lost their home and all their possessions when their house burned to the ground. Instead of feeling compassion for his family, I threw a fit because my mother's silver ring was lost in the fire. I insisted that he go back and look for it. I knew I was awful and the worst part was he was kind and sorry about it as I knew he would be. I was ready to break up with him and didn't know how. I was a real jerk.

One day at our community fair, a friend and I were walking along the gravel driveway behind the school and a large horse came galloping toward us. It showed no sign of stopping and my friend stood frozen in its path. I pulled her out of the way just in time as it ran past us.

A freakishly similar thing happened years later to another of my college friends on a sidewalk in Philadelphia. We were walking past a construction site when a man carrying a huge beam came stumbling toward us. It appeared that he had momentum and couldn't stop himself. I pulled my friend, Marilyn, who was frozen in place, out of the way, as the man with that huge beam flew past us. All the construction workers had stopped working to watch in that split second when this happened.

Our high school, though small, was divided into different social groups: I hung with the smart kids, the teacher's kids, the farmers, deer hunters, and the outcast kids. We all had something in common which was a sharp sense of humor. I seldom spent time with the athletes, though there were athletes in every group. However, none of the athletes were among the rebels or outcasts. I think we shared in common the ability to laugh at ourselves. The athletes rarely had that ability.

Mom wanted me to have fun in the summertime, so she discouraged me from working. I wasn't aware of any of my classmates who worked except on their family farms.

My first job was babysitting. I was successful at those jobs which began from the time I was twelve. The first time I babysat, I had to make hotdogs and I called my mom to ask her how to do it. I thought I should stick them on a fork and cook them over the gas flame. She told me to boil them in water. Mom and I never ate hotdogs.

The summer of my senior year, I got a job picking cherries with a crew. I lasted one day. A pickup truck came for me before dawn; I got out the door, worked all day and quit. I could not physically tolerate holding my arms up above my head long enough to pick the cherries. Mom never made me feel like a quitter. She was always compassionate and kind to me.

Incidentally, I got my license as soon as I turned

sixteen. I was a good driver because I had a great teacher, Helen Bennett. Once, though, a little girl ran out onto the street and landed on the hood of my Ford Fairlane. Oh boy, did one of my teachers make a huge fuss about that! He was ranting and raving loudly in class about me driving too fast! As it happened, I was driving slowly. I stopped to make sure she was okay, but later, her mother took her to the hospital to make sure. It shook me up. She was scared more than anything else.

The State Police came to our house because her mom reported me for reckless driving. Plenty of witnesses testified that I was driving slowly and other than my being shaken there were never any serious repercussions. I did feel a bit of resentment though, towards the science teacher who yelled and hollered that day as if I were a spoiled rich kid who was speeding around school with no regard to safety. He may have felt that way.

I mentioned that I had a bad case of acne during my high school years, and some scarring afterwards. This was complicated by Rosacea.[19] I seldom thought about this, and Mom had told me to "smile" throughout my life, which for better or worse, had worked to my advantage. Mom had tried everything to help me to overcome the acne.

She had such a beautiful complexion, but she never made me feel bad. I wonder if my struggle with acne might had stymied her. She frequently advised me to wash my face and hands when I came in from school or a trip so I would feel refreshed. I

19- Rosacea is a condition that causes redness and often small, red, pus-filled bumps on the face. *Wikipedia*

still keep this regimen into my older age, and I do feel renewed afterwards.

In the meantime, in the process of treating my acne, I took antibiotics, even birth control pills, though it never occurred to me in 1965 to mention it nor to have sex with my boyfriends. Nothing helped my complexion. The very few beauty tips mom ever passed on to me were to wash my face in cold water and to rub upwards, always upwards. My acne was far beyond those tips.

I used Cuticura soap for years, but the itchy red rash remained. Even today, when I see a teenager with a case of fiery acne, I can feel the throbbing in my cheeks. Eventually it subsided, but to this day, I bear facial scars.

Aside from that, I was very healthy during my high school and college years; I think being happy and actively engaged in life influences our good health.

Trip to Maine

VALUES

Loyalty to family was high on Mom's list of values, even as she raised me to honor God. She built up years of resentment to anyone who tried to take advantage of her and at times imagined offense when there wasn't one. She taught me to care for the poor and disadvantaged by her example, but I never heard her talk about how blessed we were. In fact, I got the impression that she felt we were disadvantaged. I on the other hand grew to place a high value on authenticity.

I wish I could say that Mom taught me more positive values, but she was relentless in her push to not let anyone take advantage of her. I sometimes got the impression that she also felt the need to take care that I didn't take advantage of her. She never called me names, though and I always felt we were a family unit fortified against the world.

As an adult, I have sometimes wondered if my presence was a painful reminder of my father's taking advantage of her and ruining her life. Sometimes, I thought to myself, "She's so nice to other people, I wonder why she's not nicer to me?" She liked to be right, and I don't remember her affirming me for having good ideas. When I became an adult and took her out to lunch, I always left a tip. Mom inevitably swept past and picked it up.

She would say, "They get enough." There was no arguing with her about it, but I tried to slip it back on to the table before we left. Sometimes she would say to me, "Believe you me," and then go on to tell me one of her "truths."

She had a way of winking at me defiantly that could send a chill up my spine. It signaled, "No one is taking advantage of me, believe you me." She implied that someone was trying to deceive her.

As Mom aged, she grew less inhibited and more stubborn. I don't remember noticing it as much when I was young. As I think of her then, she was often calm and quietly peaceful. She seldom yelled; I was the one who yelled.

Mom loved watching the birds and fed them every winter. She went around the neighborhood and interfered with the neighbor's dogs when she felt they were neglected. She didn't care if neighbors saw her feeding their dogs. Occasionally she reported them to the Humane Society. One neighbor eventually gave their dog to Mom. They interpreted her interest to her loneliness. She instead felt she was rescuing their neglected dog.

▲ ▲ ▲

Cars were a fascination of mine. I knew all the models that passed by our house. In sixth grade I told everyone that my first car was going to be a Corvette! I believed it! My mom found out through the school grapevine and told me it was not going to happen, but she thought it was a good joke.

When we finally did get our first car, it was a Ford Fairlane 500 sedan in a beautiful shade of blue. However, our second car, which we bought in my senior year, was a 1966 White Ford Mustang two-door with a black interior. Mom had the custom of keeping our cars for about two years and then trading them in before they began giving us any problems. I loved that Mustang but two years later like clockwork we traded it in for a green Ford Pinto.

Mom used to compliment me by saying I drove "like a New York City cab driver!" I felt so proud when she told me that. I don't know why. I interpreted it to mean I drove skillfully and assertively. Mom taught me to always pay attention to car maintenance; that the fluids were filled up and that the tires were correctly inflated. I realized much later this was her way of passing on her knowledge from the time she managed the filling station at Riceville.

Mom and I had fun together, most often when we were away from the house. One summer, in my junior year, we rented a small RV and traveled to Maine with Mom's best friend Lorene Byler and our two dogs. I was the one and only driver at sixteen, because Lorene didn't feel comfortable driving the RV. I loved it and loved mastering backing and learning how to manage curves.

My mom was often spontaneous about travel and when I would suggest a trip, her eyes would sparkle! She was willing to pick up at a moment's notice and go for a ride. She liked to travel especially after I got my license, and she trusted my driving. I loved that about her. Another year we traveled to Montreal with her teacher friend, Marie Patterson. Wherever we traveled Mom always speculated about the Native Americans that had lived in the area long ago. Mom and I collected rocks and seashells too. I have continued this tradition by collecting Petosky rocks in Michigan, dolomite in Palestine and dark gray volcanic rocks in Indonesia.

▲   ▲   ▲

Sometimes we walked up town to see her friend, a retired teacher, Helen Bennet who taught me to drive in her pristine cream-colored 1965 Ford Galaxie with red leather interior. She taught me defensive driving, which has remained a lifetime priority for me. Mom chose her to teach me because she felt safe when she rode with Helen. She often complimented Helen on her smooth driving and told me that she hoped I would drive like her. Mom's fear of driving hindered her all her life. She managed to not pass her fear on to me but raised me so that I was free to love driving.

Originally, we planned for me to transfer to Corry High School in my junior year so I could take Driver's Education. This became somewhat of a personal scandal. Corry High School was our school's archenemy as far as community schools went. It wasn't about athletics because we were in a completely different league. Corry had been attempting for years to get our school to merge with their school district and our little district was resisting! Mom's decision as a Spartansburg school teacher to send me to the Corry School District was akin to treason! Sparta faculty were offended. We had been fighting against consolidating with their district for decades.

I applied, transferred, and went for one day of classes. That evening, the Corry School District Superintendent telephoned to let us know that they were not going to allow me, as a single student to attend their school. It was "everyone or no one!" I was a pariah for a little while, and I know all the teachers were mad at Mom. The alleged reason I transferred was because of Driver's Education, but Mom liked to make a statement, and wanted to make a point that Sparta didn't have Driver's Ed. It was humiliating to return to school the first day having failed in my attempted transfer to a better school. Several of the teachers were happy to gloat and made a point to rub it in, announcing it loudly in class.

Mom took more than a little delight in being contrary and grew more so as she aged. If I expected her to do one thing, she often did the opposite to be ornery. This was one of our ongoing arguments. At times, I literally stood in her path, while we bobbed back and forth, she trying to get past me as I stood my ground until she listened to me, which she did do occasionally. She didn't tolerate my having different opinions from hers. She would say to me, "When you've been a teacher for thirty-six years, you'll know I'm right." In response I'd shake my head and walk away. What could I say? I wonder if she felt powerless, so she exerted herself in the one way she knew how to do.

Sometimes our home life felt stressful because Mom had such a contrary streak as did I. On St Patrick's Day, she insisted that we wear Orange to flaunt William of Orange and to protest the Catholics. We were alike in our contrary natures. I seemed compliant in comparison to Mom except when I sassed her. She was usually against the status quo. If I told her something was done one way, she tended to do the opposite. When she got her feathers ruffled, I felt conflicted over whether to be proud of her rebellion or to disagree with her views. It's not easy to be a rebel when your mother is setting the standard.

Mom could become oppositional and fired up over getting back at people who did not treat her or me fairly, though she also showed kindness and spoke nicely about her friends. She had a scary look about her where she narrowed her eyes and glared. At times, I felt she looked at me as someone suspicious.

Looking back, I think that I learned that it was okay to disagree with people because of my mom's example. I became wary, in the sense that I enjoyed people, but I was also guarded and on alert concerned that they might be trying to trick me or take advantage of me. I had good instincts and rapidly sensed when someone was insincere. This has served me well and saved me from wasting time with abusive, insincere men.

I have been in one or two situations in my life when I felt endangered, and I knew right away to look for an exit. Once, I was helping a young Lesbian woman in Philadelphia who intentionally tried to keep me from leaving her apartment by standing between me and her door. I sensed that this would happen and persuaded her to let me out without a fuss.

I never felt the pressure to have sex or grant favors to boys so they would like me. Though as a girl without a father figure, I could have been vulnerable and was indeed always on the lookout for a boyfriend. I had handsome boyfriends who never tried to compromise my ideals about sex. The one thing boys tried to pressure me to do when I was a teenager was to smoke. One of them bet me that I would be smoking by the time I was twenty-one. I laughed at him. Another, who wasn't my boyfriend, kissed me and blew cigar smoke in my mouth. It was an obsession with those boys! I always felt that I as a girl was responsible for setting the guidelines in my dating relationships.

▲ ▲ ▲

I must have become aware of fashion at some point because I remember telling Mom that something she or I wore looked old-fashioned or out of style. Her predictable reply would be, "They wear anything these days." I inevitably answered, "But not that."

Another one of Mom's phrases that lingered in my mind for years was, "beware of the unguarded moment," or the "unforeseen moment" when a tragedy might befall us. She meant, never let down your guard! This applied to losing a purse or having a puppy run over. It made me a particularly good defensive driver. She also warned me to "never marry a Catholic or a N____r."

I wondered where Mom originally got her ideas regarding race and her interest in Eugenics.[20]

Once I discovered a set of small blue Eugenics books on her shelves. When I asked about them, they disappeared, and I never saw them again.

---

20 - Eugenics is the study of how to arrange reproduction within a human population to increase the occurrence of heritable characteristics regarded as desirable. Developed largely by Sir Francis Galton as a method of im proving the human race, it was adopted by the Nazis as a means of dis crimination. It has been discredited as unscientific. *Wikipedia*

I was bothered more by my mom's unsolicited advice after I grew up and had a child of my own. I wonder if she realized as I did with our girls, that she had missed properly preparing me to be a mother until it was too late? When I became a mother myself, I didn't have much confidence that I was doing a good job and I wished that she could have affirmed me. Instead, once she said to me, "Who would think you would be a good mother?" Fortunately, she had given me her book on raising children written by Dr. Spock. I loosely followed this and advice from Jon's Aunt Helen Blauvelt in the book *Breastfeeding Your Baby*. Both books helped me grow as a new mother.

When I was younger, I had asked her to teach me how to make her delicious bread, rolls and pies. She always put me off until another time. When I asked if I could wash the dishes that were piling up or to help to straighten or vacuum and Mom would say, "Oh, no, you'll have to do all those chores when you're married." It was hard for me because I never learned how to do those disciplines of homemaking. Fortunately, we lived much of those early years with house servants in Indonesia who did the household chores.

Mom criticized me for being too strict with our daughter. Once when I got out of the car to spank Juliana for getting out of her infant seat, Mom threatened to call the police. Mom had not really been good at setting strong limits for me; she was mostly concerned about my sassing. So, I went overboard in the opposite way, enforcing rules.

Naturally, I really tried to affirm my own daughters, but I learned that even a hint of unsolicited motherly advice comes off as criticism. I so wanted to be unlike my mother, but unfortunately, they didn't see me as affirming. I wish I had been better at it. I'm thankful that our children had other people in their lives to affirm them. God knew their needs.

One thing I did differently from my mom, though, was to admit when I was wrong. I don't remember my mom ever saying she was sorry or asking me to forgive her. It just wasn't done in her generation, at least not in her family. I imagine she had never heard her overbearing father say those words. However, she spoke about her own mother as if she were a saint and talked about her a lot. Mom adored her mother, Bertha.

I am glad I was able to tell Mom that I loved her when I grew older and to sincerely ask forgiveness for all of my behavior from when I was younger.

After I had been especially naughty and was feeling ashamed and remorseful, Mom would say, "Mom loves you." I don't remember her directly saying, "I love you." I knew she did, though. Before I went to sleep each night, she said, "Night-night, love you, see you in the morning." I needed to hear her say this each night. It felt like it was necessary to say and to hear if we were to survive the night. This also felt true for our praying for protection before we left the house.

SEARCHING FOR MY
TWO DADS

LIFELONG FRIENDSHIPS

Mom had a few close friends who lived outside of our town, teachers like herself, whom we visited when I learned to drive. Betty Southwick, Marie Pattison, Lorene Byler, and Ella Augustine were her friends. Margaret Bradley was another friend from her life in Riceville. I loved to take her to visit these friends after I got my license. I sat and talked with them as if we were the same age. They enjoyed my stories, and I enjoyed their attention.

When I came home on breaks from college, I seldom visited my own friends. I had moved away from my hometown circle into each new circle of friends preserving very few of my former circles through occasional newsletters. One or two friendships lasted through the years and now others have recently been renewed. These reborn friendships are delightful.

Mom and I visited elderly women in our town regularly. Several friends stand out as unusual. Mom told me that not everyone accepted these friends as we did. Helen Bennett, a widow, and former teacher lived with her widowed friend, Dorothy May. They conveyed total acceptance to Mom and me in a way that others seldom did. They chain smoked and laughed unreservedly, called Mom "Gin," and me, "Mare." Their high-spirited banter was always interesting and I appreciated how they included me in discussing politics and other world events, even valuing my opinions.

Another couple we visited lived across the street from us. Helen Bates was the mayor of our town and her regular job was as a factory worker. Her housemate, Millie Hurlburt, was the local hairdresser whose salon was in their home. We all shared a love of animals and once I worked with Helen to rescue a baby bird that had a broken wing. Another draw for me was that Helen had a Pinto pony named Spot. I always hoped to ride him but didn't realize what an ordeal it was to get him saddled and ready to ride.

Helen, as Mayor of Spartansburg, led the yearly Fair Parade riding Spotty. He was magnificent. When they led the parade, they wore sparkling silver outfits that matched. What a splendid sight!

These four women were indeed different from our other friends. They always wore men's pants and had noticeably short hairstyles. Millie and Dorothy May had both been married with children. Now society labels women who live together as these friends did as lesbian, however, I never heard that word. Mom and I made wonderful memories as we visited with them.

I used to visit an elderly woman named Irene Kistler on my way home from school. She was one of my favorites who often invited me in to sit down and chat. Sometimes she had milk and cookies for me. I enjoyed taking time to share with her the news from town and asking her about her garden. I liked to walk my dogs down to her house for her to fuss over. Sometimes, she took me into her garden to cut flowers for my mom.

As I grew older, I was allowed to cross the dangerous curve in front of our house to visit one of my mom's oldest friends, Geraldine Brown, and her husband, Harry. I loved sitting in their front office where he conducted his motor home sales business. He occasionally unlocked one of the new models on his lot for an hour or so when he had people interested in buying one. If I timed my arrival at precisely the right time, as his customers were about to leave, he would let me sit inside and pretend it was my own perfect house for a little while.

I continued my visits to the elderly women until they all passed away. I remember sitting in Ada Rifenberick's quaint Victorian parlor as she sat in her rocking chair. With a shawl over her shoulders, she reminded me of the painting of Grandma Moses. I felt such privilege that I had the opportunity to know these women. I wish I had known how to ask better questions. This is true for my mom, too. All these older people had in common their willingness and interest to sit and listen to me, a young person. They heard my latest news and told me theirs. I will always remember this as a key to friendships with young people.

SEARCHING FOR MY TWO DADS

ENGAGED

I was engaged in my junior year of high school to a farmhand, named Eli from New York State who was seven years older than me. He drove a tractor past our house mornings and evenings to the farm up the hill behind our house where he worked. With my habit of sitting outside on the front steps every day, we saw each other, began talking and then dating.

I could tell Mom didn't like the idea, but she didn't say anything. Some of my teachers were very vocal about my engagement, haranguing me in front of the class about what a bad choice I was making, a "smart girl like you." That Science teacher who yelled about me hitting the girl with my car used to yell about me making a big mistake also so everyone could hear. The teachers felt I should have some sort of career to fall back on.

Eli and I had purchased a nice kitchen table and set of chairs, dishes and a stove and were all set to be married after I graduated from high school. I hadn't given even a bit of thought to a date, a wedding dress or ceremony, though.

Eli quit his job on the farm and began working at Rogers Structural Steel in Corry to begin building up a nest egg. Every day he would go home to the place he boarded completely covered in black grime and take a bath in Joy dish detergent to try to get it off.

Eli is the one who taught me to drive a stick shift on his 1957 Ford car, but he let me keep it before I really knew how to drive it on hills. One day I was going to pick him up from work. This involved driving up the steepest hill in the whole county. I got halfway up the hill and had no idea what to do. The car began rolling down the hill backwards. It rolled faster and faster out of control. Fortunately, I was good at backing up, even at high speed. Unfortunately, *Eli* had a lot of empty beer bottles stashed in the back of his car which made a frightful noise as the car sped backwards down the steep hill. Eventually, I figured out how to shift and recovered from my downward spiral.

Though this was the era of the sixties, and in much of the USA, young people were rebelling against their parents and having sex, I remained firm in my decision to wait to have sex until I was married. I have been glad that I made this decision and that all my boyfriends honored it, though we were very affectionate.

In the spring of my senior year, I became interested in a junior, *"Greg"* who was a Christian. *Eli* was not interested in church. *Greg* was a charismatic flirt and began to woo me away from *Eli*. We hung out at church together. His family owned a farm and once *Greg's* pony kicked me into an electric fence. Talk about romantic.

One time, *Greg* came to my back door when *Eli* was in our front room. This was quite a thrill for a silly teenage girl, but I didn't feel right being a cheater. I began to pull away from *Eli* but I didn't know how to say the words to break off our engagement. *Eli* wasn't getting my hints. It surely taught me a lesson about being straightforward and not dragging out breakups and other unpleasant conversations. I had not yet learned the words to be kind but firm. I learned from this failure. Ironically, under my high school yearbook photo, I chose the words, "To be a success at everything I try." I had ambitions I didn't fully recognize and didn't respond well to limits. From the time I was a small child I had a desire to go around the countryside in a green Volkswagen van telling people about Jesus. I seem to have temporarily lost sight of that vision.

Eli was a truly kind and thoughtful man. One time he gave me a Beagle puppy we named Jeroboam, nicknamed Jerry. Another time, he took me to see a field full of golden Daffodils. I forget whether it was him or my next boyfriend, Larry. One or the other.

On the evening of our high school graduation in June 1966, when our principal announced what each student was doing after graduation, *Eli* got the message. Our principal announced that I was going to Erie, PA to study to become a Licensed Practical Nurse[21]. I had discussed this with *Eli*, and he didn't want me to do it. He had traditional ideas about marriage and living within limited finances.

As I glanced out at the audience, I saw him put his face in his hands as the principal spoke and I thought to myself, "Well, it's over now." That ended our relationship. We had poor communication skills, and he didn't want me to be a wife with a career. I had no regrets.

---

21 - LPN's work closely with RN's to provide routine care for sick or injured patients. They have less responsibility than RNs.

Why didn't my mom try to intervene to stop this unfortunate relationship? I know she must have prayed and talked it over with her friends, but I don't remember her talking to me a lot about it probably because I had my mind set. She also may have thought about how she had resisted her own father's advice when she married my father. *Eli's* parents were both heavy drinkers and smokers. When I came home from visiting them with the strong smell of cigarette smoke on my clothes, Mom said this alone made her sick. Their home was little more than a large unpainted, drafty shack, which they didn't maintain.

I became good friends with *Eli's* sister-in-law, Deborah, and really regretted it when our friendship ended.

Eli's mother called me one last time and ripped into me for wasting her son's time and keeping the kitchen furniture he had purchased. I told her I was sorry, that it was better to break up before we got married than afterwards. He could have the table and chairs and stove if he wanted them. He said that he never wanted to see them again. My mom had provided the tiny little diamond engagement ring, so there was no loss to him there. End of story.

Before our breakup, when I turned eighteen, Mom sat *Eli* and me down to show us photos of my father and to explain to us for the first time, what had happened to him. I sat and wept. I asked her why she had never talked to me about him before and she answered, "I couldn't say anything good about him, so I didn't want to say anything."

Whenever she spoke about my father from then on she made the excuse for him saying he had been the spoiled youngest son of a large family.

Eli is the only other person besides Harriott, whom my mother spoke to about my father. No one else had heard that story before I told it.

Later, Harriott told me the rest of the story. My mother felt terrified of my father when he took her down into that distant field to shoot Skeet when she was heavily pregnant with me. When he speculated, "I wonder what would happen if this gun would go off and kill you and the baby?" he revealed what was in his heart. From that moment on she knew that she couldn't trust him and that her marriage was doomed.

Her father had counseled her against the marriage, but she told Harriott, and later she told me, that she felt it was her last chance at happiness. She had rejected a number of marriage proposals while she cared for her mother before she died from cancer. Mom feared love had passed her by.

Imagine the trauma that occurred during my time in the womb. May God forgive him.

My relationship with *Greg* lasted long enough for me to break up with *Eli*. Immediately afterwards, *Greg* went on a fishing trip to Canada with his father and I never heard from him again. I know God used *Greg* to prevent me from making a marriage I would regret.

Sadly, I also believe something traumatizing occurred on that trip that caused *Greg* to disappear. As soon as he graduated from high school, he left home and his family never heard from him again. He never spoke about it to anyone in our town. It broke his mother's heart.

After my engagement ended Mom's primary advice from my senior year onward was, "Don't settle" which I understood to mean, that I should look beyond Spartansburg for fulfillment of my hopes and dreams. She hoped I would look beyond my hometown boys for a future spouse.

The summer of my senior year, I had surgery to remove four of my wisdom teeth. Doctor Earnest came by my hospital room to say hello. He had been our family physician my entire life. It was the last time I would see him. I was hospitalized and I loved being in the hospital! This began my lifelong love of the medical field. Oddly, two more of my teeth disappeared and I have no memory of what happened to them. I have five teeth remaining on the left bottom side of my mouth.

When I went back to my childhood dentist, Dr. Amy in Corry in 1984, he asked, "What happened to you?"

I felt a bit indignant when I said, "I thought you would know."

But I feel thankful for two reasons. My mom had dentures for as long as I remember. She must have had her teeth removed in her thirties or early forties. The second reason I feel thankful is that a doctor in Ithaca in 1984 wanted to do surgery to repair my protruding lower jaw and to implant teeth in my gums. We couldn't afford it.

He predicted that when I was older, my face would sag to the left. However, the cost he quoted at that time was $4,000. My face hasn't sagged as he predicted, at least not yet, and I'm seventy-five. It is now too late to do the implants.

CHURCH LIFE

It wasn't an exaggeration to say I grew up in the church, from the time I lived with the Robbies as a toddler. I attended all the Vacation Bible Schools in our town. Mom told me that my first Bible School was at the Mennonite Church as a toddler where I saved up all my "offering money" until the very last day and then dumped the contents of my purse out into the collection plate. I did another funny thing at my first Christian and Missionary Alliance Vacation Bible school program when I kissed one of my classmates, Mark Crosby, right up on the stage. It made everyone in the congregation laugh. I have no memory of either of these incidents nor of why I did them.

When I was little I'd go to sleep at night sincerely praying:

> *"Now I lay me down to sleep, I pray the Lord my soul to keep. If I should die before I wake, I pray the Lord my soul to take."*

I never felt afraid that I would die in the night despite the words in this prayer. I had learned to trust in a good God who had good plans. Mom and the Robbies had been laying down foundations of trust in my life. Despite the fact that Mom was a fearful person, and I sometimes felt anxious, overall,

I believed that God was looking out for me with a smile on His face.

I attended the Christian and Missionary Alliance church throughout my school years and beyond. People in the Spartansburg congregation loved and accepted me. As I grew up in the church, I became friends with the pastors and their wives, began to lead the youth group and to take part in the choir. The church was a large part of my life. I took piano lessons from one pastor's wife, Mrs. Lindsay, for five years. She was an elegant, refined lady from Maine. During those years, I learned many good things and never was taught prejudice or dislike toward any other people. Our teachings centered on Jesus Christ. I think part of my attraction to church was that I was gregarious and people were friendly to me.

I carried my Bible to school every day because that was a part of the Christian culture of the day. I might have helped to establish that tradition. Mom raised me to have great dependence and trust in God and encouraged me to pray.

The Christian kids in the school attended the group called Youth for Christ or YFC. I was an officer in the group and once attended a summer YFC Conference in Ocean City MD. This was one of my first opportunities to travel away from my hometown with a large group of kids to meet thousands of other young Christian teenagers. It was the first time I heard the challenge, "Christ through you can change the world!" I embraced the concept with a passion. I didn't realize it at the time but my desire to influence the world took root that week in Ocean City, New Jersey. I occasionally stumbled into excessive zeal but throughout my life, apathy became a far greater trap.

As I grew older, I became a regional officer in YFC and attended monthly meetings in Meadville. Though I was a leader, I was still shy and not very confident. Usually I chose to be Secretary, not Treasurer. Of course, for me it was mostly about meeting guys. The more activities I participated in, the more opportunity I had to meet cool Christian guys who weren't from my school.

Even though I attended church regularly, spirituality was not yet a priority for me. I hadn't given any thought to creation or my purpose on earth. I seem to have entirely missed the idea presented by pastors and teachers over the years that it is possible to have a personal relationship with God. I did remember though, one of our Pastors, Tom Lindsay saying to our congregation, "People do what they really want to do." This statement made a lasting impression on my young life.

I continued attending church activities, leading and teaching our youth group. I loved when missionaries from around the world came to speak about their work. Two of my favorite speakers were a local couple, Dale and Opal Linebaugh, who ran a western camping ministry for kids in the area. They sang, preached, and wore western-themed clothing, but mostly they manifested love. Dale especially attracted me with his sweet manner. I wanted to be his daughter. He often complimented me on my smile.

One of my foremost desires at that time was to attend their western horse-riding summer camp, Miracle Mountain Ranch.

We never had enough money for me to go. However, I spent every summer of college volunteering as a counselor in one or another summer camp, and I spent one entire summer at Dale and Opal's camp. Our own children were able to go to Miracle Mountain Camp one summer, which was indeed a vicarious wish fulfilment for me. They loved it.

Meanwhile in high school my friends and I remained in our comfortable bubble and no closer to God until my first year at Eastern Mennonite College, in 1968.

OUR HERO

I wanted to write about our friend Troy Murdoch who had a special place in our family from the time I was a little girl. He was my loyal companion and my mother's right-hand man as soon as he could mow a lawn or lift a snow shovel.

The Murdoch family had four boys, a hard-working mother and a red-faced, white-bearded, father nicknamed, "Fuzzy." I never heard Fuzzy speak in a normal tone of voice, but only shouts or mumbles in a voice that sounded like he had pebbles rolling around in his mouth. He glared at everyone as he spoke and his reddish eyes seemed to flash with fire.

People in town felt sorry for the family but especially for Troy who always hung around outdoors. He wore very thick glasses and in today's terms might be considered in the Autism spectrum.

Frequently in the evenings he came across town to watch TV with us, he never had a curfew. He taught mom and me the word, "highlights," which were the coming attractions on TV for the following week which he anticipated with glee.

He didn't advance with his upper classmates in school, though he was fluent in the history of modern warfare and talked about it constantly.

When he talked about WWII battles his face would light up and his bright blue eyes would sparkle. My girlfriends and I decided to take him on as our project and decided that we would tutor him so he could graduate with our class.

Troy did graduate with us even though he was ejected that spring from a car in a drunk driving accident shortly before graduation. He had been drunk, riding with drunk drivers.

Troy

Troy introduced me to the first African American person I ever saw or met personally. One day as he was hitchhiking on the highway, he met a Black teenager. He invited him to my house to look over my collection of comic books. My mom wasn't at home, but I invited them both upstairs to my room to look at comics for several hours. I was a young teenager, the boys were very nice, and we had fun. When they left, our elderly, next door neighbor told my mom. She was also the one who gossiped around town about mom having nine men in her upstairs. We provided plenty of fodder for Elgie's gossip mill.

Mom took it in stride. She warned me to not have any boys visit when she wasn't at home and to not take boys up to my bedroom. As I remember, she established rules when problems arose, not before. Though she and I often argued over my disrespectful words, I was compliant with most rules that she set down, because they were reasonable.

We never knew all that Troy survived as a child; he never once discussed his home life. He was my most loyal friend who considered himself my bodyguard in many situations. We talked once about his hope that we might get married someday, but I kindly let him know that this would not happen. He survived Viet Nam, married a woman who was similarly impaired, had two children, divorced, and unfortunately died of Emphysema at a young age.

SEARCHING FOR MY
TWO DADS

ON THE ROAD IN MY MUSTANG

In September 1966, I packed up my little white Mustang to drive to Erie, Pennsylvania where I had enrolled in a program to become a Licensed Practical Nurse. My first boarding house was downtown with several other career type people. The owner of the house was a critical, older widow named Mrs. Bishoff. She complained about me from the moment I woke up in the morning until I went to bed at night. She said I made too much noise getting out of bed, and walking around my bedroom which was directly over hers. Then when I came in after school, she said I "slammed" the door to my room and stomped around. I did no such thing. It was a real trial for me because I had never been in a situation like this where someone didn't like me from the moment I met them. I tiptoed around the edges of my bedroom and still, she complained.

There was one good thing about my boarding house situation, and it was that I met another boarder, *Jake*, a Mechanical Engineer from Meadville, whom I began to date. A boy from my church, *Gary*, had asked me out and I dated him until he went into the Navy. We never really "clicked." For a while, I was dating both *Gary* from the Navy and *Jake*.

Jake had a little green Volkswagen Beetle and swept me off my feet. He showed me all around Erie, took me out for dinner to nice places. Our relationship lasted for about one year. It was long enough for him to meet my mom and for me to visit his parents in Meadville. His family were committed Roman Catholics, though and this was something neither of us talked about until we did, and we broke up. He was my nicest boyfriend until I met Jon Perry.

Eventually, a friend of mine, in my nursing class, Sharon, found another place for me right around the block from her own boarding house. This was like night and day for me, and a fantastic place for me to live. I had a spacious room with an additional sun porch extending out into the shady backyard. Mrs. Lyda Rogers was a delightful widow lady who was active and invited me to share many of her adventures.

Alice, Mrs. Rogers & Rita

She took me under her wing. I felt like her granddaughter. We watched TV together as she taught me to knit bedroom slippers with exceptionally exacting standards. "If it isn't perfect, rip out the stitches and do them over again."

Her home was spotless, and everything had its place. I discovered that this felt very restful for me. She had a light blue carpet in her living room. We girls were forbidden to eat there. Naturally, it was too tempting for us when Mrs. Rogers was out so we would bring in our food while we watched TV but ran when Mrs. Rogers' car pulled into the driveway. Though she expected me to pick up my things, I never felt pressured or criticized. When I reflect on my two years living in her home, I have happy memories of sharing my life with her.

I mostly remember her cheerful smile that lit up her entire face and her beautiful wavy brown hair tinged with gray. I never knew her age, but she was hardy. I bought a ukulele and learned to play the tune, *Edelweiss* from Anne, the first woman who lived with us. Eventually, two more of my friends, Alice and Rita moved in.

In the meantime, back in my nursing class, we elected Mrs. Jones, an African American woman, and mother of three teenagers as our class president. She was the second Person of Color I had ever met or seen in person. She was a perfect and calming leader for us silly young nursing students. She knew exactly how to help us strike the balance between being serious and cutting loose.

I will always remember when she told us, "You know, out in California, there are these young people who sit around with flowers in their hair. They call them, Flower Children.[22]"

---

22 - The name Flower child originated as a synonym for hippie, especially among the idealistic young people who gathered in San Francisco and the surrounding area during the Summer of Love in 1967. *Wikipedia*

We were wide-eyed at this news. It was 1967! She was much more aware of current events than any of us were.

At this time in my life, I do not remember being aware of the struggle for Civil Rights, or the Viet Nam War, though I had a couple of boyfriends who had enlisted during that time. All I knew was that they had put on a uniform and gone off. I was a very shallow, silly girl. Several of the boys came home with horror stories, but these normally talkative friends didn't really want to talk much about what had happened over there.

I was oblivious to the world outside of mine. I knew nothing about our government and cared nothing about politics. In 1963, I was a Sophomore when JFK was assassinated. I must have taken a cue from my mother's dislike of Catholics, when I said aloud in our school auditorium, "That's okay, I never liked him anyway."

How was it possible to be so insular in the era of media coverage of such historic events? I can't explain it, but I lived it. I kept busy learning to be a nurse, then making a living among people who were like me. No one I knew, not even Mrs. Jones, talked about these things. No one challenged me to step outside my point of view. That's one reason I try to talk about current events now. But would I have been interested back then had anyone challenged me?

I wonder where my mother's deep distrust of Catholics came from. Was it from her experience among immigrant families in Tyler, Pennsylvania? Ironically, her two best friends, Sophie and Bonnibel were Catholics and from immigrant families. Was

Mrs. Moore, the woman who had cheated us out of our money, a Catholic? Mom always warned me against marrying a Catholic. Was this a warning that she had received? I sometimes think that she would have done better to marry her childhood Italian friend and neighbor, Joe Pirralgia, who was Catholic[23], than the Protestant man, my father, whom she eventually married.

Mom read constantly, and widely. On weekends and in later years, she spent every afternoon beside her large kitchen window reading from her many piles of books, newspapers, and magazines. Often, she clipped articles to send to someone. However, she didn't change her mind about some deeply held beliefs. I wasn't aware that I had significant prejudice towards anyone. When I moved to Erie, Sharon, an Irish Catholic girl became my best friend.

I graduated as an LPN in 1967 and was honored to give the keynote address at graduation. I spoke about this moment being the beginning of the rest of our lives. *Gary* came in his Navy uniform, and Mom came with the Southwick family. Their son Curtis was the fellow I had a crush on for my entire high school life. We had never dated, but he was the most handsome fellow I knew. His mom and mine were best friends and though he went to another high school, I always wished we had dated. He went to Viet Nam as a helicopter pilot and trainer, became a Captain, then settled down to teach high school.

---

23 - See my previous book. *Grandmothers*

He died of Cancer due to the Agent Orange[24] used in Nam. What a tragic end to this wonderful young man, and what a horrible thing that he had to use such a deadly chemical.

---

24 - Agent Orange was a toxic, plant-killing chemical (herbicide) that the U.S. Military used to clear foliage during the Vietnam conflict. It was discovered that exposure to Agent Orange effects include Cancer, birth disorders, and life-threatening health complications. Production ended in the 1970s. Roughly three hundred thousand veterans died from Agent Orange exposure. *Vietnam Veterans of America*

JESUS LOVES YOU

While living in Erie, I made regular trips down to Spartansburg to see Mom. I was happy to see her developing interests outside of me. I doubt that I said this in words, though.

Mom in 1990

She ordered a Dulcimer and began taking lessons. She had been proud of her own mother who played the banjo. She collected books for the new Amish school and became friends with the Amish women in our community. This had come about in her

147

last years of teaching when she had newly arrived Amish children in her classes. In her later years she wrote letters to government officials to protest votes she didn't agree with. She always enjoyed her birds and naturalizing her yard which was beginning to resemble a forest.

During that time, I became a mentor to a couple of young people who were growing in their Christian faith. They weren't connecting with any growing believers in local churches.

This was the era of the Jesus People Movement which many theologians say was the last *Great Awakening*[25]. One of my friends from high school, Andy, became part of a Christian Coffee House ministry in Union City called, The Way In. We rode over together and talked about Jesus. I sat and talked with the kids who dropped into the coffee house. This was happening in the East at the same time as the *Jesus Revolution* out in California in the late sixties and early seventies. I never saw any of these young people showing up in our local churches, though my perspective was limited.

This proved to be a good place to talk with young people interested in spiritual things. A few were on drugs but searching for something more. We served food, tea, coffee, and friendship. I loved the candlelit atmosphere, with *Andy* and his friends softly strumming guitars and singing Christian songs in the background.

---

25 - The Great Awakening was a religious revival that impacted the English colonies in America during the 1730s and 1770s. It was a period when spirituality and religious devotion were revived. Prominent names were Jonathan Edwards and George Whitefield. *Wikipedia*

Later, *Andy* auditioned for and got into a country music quartet similar to The Oak Ridge Boys, who were popular in our area of Western Pennsylvania. After he joined the group, he came to visit me to talk about life on the road with a sense of excitement but some regret. The last time we talked I felt disappointed because he said that the members of the group told him he needed to buy a big flashy ring. This is what was expected of the performers.

Another friend I mentored was *Scott*, who played a guitar and had a band. When he came to our house, we talked about spiritual things. *Scott* married a godly woman and became a family man. He supports our ministry to this day. Another friend was *Karen*, a high school senior whom I met on her high school cruise. We spent many years talking about her spiritual life as she grew to love the Lord. It is encouraging to me that these young friends continue to walk with God decades later.

When I remember all the young people I knew who passed through the coffee houses searching for their purpose in life, I am amazed that it never occurred to me to wonder about my purpose.

I went along in my life, assuming that I could be useful, serving other people, enjoying conversations. I was talking about God, though my relationship with him was not personal or based on emotion. It was more based on actions and common sense.

Many young people were heading out to California or demonstrating against the Viet Nam War. None of my close friends chose to do that with their lives. The nurses I studied with graduated and had regular jobs.

Even though I wasn't yet a strong believer, I know my mother and the Robbies gave me a strong spiritual foundation, and the Christian Missionary Alliance Church, Reverend Lindsay, Reverend May, and their wives along with Margaret Morris added to that foundation. It probably also helped that I inherited my mother's stubborn, defiant spirit. I didn't easily bend to pressure.

The Lord guided and protected me as his partly orphaned daughter. Why? Mom used to pray for me every time I left the house, to "Lead, guide, keep and protect us." He did and he does.

I AM A NURSE!

Several of us nursing students had jobs waiting for us in Hamot Hospital when we graduated in 1967. Hamot, at the end of State Street, right on the shore of Lake Erie was a prestigious area hospital. I chose the night shift and had an exciting and exhausting year.

I am a nurse

My first position was alone on the cardiac wing, with another nurse floating from a neighboring unit. One night, I made one o'clock rounds to monitor my patient's vital signs and to make sure they were all breathing.

On my next rounds around two am I spoke with a very nice patient in a private room who was having trouble sleeping. The next hour when I made my rounds, I thought he was asleep, but I stepped further into his room to check on him and I couldn't find any vital signs. He was dead.

I was shocked. He was the first patient who had passed away on my watch. I called the attending physician, Dr. Izzo, who came immediately. His first words to me were, "This isn't your fault." He spent time sitting with me at the nurses' station and told me that the man had been in a very fragile condition, that they knew he could go at any time. He patted my arm reassuring me that there was nothing that I could have done.

I will always remember the kindness of this doctor. I wish that a nurse on the previous shift had given me a bit of a heads up about the patient, perhaps warning me of his unstable condition. However, I know from my experience that nurses can't anticipate everything that might occur when we are giving our nightly notes.

Another floor I volunteered to cover was the Alcoholic Rehab and Chronic Conditions ward. I had alcoholics who in the middle of the night would go into delirium tremors so badly that they began hallucinating. Sometimes when this happened they threw their glass IV bottles across the room, ripping the IVs out of their arms and creating a huge mess, waking up everyone on the ward.

My procedure was to call an orderly so he could restrain the patient while I called an RN to give him an injection to calm him down. I was then the one to clean up the broken glass.

We also had chronically ill patients with conditions such as MS and other Auto-Immune diseases. One patient who was in great pain with Arthritis, greeted me each morning when I did my final rounds with, "Good Morning, Glory!" She was so bright and cheery, despite her pain.

Blackie was an alcoholic homeless person who received burns over 90% of his body when some teenagers threw kerosene on him as a cruel prank. He was on our ward for months. I left the hospital before he recovered.

I had crushes during those days too. *Larry T* was a male nurse who often worked the night shift with me. We had a lot of fun together, running up and down the halls, playing tag with squirt bottles, admittedly laughing at some of the Alzheimer's patients' antics, but never in any way compromising anyone's care. A Korean Intern, Dr. Paul Han, used to chase me around and trap me in the medication room behind the nurses' station where he would coax me for a kiss.

Occasionally, I worked day shifts. Once, I was assisting on a ward when I noticed a patient slipping onto an elevator. He was recovering from brain surgery and was not allowed to leave the ward. His head was wrapped in surgical gauze, and he was wearing a hospital gown with the back open and nothing underneath.

I called his name, and for one second I thought of getting on the elevator with him, but I realized that might be dangerous.

I let him go down to the main entrance as I ran to alert security. The male nurse and I watched from the seventh-floor windows as our patient ambled up the main street into town, his head wrapped in the surgical bandages and his privates open to the elements with the security team chasing behind him.

I worked at Hamot for two years and loved it. I bought my first classy "little black dress" at the Boston Store and went out now and then to hospital parties and on dates with *Jake*. Once, I met the movie star, Claudette Colbert, who spoke at a ladies community luncheon.

I worked steadily and took on extra shifts, but one night I had a severe pain in my stomach and admitted myself to the ER. They discovered that I had the beginnings of an ulcer. Working many long nights under such stress was too much for me. I decided I wanted to begin having more fun. So, I quit my job and applied to Eastern Mennonite College in Harrisonburg, Virginia where my best friend, Alice Yoder, from high school, was a first-year student. She had been writing to me about her awesome college experience and about the wonderful young man she met and was engaged to. I was twenty and decided I wanted to have fun and find a husband too. I discovered that life doesn't work out the way we expect it to.

One of the most important lessons I learned while I was a nurse in Hamot was that I could use words to express my emotions. I learned this one day at the nurses station from a very unexpected source.

A young graduate nurse and I were talking about a boy from Spartansburg whom we had both dated. She told me, "I was upset" about something that he had done. This struck me like a bolt of lightning because I had never heard anyone say those words before. Before this, if I had felt upset, I acted out in some way, or simply got over my feelings. To actually say the words to something that I was feeling was a revelation to me!

I realized that I could use my words to express feeling rather than lashing out in anger.

SEARCHING FOR MY
TWODADS

EASTERN MENNONITES

In the fall of 1968, I loaded up my little white Ford Mustang again with essentials to furnish my first-year dorm room at Eastern Mennonite College, in Harrisonburg, Virginia in the Shenandoah Mountains. I didn't know what to expect in this new adventure, except that my best friend, Alice, had been there the year before and loved EMC. I was accepted into their nursing program. Alice transferred into my LPN program in Erie, PA and moved into my room in Mrs. Roger's house.

Alice's fiancé, Marland Miller, was the first person who met me on campus that year. Before I arrived, I suspected that I would be the only non-Mennonite at the school. There was at least one other. Another Spartansburg Mennonite girl, Jan Miller, also a first-year student, rode down with me. We became friends for the rest of our lives.

Marland greeted my roommate *Lynn* and me at our first-year mixer as if we were already old friends. What a gracious and generous person he has always been. He was an extrovert, one of the kindest, funniest young men I have ever known. He was also a bigger than life-DJ for EMC's campus radio station. Occasionally, Marland sent out an emergency call to ask me to come over to sit with him at the radio station so he could moan and groan about how much he missed Alice. I have known them both now for over fifty years and they are the same devoted couple they were back then.

Before long, I realized I was much more interested in Sociology than I was in the field of nursing, so I transferred into the Social Sciences. However, it didn't hold my interest long. It was too academic for me and didn't feel practical.

In the beginning, I focused on my social life. That had been my primary reason for entering college in the first place. I was tired of being a twenty-year old woman, working so hard that I developed an ulcer. The type of young man I was meeting in Erie was not my idea of a potential marriage partner, and I wanted to settle down. However, this didn't happen for a few more years!

I loved college life as much as I had hoped I would. The campus was beautiful, and I loved living in the temperate climate of Virginia! We had chapel every day and hearing those Mennonites sing in four-part harmony that they had been singing since childhood ministered peace to my stressed soul.

My brainy roommate, *Lynn*, and I traveled with a little gang of boys to the mountains every weekend. I don't remember exactly how we got together, they were southern boys, and *Lynn* and I were from Pennsylvania. One was a real country boy, named *Oatie*, who wore suspenders and his pants high above his ankles, but he was super smart as were the other two, *Billy* and *Daniel*. *Lynn* attracted smart people like these three. I enjoyed their senses of humor. None of us thought about fashion or material things. I sewed several dresses in preparation for attending EMC. Each one was flowered, modest and cute.

Daniel and I eventually became devoted to each other, but he was from a Conservative Mennonite family that believed women and girls should wear white caps on their heads at all times. Their men didn't wear neckties. I remember when *Dan* got his first necktie for an occasion we dressed up for.

His family didn't approve of his dating a modern girl, much less, a non-Mennonite. That was heartbreaking because we both thought the world of each other. *Dan* graduated and went on to get his PhD and to work in Tennessee at the Oak Ridge National Laboratory[26]. He visited me once in Philadelphia for a final goodbye.

I had several other crushes, but none materialized.

For my college work study, I served food in the school cafeteria; Then I took another job, working in the Mennonite Home down the road, caring for elderly people. I loved the work because it allowed me more involvement with people.

Through my years in school, Mom sold off many of her antiques and family treasures to pay for my education and also took out loans.

Around this time, I received a mysterious phone call at my dorm. A man with a deep southern accent asked for Catherine Wills. The girls on my floor came to get me. I answered and told the man that my name was Mary Catherine Wills. He excused himself and hung up. I wondered if this was my father.

---

26 - Oak Ridge National Laboratory is the world's premier research institution. It is a federally funded research and development center in Oak Ridge, Tennessee, USA. *Wikipedia.org*

I had some low points at EMC which taught me that I had much to learn. I became involved in a prison ministry which was my first time since Erie working with people who were in need. I thought that I had experience, and I made a fool of myself, by acting as if I knew as much as the leaders and even contradicting some of their ideas. This was a good lesson in humility for me and I learned another important lesson, they were very gracious in listening to my inexperienced spouting off.

Dorm life was as fun as I had imagined, raids, and water balloon fights kept things exciting. My roommate, *Lynn* was intelligent and quirky, such that I felt challenged to rethink all my preconceived ideas about religion. She got top grades with little effort. My consistent memory of her is curled up on her bed, reading. She was from a very conservative background but at the time was dating a strange, uneducated, pimply teenaged boy/man, *Phil,* whom she left school to marry second semester of our first year.

THE CULT

I didn't know about cults back then, but sure enough, their group would later be named by its members, Elohim City, City of God,[27] and by all accounts became a religious cult. When I attended Lynn and Phil's wedding in a campground deep in a Pennsylvania forest, it felt eerie. I was given a room by myself in the basement of a church where I felt deeply frightened and spiritually oppressed. I stayed awake much of the night praying. I wonder if, even then, they were forming a militia.

Lynn and *Phil* later moved with his father and family to live in Polyurethane homes in Oklahoma. One of their alleged associates was Timothy McVeigh, the man later found responsible for bombing the Oklahoma City Federal Building in 1995 that killed 168 people. The group was officially cleared of conspiracy having to do with that act of terrorism, but acknowledged that they are a Christian Identity, White Racialist Group.

---

27 - A Christian Identity group in the Ozark Mountains holding that black and brown and other "Non-whites" including Jews are "mud people." Founded by the father of *Phil*, all residents including children are trained in the use of weapons and guerrilla warfare. It became an extremist sanctuary and weapons depository. Timothy McVeigh of the Oklahoma Bombing was part of the mix. *Mother Jones*, July/August 2007 Issue

Our government had them on a "watch list" for many years because of their association with radical white supremacists and KKK members.

You can see an interview with *Phil*, the spokesman, before he passed away, on a YouTube Video. *Lynn* my former roommate is visible, sitting behind one of the speakers, in a short haircut, wearing a black blouse and dangly earrings. It has always been a mystery to me how *Lynn* could have married a kid like *Phil*, when she was so brilliant and hung out with us at EMC. I believe she was brainwashed. I never heard from her again.

A SPIRITUAL TURNING POINT

In January of 1968, with Lynn married, I moved into a large, top floor dorm room with Jan Miller and her roommate, Sharon. We were already great friends, and I loved their friends who were all Mennonite girls.

At the same time, I was developing a friendship with the other non-Mennonite girl on campus, Darlis Moyer. She spoke openly about how much God meant to her. This type of conversation was uncommon among the Mennonite kids I knew who spoke more about their home churches, political causes and social lives.

The Mennonites were Pacifists[28] and some of the young people at EMC, especially the men, were engaged in the Anti-War Movement. 1968 was the year the Moratorium[29] against the Viet Nam War took place on the Mall in Washington D.C. Busloads of EMC students joined the rest of the country in the demonstration.

---

28 - A pacificist is a person who believes that war and violence are unjustifiable. *Merriam-Webster*

29 - The Moratorium to End the War in Vietnam was a massive demonstration and teach-in across the United States against the U.S. involvement in the Vietnam War. The one in Washington D. C. took place on November 15, 1969, *Wikipedia: Moratorium to End the War in Vietnam*

There were occasional speeches in the daily chapel condemning the War. A missionary kid from Brazil, Jim Sieber, stood at the podium one day and burned his draft card. This elicited a major response, both positive and negative. This astounded and excited me, since I had never seen or heard anyone who cared about politics, especially as it related to faith. It was at EMC that I began to understand that there was a social element to the Christian Gospel.

At the same time, Darlis was talking to me about how much the Lord meant to her personally. I couldn't relate to her experience, because I had talked about God, and been obedient to the Scriptures as far as I knew them but had not given any thought to a personal experience with Him. I found a book in the campus bookstore that enticed me into a deeper spiritual experience; The book was *Prayers* by Michael Quoist, a French Priest. It was the first step that would change my life forever.

NEW LIFE IN CHRIST

I began to read my Bible out of curiosity for the first time in my life. One day, as I was sitting up on the hillside behind my dorm reading the book of Romans, I read chapter 3: 23:

"All have sinned and fallen short of the Glory of God." I could relate to that. Then I read verse twenty-four," . . . and are justified freely by his grace through the redemption that came by Christ Jesus."

As I continued to read I realized that in Adam's disobedience we all inherited sin, but through Christ's obedience on the cross, we were made right with God.

As I continued reading in the book of Romans, I began to understand how my background in legalism had turned it around. I didn't have to earn God's love. God offered it freely to us.

As I looked up at the birds flying effortlessly through the air, and the trees blowing in the breeze, it occurred to me that I didn't know God any more than they did. It made sense to me as a human being, created with so many more abilities than birds or trees, that I ought to be able to know God in a deeper way.

However, I realized that something stood in the way that hindered my ability to know God. It felt very much like a cloud. I went back to our room, got down on my knees, and talked to God. I said that I didn't want anything to stand in the way between us.

It was at that point that I identified one huge barrier that had always been more important to me than anything else. That was, to have a boyfriend! I put my boyfriend at the time, *Daniel*, into God's hands, and told Him that I didn't want anything or anybody, ever again to come before Him. I thanked Him for sending Jesus to the cross to die for my sins. I got up and from that moment was a dramatically changed person. I can best describe it as having a free and unchained heart.

How did I know to read the Bible when I felt lonely, sitting on that hill behind the dorm? I believe it came from the foundation that Mom, the Robbies and the CMA church in Spartansburg gave me. They all contributed to my conviction that the Scriptures contained the Words of eternal life. I was twenty years old.

After I asked Christ to take over my life, I felt like there were no other people on earth except Darlis and me who knew Jesus in this way. We started a Bible study on our campus by inviting an Intervarsity worker, Chris Halverson, at James Madison University, to work with us.

How did we get to know Chris? He was the son of the Chaplain of the United States Senate at the time, a godly, enthusiastic Christian man. Darlis made the connection; through having been to Bible study at JMU.

Even after my experience with the Lord, I discovered that I had not overcome my tendency towards thinking I knew a lot more than I did. Once, I was talking with *Billy* and telling him about a particularly exciting moment with God. I brashly told him that I doubted I could grow any further in my relationship with the Lord, I knew God so well! I remember saying this to him while we were standing outside the campus post office. Ironically, he agreed that he felt the same. I'm sure we've both grown far beyond those years by now.

It took many years for me to grow free of the self-assured hubris and arrogance surrounding matters of the spirit. I certainly felt like God's special girl and still do to a great extent, probably because I feel I owe Him my life. I also think that my personality doesn't lean towards meek, and my desire to influence drives me to excess.

Our little Intervarsity Chapter at EMC began to grow. Then Darlis and I attended a Navigator Conference at Virginia Tech. I had never heard of The Navigators but when we walked into the huge auditorium, I was stunned by the powerful presence of a room full of godly men singing choruses for God's glory at the top of their lungs.

I never attended another Navigator meeting or met another Navigator until I met my future husband, Jon, six years later.

I began spending hours poring over the Bible, so eager to learn more about faith directly from the source. I wanted to understand how to be a believer. Our dorm had a dedicated prayer room where I spent hours each day praying and getting to know God.

This is where I learned to meditate[30] on the Scriptures. Much of my meditation began with an emotional struggle I was having. I would look up in the Scriptures to find either the word or similar words mirroring my feelings. If I felt "hopeless or hurt" I looked for verses that taught me about "hope." I then would read and often memorize these verses and pray over them. I have such happy memories of those hours spent meditating and memorizing the Bible. I loved the tranquility of the prayer room, of knowing I could share everything with God without being disturbed behind the locked door. The appeal of the prayer room and the Scriptures were so great that I began neglecting my studies. I realize now in retrospect that some of my struggles were possibly due to emotional imbalance and excessive zeal.

My interest in classwork waned considerably. In my passion for God, I only wanted to study the Bible and decided to transfer to a school where I could do that.

The President of EMC, Myron Augsburger, called me into his office for a personal talk. He asked me to reconsider my transfer. He told me that I was exactly the type of deeply spiritual student he hoped to attract to EMC. I don't know the circumstances or how he came to know about me. But I felt honored to be singled out.

---

30 - Christian meditation, rather than emptying of the mind is rather filling our mind with God's word to replace negative or sinful thoughts.
The act of meditating on Scripture enables a deeper communion with God.
seattlechristiancounseling.com

I thought the world of Dr. Augsburger who was a well-respected author, speaker and man of God. It deeply touched me that he took the time to urge me to stay. However, I left his office still determined to transfer to a Bible College.

SEARCHING FOR MY
TWO DADS

PHILADELPHIA

In 1969, I transferred to what was then Philadelphia College of the Bible. Troy Murdoch drove down with my mom and me for a visit during the winter. We were unimpressed by the filthy streets and the ancient skyscrapers. I was however, determined to transfer so I could study the Bible full time.

Entering as a second-year sophomore was easier because we had a small group of other transfer students and an orientation leader to keep track of us. Several of these students soon became my best friends especially Marie and Lynn. My roommate, *Stacy*, on the other hand, was a nurse who felt free to diagnose me with a "Depressed Personality," because I wore a lot of brown clothing. This started us off on the wrong foot, especially as I wore the clothes that I had worn at EMC, many that I had sewn myself.

All I can say about our friendship is that I made loads of friends and was happy. *Stacy* stayed aloof and remained on the edges of school society.

Almost immediately after transferring to PCB, in January, I boarded a bus to travel to Urbana, Illinois to attend the huge Intervarsity Student Missions Conference held every four years. This became a pivotal moment in my life. I was twenty-two that January.

SEARCHING FOR MY TWO DADS

URBANA 1970

Growing up in Northwestern Pennsylvania, in my high school years I had met only one person who was not white like me. However, in high school I researched and wrote that term paper advocating for African American "dialects." I believe God planted a passion in my heart for Social Justice and Civil Rights, which came alive after I met Christ.

I knew nothing positive about MLK Jr. In my isolated area of Western Pennsylvania, I had only heard about him referred to as an agitator and a "Communist." But at Intervarsity's Urbana 70's Conference, I heard Tom Skinner, Bill Pannell, and Samuel Escobar speak about Racial Reconciliation, Social Justice, MLK Jr and the connection with the gospel. It began to click.

Once in Philadelphia I was witnessing about Christ on the street and a Black man challenged me with Psalm 37:5:

> *"I was young and now I am old, yet I have never seen the righteous forsaken or their children begging bread."*

He put his finger in my face and shouted, "That's NOT the God I know." He said he knew plenty of poor Black Christian people.

I was majoring in Bible and Social Work, I knew the Scriptures were true, that God was true to His Word. But something was very wrong. I felt ashamed that I was so naïve and ignorant of conditions that would cause someone to disbelieve in the goodness of God.

RESIDENT ASSISTING

The next year, I became a Resident Assistant, or RA for a group of third and fourth year students and I also led an orientation group for transfer students like I had been. For the next two years, I was the female RA in charge of a separate building for the older girls, Alumni Hall.

The college put a lot of confidence and trust in my ability to supervise these young women. Some of these older girls pushed the limits of school rules, especially quiet times for study, and curfew. I asked very little of them, in a situation where following rules was the standard some deeply resented them. I learned how to earn their respect and maintain good raport, rather than to demand it.

This good nature had not come naturally for me. I had been overly firm one year at a Christian camp as a counselor for little girls, one of whom had literally swung from the rafters. I resorted to yelling at this child who would not obey. My yelling at her had frightened one of the sensitive little campers and she called her mother to ask if she could go home. I felt terrible, of course. I wish I had learned this lesson much better so I could apply it later in my family.

PCB Friends

The college girls were an assortment of missionary kids, former hippies, preacher's kids, wealthy girls, and independent women. We had one Black girl among us, whom I thought then had a giant a chip on her shoulder. I would understand her very differently now. One Christmas, she and I got the idea that she would dress up like Santa Claus and we girls would ride up and down the elevator in the boys' main dorm yelling, "Merry Christmas." One thing we didn't count on was the boys pushing the buttons to stop us at every floor to pull us off.

That was quite a mishap! I got in trouble with the deans, and beyond a scolding lost some privileges. But, thankfully, my Dean of Students really liked me and chuckled about it in our private meeting.

I loved all my girls, and we got along well. I didn't stand over them with a rulebook, though I had to measure their skirts to make certain they were within regulation which was, one inch above the floor when a girl knelt down. I disliked doing this because it felt humiliating to both of us. I also had to check rooms once a week to make sure girls were making their beds and weren't too messy.

I realize now that one purpose for this room check was surely to prevent an infestation of cockroaches, the scourge of the city. I wasn't supposed to give them a warning before inspection, but I was lenient, so the girls seldom got a fine from me. I was not among the neatest girls in the dorm, and once Ms. Lewis, the Dean, came over for a neatness check on me! Fortunately, it was a day that I had made my bed and things were in decent order. But it shook me.

There were some troubled girls in my dorm and I served as their listening ear, my door was always ajar. One of the girl's boyfriends, *Todd*, was a new believer, a recovering drug addict who was angry and abusive. We suspected he hit her or might do so. She tried to break up with him, but he kept returning to our dorm demanding to see her. When we wouldn't let him inside, he stood outside her window in the parking lot loudly calling her name, begging her to come outside. He tried to break into our dorm several times, shaking the front doors to the point where I had to call security. When he was calm, I would meet him in the foyer of our building with one set of doors locked behind me, attempting to reason with him.

We sent her away to a safe place for a while and one dark evening I did a very risky thing. I took *Todd* on the subway out to the suburbs to Donna and Ken Rudy's house where he had agreed to stay to receive counseling. We were friends, and in his normal state, he would never harm me. However, that night he was agitated, and as we walked along a dark street next to a hedgerow, I didn't feel very safe. It occurred to me that he might hurt me. By God's grace we arrived with no problems.

Many of us cared for *Todd* and were praying for him to recover and learn to trust in the Lord. He eventually left school. There were many people who came to school with terrible burdens and left freed of them. Sadly, he wasn't one of them yet.

EXTRA CURRICULARS

The city exposed some of my friends to harm. Two of my girlfriends were kidnapped at separate times off the street in Philly. Both escaped their individual kidnappers by witnessing to them until they couldn't stand to hear their testimony any longer and shoved them out of the cars. Men flashing us girls was a frequent nuisance. Pimps tried to hire several of my friends.

Dangerous situations were common for me, as a student Social Worker in South Philadelphia. My first assignment was to work out of Mayor Frank Rizzo's office to try to address the truancy rate of junior high students in the public schools. At times as I walked down to South Philly from Center City, I heard rocks hitting cars next to me in the street. Somebody had thrown one at me or at least, hoped to scare me. I prayed constantly on these walks, most often from The Lord's Prayer, "Thy Kingdom come, Thy Will be done on earth as it is in Heaven," visualizing it as I walked.

I was forced to trust God to use my life and to keep me alive for His purposes, whatever they were. Each day as I walked down into South Philly I envisioned God's Kingdom surrounding me.

When I visited the homes of my students, initially, I wanted to find out why they weren't attending school. Some of them had no one at home to supervise them; others fooled their well-intentioned parents. One boy named Mark had stabbed his teacher with a pencil and was suspended from school. He never planned to go back. These kids were at most, fourteen years old.

Mark became one of my guardians as I walked down into his South Philly neighborhood. One time he abruptly shoved me into a corner grocery store when he heard a gang approaching. As we waited in the store, the gang ambled past, swinging chains and chanting. I gave Mark a big hug and bought him a candy bar to thank him for protecting me.

I didn't personally see a lot of success in my Social Work assignments, but I came to appreciate the situations these kids came from. Some families I visited had only a table in their apartments but no chairs around it, possibly one easy chair in their entire apartment.

Once, when I sat down in a chair, I laid my poncho on the floor and a line of cockroaches began advancing towards it. One family had beer bottles in the refrigerator and nothing else. They also had a large color TV.

I found comparable living situations in North Philly where we established after school Bible Clubs. We taught Bible stories, sang choruses, played games, and kept the kids off the streets for a couple of hours. While I did this, I worked part-time in Doctor's Hospital as an LPN.

I worked with a nurse whose son was involved in our North Philly Bible Club. She told me that he loved going to club and she was thankful that he had a safe place to go after school.

I also did Home Health Nursing and Private Duty Nursing thanks to my having an LPN degree. My jobs often involved sitting all night in a patient's room while they slept and helping them get up to go to the bathroom.

I loved pulling private duty assignments in the old historic hospitals in Philly, especially Jefferson Hospital. Even though there had been architectural changes throughout the years, I relished the thought that I was walking in the footsteps of historic figures. There was one factor which was not so nice which was true of every hospital where I worked. Whenever I went down to the enormous kitchens to grab a midnight snack for a patient, I would flick on the lights and close my eyes. The sound of thousands of little feet skittering across the floor was bad enough without seeing the cockroaches scampering to their hiding places.

Dr. Koop[31] the Attorney General of the United States and an elder at my church, gave me four chairs from the old Children's Hospital as keepsakes when they remodeled. I cherished these chairs and passed them on to our daughter.

Living in history was one of the best parts of studying and working in Philadelphia, especially since I was able to give orientation to our new students. Each semester I took groups to the Liberty Bell, Betsy Ross House, and Independence Hall!

---

31 - Charles Everett Koop, an American pediatric surgeon and public health administrator served as the 13th Surgeon General of the United States under President Ronald Reagan from 1982 to 1989. *Wikipedia*

Faith was uppermost in my mind and heart as I worked jobs where I had ideal opportunities to talk to interested patients about Jesus. Christ's joy often bubbled up out of me. One patient was the CEO of Belmont Psychiatric Hospital in Philly. He was the most sincerely receptive man I have ever talked with about Jesus. He wrote down what I told him, word for word and slept on it. The next day he asked me if it was too late for him to act on Jesus' invitation. He prayed with me to ask Christ into his life.

My friends and I drove out weekly to the Northeast suburbs to lead youth groups similar to high school Youth for Christ clubs. In Philly, they were called Dimension clubs and catered to a wide variety of teenagers. We learned that the schools had rival gangs. On many nights gangs from a competing school were rumored to be outside waiting for the club to be finished so they could attack our kids. These rumors caused a lot of intrigue, but somehow our students, who began with little confidence in themselves or their faith, continued to attend and grew into capable and bold spiritual leaders.

One of our students, *Gary*, who sat quietly in a corner as a first-year student, went to college, married and moved to California where he became a prominent political leader in his community.

A STUDENT OF THE BIBLE

I enjoyed studying Social Work in a Biblical context, but I confess, I loved to do research for practical reasons but never had much interest in studying doctrine. Most of the Bible courses I took were slanted towards Dispensationalism,[32] much more so than I liked.

I should have known more about PCB before I entered. My preliminary research, as I remember, had consisted of investigating the City of Philadelphia, and a bit of doctrine that I agreed with; Salvation is by Faith through Christ. I was ready to sign up. A tendency to not examine my decisions too closely has been a pattern in my life. I depended on my instinct and seldom looked back.

Uncle Robbie was not pleased when I announced I was attending PCB. He said, "That's the place where they believe, once saved, always saved."

Well, yes, that is what I believed too, but I didn't have the courage to tell him. I trusted that my

---

32 - Dispensationalism is a theological system of interpreting the Bible that was first espoused by John Nelson Darby. It maintains that history is divided into multiple ages or "dispensations" in which God acts with humanity in different ways. Among its core beliefs: A future restoration of Israel, a rapture before the second coming of Jesus after which a period of tribulation will occur. Many in Evangelical churches in the United States have followed this teaching. *Wikipedia Progressive revelation (Christianity)*

salvation was not dependent on good behavior but on Christ's death on the Cross, on Grace alone.

I enjoyed my Social Work classes; Doctor Furness and Mr. Eckert were practical professors who exemplified the values that I admired. I craved practical lessons that made sense to me, any teaching that was technical or for certification bored me. Once again, I was doomed by my preference to practice by the seat of my pants and instinct, rather than book learning. Manuals and textbooks seemed counterintuitive to my desire to get into the core of problems and help people to work things out.

I plodded through my textbooks, through my fieldwork, through my ministry assignments and working full time as an RA. In the later years, I seldom had time to work in the hospital.

I had entered into my studies planning to glean what I could from my classes, and to resist jumping on any professor's bandwagon. By this, I meant, anyone's doctrinal hobbyhorse.

One of our textbooks was the *Scofield Reference Bible*,[33] a study Bible. CI Scofield was one of the founders of our school, and we had a professor, Dr. Clarence Mason, who had consulted on the revision of the Scofield Reference Bible. I didn't know about Dispensationalism or realize that I had been raised to believe in its tenets. I learned that PCB and Dallas Theological Seminary were the central institutions where these were the common

---

33 - The Scofield Reference Bible is a widely circulated study Bible edited and annotated by the American Bible student Cyrus I. Scofield which popularized *dispensationalism*. It first appeared in 1909 and was revised by the author in 1917. It contained the text of the Protestant King James Bible. *Wikipedia*

beliefs of conservative, fundamentalist Christians of the time. We had all read the *Left Behind* series of books and took for granted that Christ would return soon, leaving planes unpiloted and pets uncared for in vacant houses. I wrestled with these doctrines and kept an open mind.

One of my favorite classes was Evangelism where we were required to memorize one-hundred verses. I discovered later that these verses were the Navigator's Topical Memory System. These verses have become the foundation for hope during challenging times in my life. Also, coincidentally, my Evangelism Professor was the father of the man who would later become our dear friend and pastor in Ithaca, New York, Chuck Tompkins.

How did I benefit from PCB if I kept my mind closed to the Dispensationalist doctrines? I would say, rather, that I guarded my mind, from committing myself to any set of beliefs without questioning them.

This may seem strange, because I wholeheartedly gave my heart and soul over to God in one time of prayer back at EMC. Perhaps because I have set God, my creator, to guard over my heart, I don't want to welcome any one creed or way of belief to take control over me above my personal belief in God and Jesus as my Savior.

Oswald Chambers said something similar in his book, *The Love of God: An Intimate look at the Father-Heart of God*[34]:

---

34 - Publisher: Discovery House, January 1, 1988

"In the realm of belief, when I become certain of my creeds, I kill the life of God in my soul, because I cease to believe in God and believe in my belief instead."

I try to be very careful that I not replace learning about God from Scripture and personal relationship, by reading people's books about God.

Devotional books and commentaries assist me in my pursuit of God and my understanding, but prayer, and waiting upon God is a much more reliable resource for me. Far from leading me to become a narrow-minded person, reading and rereading the Bible over and over has, I believe, led me to become more open-minded and balanced in loving the world that God loves and created for His pleasure. I am also grateful for The Navigator leaders who similarly seek to know God and to make Him known.

I have struggled my entire life learning to speak the truth in love and humility and to unlearn the traits of pride and selfishness.

It is still difficult for me to know when to confront and when it will benefit a situation for me to remain silent. I believe everything that has occurred in my life will work for God's good purpose.

In my years at PCB, I was learning from my two best friends, Chris and Lindsay, to look around me, to visit local art museums, sample street foods, visit the Italian Market and enjoy the city.

They were upperclassmen who lived on my wing the first year and spent much of their time beyond the beat of college life, focusing instead on arts and culture, Native American affairs and the Plymouth

Brethren[35] church they attended. Lindsay, who was Chinese, invited me to her home in Queens, New York where I enjoyed her family's generosity.

---

35 - The Plymouth Brethren are a low-church and non-conformist Christian movement whose history can be traced back to Dublin, Ireland, in the mid to late 1820s, where it originated from Anglicanism. *Wikipedia*

SEARCHING FOR MY
TWODADS

FEARS

At times, fear of death, especially from terrorism and accidents shook my confidence in God's good will, but I reminded myself that the timing of our deaths is in God's hands.

In later years, if I have not been tempted to fear for my own or Jon's death, then I fear for our children or grandchildren.

However, years ago in Yogyakarta when I worried that our children might die as a result of an accident while riding with me on my motor bike, God gave me a firm belief that He is Good regardless of what happens.

Psalm 119:68 came to my mind very clearly that day, "God is good and what he does is good." This has been the most important question in life that I've needed to resolve aside from my faith in Christ for my salvation, and that is, "Is God Good?"

I sincerely believe Satan suggests anxious thoughts to us which we then must choose whether to focus on them or not. I probably have more of a tendency towards anxiety than many, but once we have established that we no longer need to fear because we serve a loving God who always does good, Satan loses his power. Our times are in our loving God's hands.

Parents will tell you that they are only as happy as their saddest child. Each of our three children has suffered great hardship in their personal life. Few people know the full extent of their stories which are theirs alone to tell. Suffice to say they are courageous examples to me of standing strong, facing disappointment with faith and moving on with their lives through difficulties that would exhaust the average person. Our children's perseverance through pain inspire me.

A CALL TO SERVE

I tasted my first falafel[36] at a street fair in Logan Circle two blocks from my dorm at PCB. I point to that moment as the time when my eyes opened up to the world. I wonder if this might have been God's nascent call on my life to go into the world and share the good news about Jesus.

I had been trying out various Evangelical Bible churches in the area around this time and found them boring, except for one that sponsored a missions trip to Blue Hill, Kentucky for a summer Bible School. This was my first introduction to southern mountain folk, and it opened my eyes at the same time drawing me further towards missions.

I witnessed white poverty as never before. I met snake handlers, drove past cemeteries with brightly painted objects like bicycles and umbrellas dangling from trees to ward off evil spirits. Moonshine stills were in operation in the early seventies. Local people warned us not to wander into the forest because we might encounter moonshiners who would shoot at us mistaking us for Federal Agents.

---

36 - Falafel is a popular Middle Eastern "fast food." It is a deep-fried ball made of a mixture of ground chickpeas, broad beans or both. This is usually wrapped in flatbread or added to salad. It is a common Street food. *Wikipedia*

When I returned from this mission's trip, I had a calling: I wanted to serve God full time. The experience had been very much like riding around the countryside in a green Volkswagen van with my family, telling people about Jesus. A theme was developing.

THE JESUS MOVEMENT

After this experience, I traveled on ministry trips on every break from school. Mom was amazing to support me in all my trips, she understood my heart to travel and serve God. My next ministry trip was to serve at a coffee house in Portland, Maine.

One spring, my friend Chris and I met a group of Jesus People[37] in Rittenhouse Park in Philly. They invited us to visit them so we went to stay for several days at their commune in Allentown, PA.

The first night we talked into the early morning with one of the leaders called *Dave on Fire*. He told stories about a vision he had of angels surrounding them during a time when neighbors were throwing rocks at their house. We spent the night in sleeping bags on their living room floor and the next day, sat around their kitchen table teaching the Bible to the commune kids. At that time one of the marks of the Jesus movement was a strong emphasis on Eschatology.[38]

---

37 - Jesus People had a strong belief in miracles, signs and wonders, faith, healing, prayer, the Bible and powerful works of the Holy Spirit. They were said to be a "hip" form of Christianity, attracting youth with their music, street preaching, ocean baptisms and their "come as you are" vibe. *The Conversation*, September 15, 2017

38 - Eschatology is the part of theology concerned with death, judgment and the final destiny of the soul and of humankind or "last things." *Oxford Dictionary*

PCB based its doctrine on *Dispensationalism*. Many in the Jesus People Movement believed we were in the Last Days and the Scofield Bible pointed in that direction. They were like sponges soaking up knowledge.

Unlike at our Bible College, no one needed to be held accountable for evangelism, there was such a passion for Jesus, everyone wanted to tell others about Him. They shared my belief that God wanted to change the world through them.

One night, I went with Dave to the local Allentown Hospital to talk to the patients about Jesus. We only lasted a few minutes before security told us to leave. As we walked down to the pier, a motorcycle gang pulled up blocking our way. Dave was excited to share Jesus with them but I felt nervous. The gang was very antagonistic and armed. Dave began sharing about Christ and his hope of eternal life.

The hefty gang leader took out his knife and held it to Dave's throat and said, "If you're so excited to get to heaven, how's about I send you there right now?"

Dave bared his neck, answering him with a look of pure peace on his face saying, "Sure, go right ahead!"

I was observing all this, in a bit of shock, knowing the truth of Dave's hope, but still hesitant to be sent to heaven on the spot. I also wondered what my next step should be if the gang leader made good on his promise.

Well, nothing happened. The gang listened respectfully and possibly some prayed to ask Jesus into their hearts. I know Dave gained respect that night. We went back to the house where Chris and I stayed two more days.

We discovered that some of the commune members' enthusiasm could be misplaced. One young fellow felt he was called by God to break and burn their leader's LP record collection while the leader was out of town. The rest of the group weren't on board with smashing them without consulting the leader, but this naïve young fellow was convinced the leader would appreciate it.

We watched in dismay as he broke the records and tossed them into the burn bin in the backyard. When the leader returned from his trip, he was obviously traumatized over the loss of his valued collection. He struggled with this younger brother in Christ who had taken this decision into his own hands. He openly grieved but at the time, controlled his temper.

Years later, I learned that the Forever Family[39] as they eventually became known, with one of their leaders, Dave, became a cult.

When Chris and I boarded the bus to return to Philly, two of the younger kids came down to the bus station waving us off with tears in their eyes. It was a memorable weekend for all of us.

After these experiences with coffee houses, the Jesus People and seeing the way Jesus was transforming lives, I was never fully able to return to traditional church life. The Holy Spirit stirred

---

39 - A Christian communal group who lived together in the 1970s in Allentown, Pennsylvania. They taught evangelical Christianity and were very strong on sharing the gospel of Jesus. They participated in Christian coffee houses in Allentown.

a generation of us to witness God relating to the real world. I was revived and renewed and found it difficult to settle into conventional ministry. Transparency and vulnerability became the standard for my attitude towards other people. I began to feel that rejection was not the end of the world in a relationship, but I wanted people to reject me for who I really was, not for some false version of me.

At this same time, I was reading Francis Shaeffer's books which opened my eyes and heart to learning about higher culture and to understanding intellectual freedom in new ways. These were the days before he was involved in the anti-abortion movement. I felt privileged to hear him speak once at Westminster Seminary, though he was always far ahead of me intellectually.

WORD OF LIFE

Another summer, I was selected for the Counselor in Training Program at Word of Life Youth Camp[40] in Schroon Lake, NY. At this time, it was one of the best known Evangelical non-denominational Christian camps for kids on the East Coast. As a Counselor in Training (CIT) for the summer, I received counselor training, and then helped take a group of highly motivated kids on adventure camping trips into the Adirondack Mountain wilderness for weeks at a time. We were to help the kids learn survival skills such as how to start a campfire without matches, how to build shelters and survive alone in the forest. Each of us counselors had to learn these skills first. We learned to scale cliffs and rappel down them and I loved doing that. The students grew in their confidence and courage and so did we.

Though I had always considered myself brave and successful in everything I put my mind to do, I faced several difficult challenges that made me question my courage and abilities. On our long portages, across country from lake to lake in Northern New York State, we carried our canoes over our heads in a portage for one or two miles. I had never been able

---

40 - A Bible Camp on an island in Schroon Lake, New York offering opportunities for spiritual growth and adventures. *Word of life website*

to hold my arms over my head for long before they began aching so I didn't think I would make it. At times I felt like an imposter trying to fit in.

Something I regret was when I failed at my first real nursing challenge. We were far out in the forest when one of our campers fell and knocked her elbow out of joint. We had to call in a seaplane to come to pick her up. However, our group had to hike several miles to get to one of the lakes. My first real emergency rattled me so much that I forgot to make a splint for her poor arm. I cleaned the wound and put her arm into a sling and told her to hold it securely as we hiked.

One of the kids asked if we shouldn't make a splint to put on it. I covered for myself, saying it was enough if she held it in place. It was the first time I had thought of the splint. We reached the lake, and the seaplane took her to the hospital. I worried for the rest of the summer about her arm, that it might have required surgery and that I might hear back from her parents, but I never did.

Another time on our trek I faced a daunting challenge. We had to cross a stream over a deep ravine by walking down a narrow log which slanted from high up on one side down to the other. It terrified me, and after everyone else had done it, I sat on the top of the log and couldn't make myself do it.

Our leader, *Bob Lee*, sat down at the bottom of the log, across the ravine for several hours until dark, telling me repeatedly he knew I could do it. Finally, I gained the courage I needed to overcome my fear and I made it across. I will always remember *Bob's* kindness and patience with me. He never made me feel embarrassed or ashamed, though he was better known for being a tough guy than for having a tender heart. He was always especially sweet to me.

Predictably, I had a crush on all the leaders. A highlight for me was the weekend when *Bob* took our staff to his parent's home and gave us rides on his large motorcycle. Speeding around the curves up on those Adirondack New York highways permanently replaced my childhood passion for horseback riding.

SEARCHING FOR MY
TWODADS

MY LIFE CHANGES AGAIN

DISCOVERING GOD, MY PERFECT FATHER

Two remarkable events occurred at Word of Life that transformed my life. The first was that I began to understand that God planned for me to be born, even though my father didn't want me.

Woody Lewis was *Bob Lee's* colleague in training and leading us. He was newly out of Princeton Seminary and serving as our Bible teacher as well as the one who brought humor into most situations.

We were riding the camp bus up to one of the lakes for a canoe trip. Woody was standing up in the front of the bus entertaining us, singing silly songs, and making jokes, when, in his natural way, he began teaching us about the verses in Psalm 139: 15-17:

> *"My frame was not hidden from you when I was made in the secret place. When I was woven together in the depths of the earth, your eyes saw my unformed body. All the days ordained for me were written in your book before one of them came to be. How precious to me are your thoughts O God! How vast is the sum of them!"*

These words hit me like a brick, and I became aware for the first time that I harbored feelings of rejection because my father had not wanted me and had wished I were dead. What a relief to know that God circumvented my father's plans and brought me to this earth! Words are inadequate to explain what joy and wonder I felt as I sat there on the bus pondering these truths!

This was true, but also God thought I was precious! Though my earthly father didn't seek me out, my heavenly Father thought about me often and his thoughts towards me were precious! From that moment on, peace flooded over me as though some great puzzle had been solved. I have often reminded Woody of his part in my spiritual growth.

▲   ▲   ▲

A second significant event occurred in the town of Schroon Lake which convinced me that angels are real.

I was taking a group of our students into town to go shopping. We were walking along the sidewalk when a fire siren sounded. An old car came speeding along the street going in the opposite direction from us. When it came even with our group, the driver slammed on the brakes and did a one eighty turn right in the middle of the street. The car went out of control and began fishtailing at a high speed towards us, as we stood on the sidewalk staring at it. I began pushing the kids into a hedge as the car barreled toward us. Just as we toppled into the hedge, the car jolted to a sudden stop a few feet before it should have hit us!

I remember seeing the look of horror and shock on the driver's face. What had caused that out-of-control car to halt so suddenly to a stop before it hit us? I will always be convinced that an angel stood on that street between us to stop that car.

SEARCHING FOR MY

TWODADS

YEARNINGS

In the meantime, back at college, the yearnings in my heart for a solid relationship continued. I had several steady boyfriends but when they became serious, I would end them; *Nick*, who was a charming, Irish, local policeman's son, told me that if I broke up with him, he would leave school and join the Philadelphia Police Force. He did.

Patrick was an energetic Irish kid with green eyes and a contagious laugh who became the President of our Missions Society. I was elected Secretary. *Pat* took this much more seriously than he should have, considering me his personal assistant. He walked around school at a fast pace carrying his briefcase, his mind working overtime. He slipped me notes asking me to meet him in the chapel or library for quick meetings. In our meetings, he had me take notes on his constant stream of ideas. As we sat there, he remembered assignments, and I wrote those down while he talked a mile a minute.

I went along with it for a while because he fascinated me. In the beginning, I spent time with him as a joke. I don't remember one single thing that he dictated to me. After I decided to step down from my position because I wasn't getting my own work done, another girl, Nancy, took over for me.

I have searched my college diaries to see if I mentioned my time hanging out with him and found that I confided in Pat as a friend. I wonder what he did in the future. His college life was full of himself!

I had my usual crushes on cute boys. Not one of them was a typical college guy who was into athletics or even music. They were usually social worker majors, but one, *Terry*, was a senior education major with red hair and freckles who noticed me when I first arrived.

He and another senior fellow, *Toby* had an apartment off campus. I often spent time there with them though I suspected, as a freshman it was off limits. I never asked about it, though. They made theological jokes all the time and though I didn't always understand what they were discussing, I loved their wittiness and intellectual banter.

Toby came from Cranberry Township in Western Pennsylvania and began asking me for a ride home whenever I was going. We began dating. *Terry* was probably dating somebody else.

When *Toby* graduated from PCB, he went on to Reformed Theological Seminary and wanted to continue dating. I was creeped out because he reminded me of an actor who played a part called Mr. Peepers and also, Woody Allen because he was small and wore glasses. *Toby* took me to Reformed Episcopal Services and I resisted, saying I could not stand the liturgy and praying rote prayers. I behaved like a brat. Instead of breaking up with him, I let our relationship drag on until I had several nightmares about standing at the altar ready to marry him. Finally, I made the break.

Driving into the city became impractical because I seldom used my car, and I didn't want to pay for parking. I began taking the Greyhound bus from Center City Philly riding for twelve hours back home to Erie or Corry where someone picked me up.

The bus had a layover in Scranton, PA until 3 am. Many a late night I sat down, put my head down on my bags, covered my head with my poncho and slept like a baby until departure. I never felt any fear because I knew God was with me. There were a lot of dodgy characters hanging around at that time of night, though. This was possibly one reason I felt confident to let our girls go off on independent adventures by themselves to Europe because I trusted their judgment and the Lord's care and protection over them.

I always carried an orange with me because these long bus trips made me nauseous. Often, the buses were empty except for three or four people who seemed to smoke the entire time. My emotions were always tender on both ends of the trips.

At the beginning, I teared up and cried a little at the thought of leaving all my friends and activities behind, then about halfway home, I began to anticipate relaxing at home, eating Mom's tasty food, and having long talks with her. On the return trip, I would cry a bit, missing my mom, the pets and the freedom of no schoolwork. By the time I had arrived back in Philly, I was eager to dive in again to be a student, school counselor, and guide to new students ready to explore the City of Brotherly Love.

Naturally, boys had a prominent place in my life. One day, as I sat across a table in the school library from my friend, a handsome, French transfer student, Jacques, I remember bemoaning the fact that I would never find a godly man to marry me. He took my hand in his, looked deeply into my eyes with his baby blues, and said, "Mary, nothing in life is sure, but God."

This is a phrase that I often remember and thank God for Jacques who delivered this word in due season when I needed it. Jacques became a missionary in France.

▲   ▲   ▲

I kept busy advocating for my students who were feeling fed up with the rules they had to follow in the increasingly enlightened age of the seventies. The school required men to wear their hair cut above the ears and never longer, while girls had to wear their skirts at the knees or longer. Girls were not yet allowed to wear slacks to class. As I remember the men were not even allowed to wear jeans. When these rules became untenable for us, I went to the deans to protest on behalf of my girls and to ask their rationale. They told me frankly, that the reason they kept these rules was because of PCB's "constituency." That is the people who supported the school financially. I appreciated the administration's transparency with me.

Not long afterwards, the administration asked all of us students to sign a pledge that we would *never* speak in tongues while we were students at the College. I refused to sign, telling the deans that I had no idea, but that God might send the gift of tongues on me at any moment. Who was I to dictate to the Holy Spirit? In the past, I had prayed and asked God if He wanted me to speak in tongues and told him I was willing. I was sincere, but not eager. It did not happen. This blew over within three days and I never had to sign the statement, in fact, they rescinded it. This gave me confidence that I might have influence within the school, as an older transfer student who sat in a position as a Resident Assistant with the administration, and the deans.

I continued counseling girls who were going through many issues. I advocated for them with the deans. Life was intense, and I enjoyed my studies. Every Friday afternoon though, I was experiencing letdown migraines. These continued for thirty years until I found a Neurologist who helped me

SEARCHING FOR MY
TWO DADS

HEARTBREAK

I have been wondering how I will approach this chapter and dreading it. So here goes. I met *Brad* at PCB's welcome reception for new students. He arrived like a shooting star in the second semester of my junior year. He was my age and had been a hippie and involved with drugs. He met Jesus after some bad LSD experiences while he was attending the famous Woodstock Music Festival in 1969. At one point he had stayed in a motel during a drug trip, opened a Bible he found in a bedside stand and read it. This is when he met Jesus.

Brad was tall and handsome, with blond, curly hair and piercing blue eyes that looked deep into my heart whenever we spoke. Whenever I see the film star, Tom Hiddleston, who plays Loki, he reminds me so much of *Brad*. His charming smile and mannerisms are similar. When *Brad* arrived at PCB, he told me he was still having flashbacks and struggling with living an uneventful, average lifestyle. He was the center of attention and accustomed to an audience.

I fell into his orbit of charm and childlike innocence. To watch him awaken to life, without depending on drugs was delightful and I loved that he wanted me to walk with him on his journey. He discovered new things in his classes every day and came over to sit with me on the steps of my dorm each evening to share his excitement with me. I loved to see the joy and pure pleasure in his face as he grew in his relationship with God.

Soon, we were walking the halls to and from class. Everyone knew we were a couple and commented on how we glided through the hallways in step. We sat together in chapel, at lunch, shared notes, and walked the streets of Philadelphia making memories. I was smitten, and he seemed to be as well.

We passed Scripture verses back and forth, sometimes on our meal trays when one of us was working in the school cafeteria. Our special place was the Logan Circle Fountain on the beautiful Franklin Parkway. I don't remember kissing *Brad*, or any of my boyfriends, even *Eli* when I was engaged. I know we kissed, but I only remember kissing one person whom I will write about later.

I went home to spend Christmas break with Mom. It seemed strange to me that I didn't hear from *Brad* since he was such a relentless communicator. He often drew me out about my feelings and talked about his. This was a completely new dimension for me and caused problems at home when I began asking my mom about her feelings.

She blamed *Brad* for teaching me about feelings. "Feelings," she cried out once, "If you had never met *Brad*, you wouldn't always be talking about feelings!" She also said to me once, "If I had had feelings, I'd be dead by now!"

Despite receiving only one letter from *Brad*, I labored to sew him a wool necktie made from his Scottish clan/Tartan plaid. When we returned to classes, he avoided me for several days. When we finally got together to talk, I gave him the necktie. At the same time, he told me that he had met another girl over Christmas break.

Brad told me *Sweetie* was a model, and a new Christian. He told me that he knew I would make the perfect wife and mother, but he wasn't ready to settle down. He wanted somebody "sleazier." This is the exact word he used. I had to look it up because it had a bad connotation for me. I know he was misusing it, but I got his meaning. I wasn't pretty enough.

My heart broke. I spent days and every free hour in my room between classes in anguish, crying and praying. I felt like I was under a heavy blanket, so thick that I couldn't breathe. I felt rejected but this was also the first time I had been so certain of God's direction for my life but misunderstood it. Or had I? I was bewildered.

My good friend, Pam, was a pastor's daughter and had suffered depression. I spent a lot of time in her room sitting listening to music and mourning privately. No one would find me there. She played Frank Boggs records for me. I especially related to his song, *How Tedious and Tasteless the Hours when Jesus No Longer I See*. She also shared with me the works of her favorite English poet, an Anglican hymn writer, William Cowper,[41] who himself suffered with depression. A portion of one poem meant a lot to me:

---

41 - Cowper was an English poet and Anglican hymnwriter who changed the direction of the 18th century nature poetry by writing of everyday life and scenes of the English countryside. He was one of the forerunners of Romantic poetry. *Wikipedia*

His purposes shall ripen fast.
Unfolding every hour
The bud may have a bitter taste.
But sweet will be the flower.

The final straw was when Brad came over to ask if I would please befriend his new girlfriend, *Sweetie*. He told me that whenever he brought her around school everyone who knew me snubbed her. He thought that if I set an example, others would follow my example. I said I would not be able to befriend *Sweetie*. Period.

Brad and I continued to travel together to Dimension Clubs, trying our best to be normal, but all the kids could tell there was something terribly wrong. I was suffering a spiritual dilemma because I had been certain that *Brad* was the person God wanted me to marry.

When he broke up with me, I felt certain he was wrong, and that God planned to bring him around. I had verses!!! When he began dating Sweetie, I thought surely, they would break up. Then, they got married!!! I couldn't believe that God allowed this to happen. Yet, I still didn't question my conviction that *Brad* was the man for me. I was so certain about God's will that I assumed that *Sweetie* would die in an accident. However, when I heard she was pregnant, my certainty began to falter. I finally began to allow myself the slightest sliver of doubt that I might be wrong. I doubted that God would allow *Sweetie* to become pregnant and then kill off this woman and her baby. I realize how misled I had been by my emotions.

I never doubted God's Word, but I began to question my own ability to understand it. For the first time in my life, I realized that my interpretation of what Scripture is teaching might not always be the correct one. It was an exceedingly difficult and humbling time for me because I didn't have another love interest. I went a little off the deep end, purchasing a beautiful purple suede coat (on sale), and a couple of cute new fashionable dresses. I began to dress a lot more stylishly.

I sincerely thought it was not to win *Brad* back, because I accepted that it was impossible. I fooled myself into thinking I wanted to change my look or so I convinced my wounded heart. I imagine subconsciously, I was wishing he would regret his decision.

Brad continued to want to spend time with me popping up in my day from time to time. He still wanted to talk and debrief. He said he was concerned that I was changing my look. I told him that I needed to have a complete break from the past. I needed to move on. Eventually, *Brad* left day classes and began night school and I missed seeing him. I didn't see him until years later when I was engaged to my husband Jon and introduced them.

During this time, I stopped attending the traditional Evangelical churches and attended a house church, Church of the City over at the University of Pennsylvania. I loved the informal atmosphere, the leadership by seminary students, and that it was comprised of university students.

SEARCHING FOR MY
TWODADS

A CHURCH TO CALL HOME

In 1971, I was twenty-three. It was my junior year of college. I had visited many churches and was drawn to the casual house church. The leaders were seminarians from Westminster Theological Seminary, one was Edmund Clowney Jr. I loved the informal atmosphere, families together with students, sitting on the floor, hearing powerful teaching. Eventually, though, I joined Tenth Presbyterian Church in Center City. I was drawn to Tenth by the depth of the Scriptural teaching of my Pastor, Dr. James M. Boice. I began to respond to the more formal worship, to the older Scottish hymns, and classical music.

At Tenth, I met a successful, single professional artist, Paul Rickert.[42] We often sat together in the balcony and of course, I developed a crush on him. I attended his art shows and began to learn about art for the first time in my life. I often visited the Philadelphia Art Museum for fun and enjoyed seeing some of the more famous paintings, so it was thrilling for me to get to know a real artist. I didn't know that God was preparing me to marry one.

---

42 - Paul Rickert is an American artist, known for his watercolor paintings of urban and industrial scenes. *Wikipedia*

I was interested in several of the younger elders at Tenth. One man who liked me was a seminary professor, *Jason*, at Westminster, but I was not interested in him at all. The other was a shy Philadelphia City Detective, Stu Houston. He was on the Board of Philadelphia House, and we had a friendly relationship, but I didn't want to pursue anything further. He later married one of my PCB classmates.

During this time, my relationship with Mom was relatively peaceful. I spent much of my vacation time on mission trips, and when I returned home, we travelled around doing things she looked forward to doing. One of our favorite treats was to eat at the Corry Hotel where I learned to love the Crème de Menthe Ice Cream Sundaes. I have another story about that hotel which I want to tell later. Mom loved hearing about my mission adventures. I took her around to visit her friends where I retold these stories. I lost track of all my high school friends during the early seventies. At one of our dinners, I encouraged her to have a glass of wine. She sampled it and felt guilty for years afterward.

CANCER

In 1972, the winter semester of my senior year in college, Mom drove with me to Michigan so I could be a bridesmaid in my friend's wedding. While we were staying in our hotel, I noticed blood on the toilet in the bathroom. When I asked Mom about it, she told me that she had been having blood in her stools for quite some time.

This was a shock to me and of course I insisted Mom go for a check-up immediately on our return home. The doctor discovered a tumor in her large bowel, it was advanced malignant colon Cancer.

Shortly afterwards she entered Hamot Hospital in Erie for surgery. I took a break from PCB to stay with her. I felt all alone and didn't know anyone whom I could call for help except Harriott. When I called her, I told her about Mom's condition and asked her to go to our house to care for our dogs. I felt desperate because I couldn't take care of Mom's needs up in Erie, and care for our dogs back home over an hour away.

She was reluctant because she seldom drove in winter, the roads in western Pennsylvania were treacherous and she already had three dogs of her own. Besides, she was already in her late seventies. I knew this was a big favor to ask. She told me all the reasons she couldn't, but like a true family member, she agreed.

After Mom's surgery, the doctors gave her six weeks to live. She told me afterwards that during her operation she had a sensation as if water was running out of a tub when suddenly someone put in the plug and the water stopped going out. She said she felt sure that she was dying, but God gave her back her life. She had a colostomy for the rest of her life, which she handled very well for such a nervous and lovely woman.

It was a messy, dirty bag, constantly reminding her of her condition. As she aged, it became more difficult to handle, giving off lots of gas and limiting her eating.

Mom lived more than six weeks! She lived for thirty more years to see me get married and have children, and to see the two girls get married!

While Mom was recovering in Hamot, Harriott I got the idea that we would help her by cleaning out one of the junk rooms. I suspect both of us were curious to see what was in there.

I look back on Mom in her older years as mostly melancholy, for some valid reasons that I've mentioned. She reminisced and talked to me a lot about her happy memories as a young person, of having eighteen cousins and happy celebrations centered around her grandmother's home. None of her close relatives survived. She hoarded things and made no distinction between family treasures and pretty dishes she found at yard sales.

She held onto tangible memories of her Grandmother Lucy's, her Mother Bertha's, Father

Harry's, and my own baby things. She let me play with some of these treasures. She had her father's stereopticon[43] with many slides. Also, her mother's simple telegraph instrument or Morse Code Telegraph Key. I spent one entire winter as a child mastering the Morse Code.[44]

Our eight-room house was crumbling around us despite Mom's efforts; five of those rooms plus walk in closets and an attic were filled with huge garbage bags and boxes of things belonging to relatives I had never known. I was constantly fascinated with all the hidden treasures in these rooms, but Mom kept track of me in the house. Whenever she heard me open the doors to one of those rooms, or if I set foot in one of them no matter how silently, if she heard me, she would call out to distract me, often giving me a minor task to do.

I knew I would inherit many of the things in these garbage bags; Harriott and I decided to get a start at sorting them. We found vintage *Life Magazines* with my Grandfather's personal letters stuck between the pages; we also found valuable heirlooms, my Great Grandmother's beautiful China dishes among some junk. There were lace curtains from generations of women before me. There were clothes, sometimes rags. After several weeks, we brought Mom home to Spartansburg, and Harriott stayed on with us for several more weeks to help.

---

43 - A Stereopticon is a slide projector that combines two images to create a three-dimensional effect or makes one image dissolve into another. A "Magic lantern." *Wikipedia*

44 - Morse code is a method used in telecommunication to encode letters of the alphabet, numbers and punctuation marks by arranging dots, dashes and spaces. *Wikipedia*

Mom suspected we had been doing some clearing of her junk rooms and became irate. There was no reasoning with her about her hoarding. I imagine she felt she had lost all control of her life. Her hoarding had become so much worse the longer I had been away. I mentioned before that there were two or three layers of stuff lining the walls of our bedroom. The windows were unapproachable because of the layers of stuff standing in the way. Window blinds were always closed making it pitch dark during the day. Clothing covered chairs, and drawers overflowed with sundry pieces of beautiful cloth.

I discovered Mom had been collecting dishes and pretty treasures from thrift shops for years. She also saved gifts her friends had given to her over the years, new towels, sweaters, sheet sets, knick-knacks. She was saving all of these to give to me or to someone else who was nice to her. She always wanted to give gifts to people who treated her kindly. She tucked these nice things away into her chests of drawers with bars of Yardley soaps to give them a pleasant fragrance.

Sadly, I also discovered that some of her heirloom jewelry was missing. When I was a little girl I would explore her jewelry box and admire her pretty rings. One in particular was a black Onyx with a Diamond in the center. I looked forward to wearing it someday. Somewhere along the way, she had either sold it or unscrupulous visitors had stolen it.

I determined that I did not want my children to bear the heavy burden of sorting through our "storerooms," I would be faithful to simplify. But as I age, I am finding it much harder to downsize than

I realized. I can now sympathize with my mom. She had no living relatives to talk to about her memories. It's no wonder she held on to their possessions. I grieve over my lack of understanding.

I want our children to carry a legacy of a few valuable character traits from me. "The best of me goes on in you," as Grandmother Violet said to Lady Mary in the film series *Downtown Abbey*. My daughters and granddaughter carry the positive legacy of the women in our past. They are examples of the Proverbs 31 woman.

SEARCHING FOR MY

TWODADS

REST & RECOVERY

Harriott returned to her home in Oil City and Mom and I managed to weather a few months together. I returned to college to finish my final semester. I took several summer courses and became friends with *Nancy*, a student, who was the daughter of the President of a Seminary in Philadelphia. Her family was well known in Christian circles and *Nancy's* boyfriend happened to be best friends with *Brad*, my former boyfriend. She understood how devastated I had been and then on top of all that, having to drop out of college because Mom had terminal (we thought) Cancer. That summer she made it her aim to encourage me. I spent many hours in her sunny, beautiful home, healing, relaxing, reading her favorite writer and missionary to India, Amy Carmichael, and talking while *Nancy* listened.

I grew in my faith during this time, deeply grieving, deepening my understanding of how to journey with God. I did not know what my future held. I had a passion to tell people about Jesus. I had already applied and been accepted by Greater Europe Mission to go to France. I questioned whether this was the best time to leave the States to become a missionary while my mother's health was uncertain. It was during this time that a professor from PCB whom I admired, told me that he saw a

225

light on my face, he interpreted as "guileless[45]." I had to look up the meaning of the word, and considered this as a gift from God, relishing the evidence that He was at work in my life to repair my broken heart.

Nancy provided me with a much-needed spiritual oasis at a time when I felt bereft of anyone who understood the pain I had experienced. I continued to attend Tenth Presbyterian Church in Center City Philadelphia and through them, met Reverend Young Son, a Korean Minister affiliated with Inter-Varsity International Students. He and his wife, Mary Lou and their five children lived in a beautiful mansion called Philadelphia House[46] in Overbrook, a suburb of Philadelphia. Young and I met at Tenth's Sunday night coffee house, The Catacombs, where he recruited me to join him and his family in their ministry to international students at the universities in the Philadelphia area. I would live here after I graduated college and before I met my husband.

This ministry appealed to me because I had missed the departure date to go to France with Greater Europe Mission that year.

I didn't march in my PCB graduation. I had been a transfer student and many of my best friends were older and had already graduated. A friend and I watched from the balcony of the ballroom in the Sheraton Hotel in 1973 as my graduation class marched up the aisle to receive their diplomas. I had mine mailed to me. I was done with PCB.

---

45 - Guileless adjective, devoid of guile: innocent and without deception. *Oxford Dictionary*

46 - Philadelphia House: Non-Profit organization serving international students and foreign professionals in Overbrook, Philadelphia, PA

PHILADELPHIA HOUSE

The next week, *Gary*, one of the kids from our Dimension Club, helped me move into a sunny third floor room in Philadelphia House. I called this wonderful place home for two years with Young and Mary Lou Son, their family and ten students from around the world among them: Japan, Estonia, Brazil. We also housed career people and artists from the area.

I grew close to one young artist named Robert Montoya, we often drove out to Chadds Ford where we shared a love for the artists Andrew and Jamie Wyeth. I also grew to appreciate Bob's love of simple things such as the skeletons of trees in winter. This was around the time I met my future husband Jon Perry.

Next door to Philadelphia House was another beautiful mansion nicknamed, The Hidden Matzo, where our Messianic Jewish friends lived. Several blocks away in another large mansion, Young Myung Moon and his cult, referred to as The Moonies, lived. This was the time of cults, of Jesus People, and communes. We were affiliated with a legitimate church as were the kids next door. This often provided an opportunity for me to distinguish my beliefs from the "Moonies," especially since both homes in the neighborhood were headed by

Korean ministers. The primary difference was that we believed Jesus had died on the cross for our sins, that He alone was the way to God. Their leader on the other hand believed he was Jesus.

I often attended Pastor Herb Link's Messianic Congregation[47] down on Chestnut Street in Philly. For a while, I thought I might have a calling to minister to the Jewish people. To be honest, I also thought the Jewish boys I was meeting were handsome. Pastor Herb had challenged me with the verses in Genesis 12: 2-3:

> *"I will make you into a great nation and I will bless you; I will make your name great, and you will be a blessing. I will bless those who bless you, and whoever curses you I will curse, and all peoples on earth will be blessed through you."*

He suggested that if I gave one or two years to minister with the organization, Jews for Jesus, I would have God's blessing on me. I considered doing it. I loved the Jews, their music, and the Jewish believers. The history of the Holocaust was compelling. It was thrilling to sit in the prominent storefront church on Chestnut Street during the time when the Jewish Defense League or JDL was threatening Messianic Congregations. Each time someone came in the door during the service, heads would turn. There were threats of a bombing. Violence had occurred in California.

However, I was committed to being Young Son's first staff member, and soon recruited my best

---

47 - Worship using Jewish. *www.chosenpeople.com* music Jewish people who are sharing the gospel and proclaiming salvation through Jesus to other Jews while maintaining their Jewish identity.

friend, Chris, to join us. She moved from Wisconsin and became a major help to Young in the office as well as a blessing to international students. Soon, we opened an office on the campus of University of Pennsylvania, and another one up on North Broad Street across from Temple University. We held our Friday night meetings and international dinners at Penn and had drop-in hours at Temple. One regular attendee was "Hudsie," Hudson Taylor's[48] grandson, a vibrant and charming fellow.

Though we liked living at Philadelphia House, and loved Young, Mary Lou and the kids, Chris and I were ready to be independent. We made the case to Young Son that we should get an apartment closer to U of P campus.

Young was like a father, reluctant to have his grown daughters move away from home, putting forth all his arguments for why this wasn't a good idea. He seemed suspicious that we wanted to get out from under his watchful eye. This was partially true, especially for Chris who was one year older than I and often felt irritated by what she viewed as Young's sometimes irrational ways of thinking. I viewed his quirks as typical of older generation Korean men and was able to cope better with them. This was true, even when he ordered me once to jump over a small fence in his yard. I knew it was a ridiculous order, but because he jumped, so did I, cutting my leg.

He told me once that I irritated him with my "clarifying" questions. I did this to be sure that I

---

48 - James Hudson Taylor was a British Baptist Christian Missionary
to China and founder of the China Inland Mission. He spent 54
years in China. *Wikipedia.org*

understood his instructions. He told me that when I got married this constant checking would annoy my husband. I on the other hand felt insecure, because when I didn't understand him, he sometimes smiled a very Asian smile which conveyed his anger. No one in the house was happy when Young was angry.

I learned how to become a more involved mother from Mary Lou, as I watched her interact with her kids, sitting at the table ready for a chat when they returned from school, preparing big meals, and supervising chores. Our household was a lively and creative group, and there was never a dull moment in the house when Mary Lou was around. I learned from Mary Lou's transparency that I didn't have to act like a perfect Christian to do good. It is okay to do the best you can and move ahead. I also learned that few of us appreciate the mothers that God gives us.

Chris and I convinced Young that moving closer to campus was a good idea so we moved into a second-floor apartment on Forty-Second Street. It had one large front room, a tiny kitchen with a table that folded out from the kitchen door, a good-sized bedroom, two closets, and a bathroom. The woodwork had thick layers of fluorescent orange paint.

Young never really trusted us to live apart from his watchful eye. He used to call us at random times, especially early in the mornings when he suspected we were sleeping in! Occasionally, we were, and we would scramble out of bed to put on our best wide-awake voices. Sometimes we had been out late the night before in ministry on campus at the University of Pennsylvania International Center or had students in for dinners. Young had trouble with delegating, trusting, and above all he disliked laziness.

Ironically, Chris and I were very conscientious and sincere in our hearts to serve God and we loved the international students. We never considered shirking our responsibilities.

Gradually, I became tired of Young's strict scrutiny of our every move. I was restless and wanted to move on, but a principle that I had developed in my life guided me. I didn't want to move out of a situation to escape it until I had some place to move to. I didn't want to run away or avoid a difficult situation, to escape without a positive place to go next.

One funny incident happened between Young and me during a Philadelphia House board meeting at the Boice's apartment. Dr. and Mrs. Boice served us sherry but Young had taken a vow of abstinence from alcohol as a young man. When they passed around the sherry, I could tell that Young was embarrassed. The next thing I knew, he secretly passed his glass of sherry to me. I had never had a drink of alcohol in my life and didn't like my first taste of the sherry. So, I dumped both of our glasses of sherry into a large plant between us. Philadelphia House, Young and Mary Lou and their family will always be very dear to my heart.

Jon when I first met him

THE REAL DEAL

In the winter of 1973, when I was twenty-four, Young Son, our co-worker Chris and I organized an annual Christmas Conference in Bethlehem, Pennsylvania. International students from University of Pennsylvania, Temple, Drexel, and Villanova had a homestay in local Christian homes. They would tour Moravian sights including the Nativity Scenes, for which the town of Bethlehem was famous. We also planned for students to tour Bethlehem Steel, which was still flourishing at that time.

While there we met Jon Perry who was Navigator[49] staff at Lehigh University in Bethlehem, PA. He was volunteering at this Christmas Conference as a favor to a professor at Lehigh who hosted the yearly conference.

I first met Jon on a bus when we were touring Bethlehem Steel. We were wearing hard hats and safety goggles. The first thing I noticed about him was his vibrant smile.

He sat in the seat behind me, and as we talked, I checked to see if he was wearing a wedding ring,

---

49 - An international, interdenominational Christian organization working globally to help people know Christ and to help them grow in their relationship with Him. *Navigator Website*

but he wasn't. I assumed he was married because he was a little older than most of the single men I knew and very attractive! I thought that he should be bringing up his wife in our conversation.

I soon realized, to my delight, that he was not married. We stood in line together while touring a candle factory and he flirted. My friend Chris, pointed at Jon from across the room and said, "You know, if you married him, your name would be, Mary Perry!"

I laughed. He remembers me surrounded by the Japanese women from my English language courses. They were the wives of medical doctors who were in continuing studies at the University of Pennsylvania.

Just before we broke up the conference, Jon came over to say good-bye and I gave him my phone number and casually said he should come down to visit me in Philadelphia if he were ever to pass through. Happily, he "happened" to be passing through a short time later and called me to make a date.

Young and Mary Lou were delighted when they met Jon and noticed that we were talking. Young counseled me, "When Jon asks you to marry him, wait two weeks before you say, yes!"

Young had been concerned that I was spending too much of my free time with the artist, Bob Montoya, and he didn't feel we were a good match. He was several years younger than I was, and an artist without a reliable plan for the future. Young spoke to me several times about it and felt that Jon and I were a great match.

I had told Bob that Jon was probably going to ask me to marry him. I told him that one reason Jon would be a good husband for me was because he had high expectations. Bob sweetly told me that if I married him, he would never expect anything from me. It was close to a proposal but not quite.

▲　▲　▲

How did I know that Jon was the one? Well, I had been madly in love with *Brad* and that didn't work out. When I met Jon for the first time, I was attracted to his looks of course. But this time, I depended on my mind to lead me instead of my emotions when I chose a boyfriend/mate. I had been sitting under the teaching of godly men my entire life. These men were examples to me of the type of man I wanted to marry.

Earlier at PCB, after recovering from the whirlwind romance with *Brad*, I realized that I needed to consider more seriously the character that I wanted in a lifetime mate.

Sometimes as I sat in chapel listening to missionary speakers I'd think about the qualities that I admired in them and desired in a husband. At the same time, I realized that I needed to have qualities in my life that were attractive and a good match for someone who was as solid and stable as they were.

I also realized that I wanted to marry a man who was not on an emotional roller coaster, up and down like *Brad*.

I chose to focus on the qualities of the overseers, deacons and elders set forth in the Scriptures as my pattern for the man I wanted to marry. One example comes from 1 Timothy 3:2, 3,7 New International Version Bible

"Now the overseer is to be above reproach, faithful to his wife, temperate, self-controlled, respectable, hospitable, able to teach, not given to drunkenness, not violent but gentle, not quarrelsome, not a lover of money . . . 7 He must also have a good reputation with outsiders, so that he will not fall into disgrace and into the devil's trap."

When I eventually married Jon, I liked to say it was the first logical decision I had ever made in my life.

On our first date, I took him on a walking tour around the city of Philadelphia. While we were out, the chicken I was baking for him in my oven collapsed into a crispy heap in the baking pan. He claimed it still tasted good. He had an even temperament.

On Jon's second visit to our apartment, *Betty*, a friend from high school, was staying with me. She had struggled with mental health issues her entire life and was just recently released from a mental hospital. When Jon arrived at our door, she welcomed him by planting a big kiss right on his lips! This happened before Jon and had I kissed for the first time. He had a good sense of humor and was kind.

I knew that Jon was interested in marriage from our second date when we went to Bookbinder's, Philly's famous seafood restaurant. A collection of beautiful China plates made up the décor around the walls in every room, and when I made mention of it, Jon grinned across the table and asked, "What shall we collect?" That was when I knew he wanted to marry me. It was a very romantic moment.

▲   ▲   ▲

Jon asked me to marry him after we had known each other for three months. We were married within six months of meeting each other. He kissed me and told me he loved me in the foyer of my apartment in Philadelphia. This is the one kiss that I remember from all the boyfriends I have ever had. I simply don't remember a single other kiss.

He gave me my engagement ring in a gazebo on the lake in America's Keswick, a retreat center in New Jersey which was a meaningful place for him.

My ring is rose gold with a tiny Tiffany diamond in the center from the store in New York City. It was originally a *sweet sixteen* ring inscribed with the name of a young girl by the name of Minian P Barr 1876. Jon's dad provided it. I recently discovered that her middle name was Patience, and she was a relative of Jon's mother.

▲   ▲   ▲

What was it that attracted me to Jon? I first noticed his authenticity. His sense of humor and smile reminded me of my Uncle Robbie and my favorite Cousin Billy. He was good natured, and he often winked at me. He proved himself dependable and was happy to meet my friends. He was optimistic and affirming, eager to try new things. Soon I could tell that his faith in God was the most important part of his life as my faith was for me. His commitment to Scripture informed his life. He was warm and welcoming to strangers. He never belittled me, always believing the best about me. I enjoyed helping the poor and needy and I trusted that he would also. In fact, in our lifetime, it turned out that his insistence on helping the needy exceeded my own at times resulting in negative balances in our checking account. I had one further criterion for a man. If I couldn't trust and respect him enough to follow him across a busy Philadelphia intersection, he wasn't the man for me. I trusted Jon to guide me across the street, even with my eyes shut.

Jon and I went to Spartansburg to ask permission to marry from my mom and talked it over with Young Son and Mary Lou. He also took me around to visit several of his valued friends, Bob and Jan Lewis who were Navigator Area Directors and his best friends in the Navigators, Al and Elaine Cox who were in ministry at Rutgers University. We hit it off! I never could have predicted that the Cox's and we would become lifelong friends living in The Philippines and Indonesian cities together!

Jon was the first Navigator I had met since I had heard those young men singing at that Navigator Conference when I was in Eastern Mennonite College soon after I began to follow Jesus in 1968. In May 1975, Jon and I drove cross-country to a US Navigator Staff Conference at Glen Eyrie, The Navigator's headquarters, a beautiful castle in Colorado Springs, Colorado.

Jon was a veteran Navigator, well known by the US staff at Glen Eyrie because he had spent time working there, so we were kind of celebrities. Apparently, Jon was one of the most eligible bachelors among the staff men and people had been praying for him to find a wife for years.

I enjoyed the Bible teaching at the conference, and of course, the singing, but I felt very much out of place among most of the staff wives. I valued authenticity and found Elaine Cox very down-to-earth. I noticed a pattern about the wives I met in Colorado, they all seemed a bit like they were fitting into a mold. Not exactly cookie cutter wives but many of them had hair the same and smiled and talked alike. I guess this makes sense because many of them had been through Navigator homes and college training programs. Admittedly, they were all attending a conference where they may have felt they were being observed and tried to be on their best behavior. I didn't see much individuality.

One activity that I enjoyed was sitting in a group together to consider what we would like to have written on our tombstones. I loved that, but I don't remember what I wrote. I probably chose something about making a difference or influencing people.

We drove back across the country, getting to know each other better. I remember that it snowed at Glen Eyrie, in May! In the meantime, Mary Lou Son had been busy organizing and planning our June wedding.

My mom told me that she didn't know anything about weddings. I wasn't surprised, nor did I expect anything from her. She lived far away in Western Pennsylvania. My friends from there gave me a wedding shower as did several groups of my friends in Philadelphia.

In the meantime, Mary Lou was taking care of the wedding details.

HS Friend's Wedding Shower

PCB Friend's at Shower

Mary Lou's and my ideas were radically different, however. I had never dreamt of a fancy wedding, or any wedding at all. I just wanted it to be as simple as possible, but Mary Lou assured me that I would regret everything I left out. As I remember it, I wanted to get married in my bare feet. I had no expectations for a wedding dress. My one wish for my wedding was that I wouldn't be an ugly bride. Once again, my perception of myself as homely returned.

My Friends Before Our Wedding

Jon Perry and I were married on June 21, 1975, at Philadelphia House in Overbrook, Pennsylvania! My Uncle Robbie gave me away and Young Son officiated. Young Son's kids, Megan, Jennifer, Sarah and Elizabeth were in the procession, Chris was my Maid of honor and David Son was our ring bearer.

The Young Son Girls

241

Mary Lou baked us a beautiful three-tiered frosted wedding cake, and hosted a huge reception in Philadelphia House, inviting our many friends.

This included our international friends, Jon's Navigator friends, my PCB and Tenth friends, Young and Mary Lou (and my Amish/Mennonite friends) my Dimension high school kids who all came together.

Grandpa Robbie & Me

Grandpa Robbie gave me away. He had been the one consistent father figure in my life from the time I was a little girl! He lived to hold and pray for our first daughter Juliana and to dedicate her to the Lord.

My Japanese English student played the piano on the back porch and guests sat in folding chairs on the back lawn. I wore platform sandals, and a simple ($85) white, smocked, peasant dress created by fashion designer, Anne Pakradooni. Anne had just opened a new little shop on the Main Line.[50]

---

50 - The Philadelphia Main Line is an informally delineated historical and social region of suburban Philadelphia known for historic homes and wealthy towns. *Wikipedia.org*

She was beginning her business but eventually became world famous serving film stars and politicians. My friend Zaga Sain, an ESL student wife from Montenegro, embroidered tiny green vines and pink flowers on the bodice.

After the wedding as we walked down the back porch steps and around into the front yard, we had our pianist play the ragtime theme music, *The Entertainer*, by Scott Joplin, from the movie *The Sting*[51] which we had recently watched. Everyone laughed in surprise.

Japanese Friends at Our Wedding

The reception was exhausting, but everyone held up well. It was that day that I first felt the extreme exhaustion that was to become so familiar for the rest of my life. This exhaustion arose out of my giving so much emotionally that I had nothing more to give.

I was proud of Mom and her gracious people skills. She stood behind me for part of the time and once when a friend of ours told her he was just in

---

51 - The theme music was from the 1973 film, *The Sting* starring Robert Redford and Paul Newman.

the background taping our conversations she said, "A very important background, I'm sure." That was Mom. She looked very pretty and charmed everyone.

Our Wedding

The photo of Mom and Grandpa Robbie, sitting together on the porch swing with Young, Mary Lou and Megan on the front porch of Philadelphia House shows them as we took off for our honeymoon. Mom told me afterwards and I could tell that she had been hurt and worried because Young had said to her "Now Mary will have to look after Jon's Mother as well as you."

Jon's Dad & My Mom at the Wedding

I cannot imagine anything more upsetting that Mom could have heard.

Mom on the Front Porch

SEARCHING FOR MY TWO DADS

THE HONEYMOON WAS OVER

GOD'S TRAINING PROGRAM

Jon and I headed out to Ocean City, Maryland to Navigator staff Harv Oslund's Cabin. Jon had designed and built the cabin with his Navigator friends while he lived with Harv and Maydelle.

For the first time, I felt that I was finally a grown-up! Our options were ours alone to choose. However, I soon realized that I had not given any serious thought to what marriage required. I had never dreamed about my wedding. I had not learned how to intimately partner with a man. I had never thought about the logistics of sex. I spent so much time and energy avoiding it with all my boyfriends, that I never once gave a thought to the actual act of having sex.

Though I was boy crazy in a romantic way, I wasn't prepared to have sex. This would present difficulties.

On the way we stopped at a hotel where we had our first disagreement. It was at that point we realized how little we knew each other. As we drove into the parking lot, I pointed to an empty space near the office entrance and casually said, "Park there."

I don't know exactly how Jon reacted, he may have stiffened, probably his pupils widened, he set his jaw, or he got silent. It was clear to me that he didn't like me giving him a suggestion, or was it the tone of my voice? This type of situation would become a sore point between us for many years. I was astonished that he was upset by my suggestion.

I should have been better prepared when earlier in our engagement he had given me the following list of requirements:

- I should not watch soap operas.
- We should live far away from my mother.
- I should do whatever he tells/asks me to do first before other jobs around the house.

I eagerly and foolishly agreed to these, with no context, no discussion, even though I didn't watch soap operas. Jon and I hardly knew each other at all. I began to feel angry about how Jon came into our marriage expecting it to work like a formula without any understanding of communication or connection between men and women. I began to realize that he might be good at teaching principles and illustrations but did not appear to understand human relationships. I expected him to be like other men I knew, who were natural communicators, but he was very different.

I had no experience living with a man aside from living in Philadelphia House with Young Son, Bob Montoya, and several of the Japanese international students there. I had no experience at all living on an intimate level with a man, definitely not with a man settled in his ways as Jon was at 33 years of age. We were direct opposites in most ways.

▲ ▲ ▲

Jon's parents were older, and when they were upset with him as a child, they responded with silence. He had one brother eight years older than he was. He told me that they never argued.

Jon & His Brother Win

Winston, his brother seemed like more of an admirable father figure who graciously taught Jon many skills like sailing and was sometimes willing to have him tag along on dates. My mother and I yelled and argued like two cats and then asked forgiveness and were back in communication. I never had to get along with a sibling.

When I became hurt and angry, I didn't know how to channel or voice my anger in respectful ways. As a happy young adult, I was seldom angry, and now, I was angry with my husband just hours after I had made a lifelong commitment to love him.

None of the marriage books I found had information about this. The problem was, I didn't know how to behave respectfully at home. I respected Jon, but I was accustomed to speaking my mind. The more he reacted woodenly against my ideas, the more I persisted and raised my voice. Here he was practically a stranger who actually asked me once if I could "think less."

249

Jon became offended with me saying that my tone of voice and even my look seemed "bossy" to him. I got along well with everyone I knew. I had been living with Young Son's family and got along with him. Surely Young Son, the ultimate Korean man would have coached me on how to be more polite. No one ever complained that I used an objectional tone or that my face looked "bossy."

My hospital patients and co-workers thought well of me. I worked well with authoritative people and with students who were rebellious and with shy, timid people. I felt terribly disappointed that my husband didn't seem to like or accept me the way I was. On the other hand, admittedly, marriage felt like it had turned on a switch in me, where suddenly, I reverted back to my original angry self.

Getting back to sex. Of course, my emotions, plus my failure to have thought through on sex in marriage affected us for a long time. This was surprising to Jon who expected sex to be as natural for me as it was for him. For me, who had been hugging the opposite side of the bed from my mom most of my life, it felt most unnatural.

On Jon's part, he assumed that his ideas were right and wasn't prepared for discussion or conflict. He felt that apologies meant he was wrong, rather than caring whether he had wounded me. I was willing to admit when I was wrong, which only confirmed to him that he was right. This hurt me for many years.

I felt unaccepted and unappreciated because he was so frequently offended by my blunt answers. This continued into the nineties. Though he worked well with strong women over the years in Indonesia and at Cornell, he told me that it was different with me. My good opinion mattered more to him and hurt him more when I disagreed. He wanted my approval and for years I was unable or unwilling to learn to give negative feedback with tact and kindness. It felt like he only wanted positive comments.

Sometimes, I compared my life with Jon as if I were a raw egg being cracked on the edge of a bowl. I was the raw egg; he was the bowl. He had rigid ideas and I had to conform to them. This isn't the way a normal marriage works, but Jon and I weren't normal marriage partners. I think our seven-year age difference worked against us.

Our First House

I realize that I, who was so often oppositional, had much to learn about cooperating with Jon. It wasn't easy. He also had important things to learn from me. God brought us together for His purposes. It has taken most of our marriage for us to learn these lessons. We both believed that God was doing something even more important than our marriage through our difficulties. We believed that He wanted to shape us into better human beings, and closer to the example of Christ Jesus.

My blunt, feedback hurt Jon's sensitive feelings. I felt shackled, unable to express myself honestly, it was dampening and stressful. I felt like he preferred me when I was weak, sick, or depressed, too feeble to exert my opinion. On the other hand, I thought he should toughen up. We were at a hopeless checkmate.

I have read that when we don't learn important lessons in our childhood, God continues to teach us these things into adulthood. This was true for us regarding my brashness and what I saw as Jon's hypersensitivity. I now realize that both of our families in the past were influenced by great trauma and loss. Jon's father had lost his parents when he was a little boy, and Jon's parents grieved the loss of two baby boys before Jon was born. I was rejected by my father and my mother was traumatized herself.

Because of these issues, we came into our marriage with coping skills that we weren't aware of but which hindered our communication and intimacy. We had learned to protect ourselves from further trauma. Sadly, we didn't learn valuable lessons in time to model a loving marriage for our children. They grew up to believe that marriage is a commitment and hard work, which it is. However, it wasn't until after they left our home that we had learned to model a marriage that was also happy and loving.

I marvel that God guided me out of potentially disastrous relationships and led me into a stable and dependable marriage with a husband like Jon Perry. I knew he was reliable and had integrity, qualities of the overseers, elders and deacons, that I had been looking for since PCB.

My mother liked Jon immediately, and his dad liked me. I seldom felt approval from his mother, and I understand why. Mothers have grand expectations for their children. Jon was an exceptional person, and I was not emotionally stable. I think most mothers have protective radar when it comes to their children's prospective mates. I had a quick temper; a blunt tongue and I was not educated to their standards. I used to joke to my friends that Jon's family sat around the dining room table chatting about Chaucer, but they really did.

Each member of his family was talented, highly intelligent and well educated, many in Ivy League schools.

This was true of Jon too, however, I never felt anything less than equal to him. In fact, he often told me that I offered things that he did not get from his family, such as understanding of people, and empathy. Jon's mother didn't attend our wedding and never visited our home. Understandably, she also had a painful case of Shingles that lasted most of her old age. However, I wonder if she simply didn't want to visit us.

The Happy Newlyweds

It took thirty years for our marriage to become peaceful. I admire Jon because he was always willing to receive counsel from others and he remained faithful to me. I have never heard Jon say a mean word other than his criticism of me, which seemed more like self-defense.

It took us many years for us to become self-aware, and I believe if I had been more prayerful and less argumentative, this would have occurred sooner.

We requested marriage advice from every counselor who visited us in our homes in Indonesia throughout the years. We both went to counseling, read books and attended as many marriage seminars as possible.

Nothing seemed to help us. The advice seemed aimed at so called, "typical couples," where the man was assertive, the wife was quiet and demure. Indeed, we were reading books and receiving counsel that seemed to be left over from the culture of the fifties, of what remained of the "Leave it to Beaver" family.

Christians were writing books aimed at traditional couples. We were the opposite. Jon, with his artistic temperament, rarely thought about asserting leadership, yet he insisted that I wait and follow his leadership whenever I asserted myself! It was a conundrum.

I respected Jon and also had a passion to shake up the world, to change it where I could influence people that I met. I was eager to confront problems. Confrontation signaled conflict and chaos for Jon and was the last thing he wanted to be involved in.

This was such a source of frustration for both of us. Jon was so often offended by what he perceived as my criticism that he rarely if ever asked for my opinions.

If I differed from him, the blunt way I volunteered my opinion hurt his feelings and felt so offensive to him that he could not receive it as anything other than hurtful. I used to hear great preachers say that their wives were their best critics. How I envied those wives.

We persevered and at last, one year we attended a weekend marriage seminar where we discovered the problem. Roger and Shelly Iishi suggested we try the seminar called, Dynamic Marriage: A Seminar for Transforming Relationships, developed and written by Joe Beam. His organization was Family Dynamics.

Whether another seminar would have been as successful, I don't know. Possibly, it was the right time for us. Jon realized that he had never truly listened to me. I had not been listening to him, either. We learned that it was important to hear what the other thought without reacting negatively.

We realized that we had been forcing ourselves into traditional roles because of our flawed understanding of Biblical teaching. Even more damaging, I had been foolishly trying to force Jon into my image and Jon had been trying to force me into his. It was that simple.

We had stubbornly refused to accept or appreciate the ways we were the exact opposites of each other and of all the examples in Christian marriage books written in the 1970's.

Until we decided to accept one another for who we were, we would never be happy.

Our unique qualities were created by God. I remember the exact place we sat under a tree in our car after the seminar as we discussed this discovery which transformed our marriage.

CHILDREN ARE A GIFT FROM THE LORD

I wish that our marriage had been better before we had our children, but I would not have wanted to miss the wonderful children we have.

Our first daughter, Juliana Blauvelt was born, May 9, 1976, in Bethlehem, PA, eleven months after we were married.

I remember the music they were playing in the delivery room, and for years tried to find out what it was, because it was memorable and calming. I finally discovered that it was "Send in the Clowns" by Judy Collins. Interesting "walk on music" for our tiny, beautiful Juliana. She has always had a great sense of humor.

She was born after seventeen hours of labor. She came out with an anxious look in her big brown eyes! What a joy to see her solid, round head, hard as a rock and barely molded. A large Perry head, I thought! The doctors had given me an epidural, which caused back spasms afterwards.

Giving birth gave me a new perspective on the unsurpassable value of life. Each human being comes into the world through pain and suffering, a high price paid for each one. I grew more sensitive when I heard of children having accidents or suffering with disease. It was heartbreaking to consider all of the effort expended in bringing a new person into the world, and then to have their lives lost.

Between the spasms and my anxiety, I held Juliana for a very few minutes and then they didn't let me hold her for many hours after her birth. I became very anxious about that. How I wish I had the reassurance of a mid-wife to sit with me and calm me down during my first experience as a birth mother. I'm sure Jon tried his best, but we weren't connecting very well emotionally.

Our birthing story was so different from the stories of all my friends in the Lamaze[52] birthing group. Many of the mothers had given birth to their first babies several weeks before me. They talked about how easily they had pushed them out. Most of their babies were huge. I was unprepared for seventeen hours of labor. Tiny Juliana went into distress and had a monitor put on her head. I also became distressed. I had terrible back spasms afterwards. No one talked to me to calm me down.

Jon tried to be supportive, but given our relationship, neither he nor I knew how he could be of help. He tried to say all the right things, but he couldn't calm my fears. When the nurse eventually brought Juliana to my room, I requested that she sleep beside my bed in her little portable crib. The nurse was openly disapproving of this new concept they called rooming in and said they discouraged it because mothers couldn't get enough sleep.

---

52 - Lamaze is a method of childbirth that involves building a mother's confidence in her ability to give birth, through classes that help her cope with pain in ways that facilitate labor, including relaxation, breathing and massage. *Wikipedia.org*

After about a month, my pediatrician also told me that I didn't have enough milk for my baby to thrive. While I was adamant that God made me her mother, so it made sense that I had had enough milk for her, he became indignant and said there is a condition called, "Failure to Thrive Syndrome."

He inferred to me that my skinny little girl might have it. I stubbornly resisted supplementing my breast milk with bottle-feeding, though she cried so much and grew slowly. It took two years for me to overcome my feelings that I was a failure and a bad mother. We were into eating healthy food and we discovered later that some of the good food, like whole wheat bread and bananas that we fed her gave her stomachaches.

I compared tiny Juliana with other children who were larger, and walking. However, I was proud of her because she was especially charming and crawled around talking. I worried for a while that she might have "Dwarfism."

One of my older friends unhelpfully told me that you can't really predict whether a child will become a midget when they are babies.

As I look back now, I realize that despite Jon being in my corner, there was no one else hearing my concerns. No one was assuring me that I would succeed as a mom. I don't think Jon understood how seriously I doubted myself.

When mom said to me once, "Who would ever think that you would be a good mother," it was typical of her mothering of me throughout my life. She didn't consider how to instill confidence, but instead gave her frank opinions, I had been following her pattern. It seemed that our life was more centered on stories of her life and her wonderful parents, than about understanding me. Maybe that's one reason I became so angry. I also became a realist, but I have tried to be more affirming to my children than Mom was.

During my relationship with *Brad*, I had begun learning what it felt like to share my feelings, to have someone listen and be empathetic. We had a natural connection. We clicked. That is one reason our relationship meant so much to me. Now, I was in a marriage with Jon that felt shallow and unsatisfying. I vowed to love Jon, but I worried that my decision relegated me to a life of loneliness of spirit. I had tasted depth and now I felt unsatisfied and sad. But we were committed.

Juliana brought immense joy to our lives which revolved around her. Everything she did was new and wonderful to us!

We often said that we had practiced being parents with our puppy, Gretchen, a fluffy little black terrier we adopted soon after our marriage.

Gretchen & Juliana on Her First Christmas

Early in our marriage, Jon told me that we couldn't have a dog because he felt concerned that I would pay more attention to it than I did to him. I accepted this as just another of his rigid ideas. Looking back now, I realize that I wasn't meeting Jon's needs for affection, and he didn't know how to talk about it or what to do about it other than to set down a rule.

Jon soon grew to love Gretchen even more than I did. Every afternoon when Jon walked home from work, our little Gretchen would race like a bullet train down the sidewalk to meet Jon and jump into his arms.

I stayed home with Juliana while Jon, who was an architect, worked in an architectural office in downtown Bethlehem. We were in ministry to students at Lehigh University, and we had a Bible study with some local married couples. Before Juliana was born, we also led a junior high Sunday school class in the local Episcopal church. It was a happy time, because we were busy, and we didn't have too much time to dwell on our relationship.

My new role as a mother was as enjoyable as I had expected. I loved carrying baby Juliana around the neighborhood teaching her new words and pushing her in the stroller pointing out trees and colorful flowers. I relished the luxury of quiet, late-night breast-feedings, reading Upton Sinclair's book, *The Jungle,* while rocking her. I nicknamed Juliana, Una, after one of the characters in the book. Jon called her "hockey puck" because of some baby words she had uttered.

An older Navigator staff woman recently told me that I have changed so much since the seventies when she first met me. She remembers me silently taking care of my young child and smiling all the time. I remember that I was trying to fit The Navigator wife mold. But, I had not yet learned who I was.

We drove out to Glen Eyrie, The Navigator's headquarters, with Juliana for a Navigator training program for college students the summer that she was one year old. I had such a wonderful time getting to know several other young wives. I did worry about Juliana because she didn't walk until seventeen months old, though she talked early. It was really cute to see her crawling around chattering in full sentences.

OUR CALLING

While we were at Glen Eyrie, we met missionaries from all around the world and we concluded that the Lord was leading us to go overseas. Jon admired the evangelist, Brother Andrew, who smuggled Bibles into the Communist Eastern European countries, and wanted to do this too.

After PCB I had made plans to go to France. God had given both of us the verses from Matthew 28:19, 20 "Go ye into all the world, and preach the gospel to every creature..." We didn't feel we needed specific verses directing us to go to missions, though some of our friends did want this additional call. This was not a new idea for me. My childhood vision of my future had been to travel around the United States with my family in a green Volkswagen van telling people about Jesus.

The Navigators asked us to consider going to Indonesia. Neither of us knew exactly where that was. I personally had never heard of it, and thought it was in the vicinity of Vietnam, Southeast Asia. We both readily agreed, even when the Navs told us it would be a difficult assignment. They told us we should be prepared for earthen floors, and no dependable electricity or water supply. I naively jumped at the chance to serve the Lord and see the world!

After the training program, we moved to Spartansburg to stay with my mom for the summer while Jon went to Toronto School of Linguistics (TIL) to learn principles of language learning.

The Navigators intended me to go to Toronto too, but I, yearning for a better relationship with my mother, took the opportunity to go back to Spartansburg to stay with her. I wanted so much to try to heal our relationship before going overseas. I was good at learning languages but felt like a failure in my relationship with Mom. However, we continued to argue whenever we were together.

Juliana, Gretchen, and I stayed with Mom while Jon went to language school. It was a terrible time with me and Mom arguing, and bickering.

I felt terrible for the baby (Catherine) that I was carrying. I failed miserably in my desire to get along better with Mom. In fact, I realize now that I was vulnerable to her baiting me, whether consciously or not. Maybe she didn't intend to bait me, maybe I was easily triggered by the things she said. I felt as if she was more comfortable in a combative relationship with me than she was in a peaceful one. Maybe, also, she was bracing against the loneliness of our leaving and moving so far away.

I wish that I had realized then that desires are different from goals. A goal is something I alone can carry out. A desire is a wish that depends on others. We were back to my childhood patterns, I apologized often and felt terrible. I desired to get along, but my goal was hindered by our patterns of arguing.

Jon, Juliana and I returned to Bethlehem, PA in the fall, sold off our things and gave away our beloved

Gretchen dog to a couple in our Bible Study. We assumed that they would include her in their family as we had. One of our greatest disappointments happened when we returned home on our first furlough in 1984 to visit our darling little Gretchen. We found her tied outdoors to a doghouse. She had grown dumpy and fat from little exercise. The spark had gone out of her eyes, and she showed no recognition of us. We couldn't say anything to the couple who were clearly kept busy by their large extended family, but we both cried when we left. It's a good thing we can't see the future.

At the end of summer, we rented a U-Haul and moved to Colorado Springs. We drove cross-country in what felt like the hottest season on record. We had no air conditioning in the truck, Juliana slept at my feet, and I poured cups of water over us.

On November 1,1978, our second daughter, Catherine Hammond was born in Colorado Springs. I had been dreading childbirth because my first experience had been upsetting. I felt like such a failure.

Though I was fearful about giving birth to Catherine, her birth was fast and easy. She was larger than Juliana had been, calm, slept well and took to breastfeeding right away. I spent the late-night hours with her after Juliana was in bed. Juliana as a toddler understandably required every minute of my time during her waking hours. She was curious and full of fun ideas and questions.

Giving birth to Catherine in Colorado Springs was a pleasurable experience compared to my ragged experience in Bethlehem, Pennsylvania. "Rooming in" was expected, and Jon and I were given red wine and a steak dinner to enjoy in the privacy of my room. We brought Catherine home and enjoyed taking walks in the Colorado sunshine together with toddler Juliana. My mom flew to Colorado Springs to spend time with us, which helped to keep Juliana entertained. It was a peaceful time together.

We were living in an apartment complex on Nevada Avenue where many Army people lived. Our neighbor across the hall, Linda, told me that sometimes, she was afraid for her life because of her partner's temper. She brought his pistol over for me to hide in case he came in angry and drunk one night.

As I rocked baby Catherine each night, I read the book, *The Awakening Land* by Conrad Richter. I often glanced up at the gun in our closet praying that our neighbor wouldn't demand to know where Linda had hidden it.

One time, Juliana's blanky disappeared from our community dryer. Though we substituted another one which she accepted, I wanted to track down the thief. I was in the laundry room one day when a little girl named Brandy walked in dragging Juliana's blanky and chewing on a huge turkey bone. I coaxed her to give me the blanket by handing her another treat. Brandy was a pale, wispy, neglected girl whose mother often let her play outdoors in freezing weather without proper clothing. Jon and I argued about whether I should report her mother to the authorities. Jon said no, but I thought I should.

At that time, Jon believed firmly that we shouldn't get the government involved in families because they might take the children away and break up a family. This was the predominant Evangelical thinking in the seventies. I went along with him but against my better judgment. Several times I had to go into Brandy's mother's apartment to wake her up from a drunken stupor so she would take care of her children.

Virgina & Catherine

We were waiting for our Visas to go to Indonesia, which were taking a long time. Finally, the Navigators suggested that we should get over to Asia and wait there. I had opted to wait nine months to give birth to Catherine in the west to avoid inoculations that I worried might harm her. My primary concern had been the effect of the Smallpox vaccine. The timing worked out perfectly.

▲   ▲   ▲

The time came to return to Spartansburg, and Nyack, NY to say our goodbyes. Jon found twenty-six barrels that were discarded by the Colorado highway department which we packed with all of our possessions. The insides were thick with dried yellow highway paint. We shipped them to Indonesia from Colorado Springs and drove back East in our golden Plymouth Valiant with the two kids.

We stayed with my mom and then went down to Nyack. Mom and Jon's parents were wonderfully supportive regarding our decision to leave though it was very difficult for Mom. We were taking her only remaining family away across the world. She cried when we left.

Leaving our parents felt sad, but I confess we were largely oblivious to how difficult it was for them. We departed from JFK Airport with twenty-six suitcases, destination Hong Kong, Japan and then Manila. It was an easy trip with Juliana already two years old, excited about learning new things. She carried her little go bag full of interesting things to do.

ASIA

We spent two weeks traveling across Japan by bullet train, visiting Jon's niece, Susie, who had married the Japanese writer, Tomo Matsui. We also visited many of the Japanese women whom I had taught during my time at Philadelphia House.

Juliana and Catherine, who was eleven months old, were easy travelers. The difficulty was when we slept in a room on tatami mats. Catherine, who was used to sleeping in a crib crawled all over us throughout the night.

We carried both girls in backpacks. The Japanese families were very hospitable, treating us like royalty. We traveled from the Northern to the Southern parts of Japan. This gave us a wonderful experience in another culture. We visited an elementary school on Children's Day. Juliana became a little celebrity, running on the playground with the Japanese children. We experienced our first Typhoon in Japan which was fierce and thrilling, but we took our cue from the family we stayed with and avoided panic.

SEARCHING FOR MY TWO DADS

MANILA, PHILIPPINES

In Manila, Geoff Garton from the New Zealand Navigators picked us up at the airport in his open-sided Jeep. It was culture shock from the beginning as Jon chatted with Geoff up front and I held on tightly to two babies to make sure they didn't fall out the sides. Geoff and Jon were oblivious to us in the backseat as Geoff swerved around curves. The heat was oppressive, and I was exhausted. Juliana felt such joy at riding in the jeep, as if she was in a carnival ride.

That night we went out to an authentic Filipino restaurant where between the sweltering heat and the unusual odors and tastes, I got my worst migraine ever. I spent much of the evening in the filthy restroom leaning over the squat pot toilet throwing up.

After a good nights' sleep, I felt better. Geoff and Joanne Garton's home was comfortable and we felt welcomed. Conversation with them was easy. Juliana had an instant playmate in their little girl. The young men who studied in their home were so sweet to Catherine and Juliana and loved practicing their US English with us. Juliana gave them plenty of practice with her current question, "Because why?"

We soon moved into a four-room house on K-8 Street near the University in Quezon City, a suburb of Manila. This was a typical Filipino home with tile floors; we had a living room which opened into a step-down dining room. Next came a small kitchen. Outside in the back we had a slab of cement with clotheslines and running water which served as our laundry area.

Upstairs we had two bedrooms. We had a front veranda and a very small, fenced yard. The traffic in front was primarily motorcycles, bicycles and sometimes oxen driven carts, rarely cars.

We opted to rent this house in the type of neighborhood where a public-school teacher would live comfortably. We wanted our children to have the experience of knowing children from all economic levels so they would not consider their privileged Western lives to be the norm.

Compared to many of the Westerners living in the Philippines and later, in Java, our family lived quite simply. Many of our Filipino neighbors lived in poverty.

We spent Thanksgiving with our friends, Al and Elaine Cox and their children at the Missionary School where they were serving as temporary house parents. This was the day I looked down at our baby Catherine's blond head and saw lice crawling around on it.

What a shock! I called Elaine to warn her, and she assured me it was no big deal, her children had them too. We spent Thanksgiving afternoon treating all the kids for lice!

"If your children have friends, they will have lice," this was a quote from Doctor Kevin Lehman and it was confirmed in Manila. The little neighborhood kids played at our home all the time. I got lice also, though mine may have come from the neighborhood salon where I got my hair cut.

I was so grateful we could spend our first Christmas in Southeast Asia in the Philippines. I'm convinced no one celebrates Advent as well as the Filipinos do. Beginning in October, Christmas carolers stroll from house to house with guitars each evening singing carols. The Filipinos decorate the streets with lights and displays throughout the cities and suburbs.

Christmas in a foreign culture held some fascinating contrasts for me. I remember the hot Christmas Eve as I sat in my neighbor's home, I looked out at the palm trees swaying in the breeze and saw a little goat bleating in the front yard where he was tied. He was to be slaughtered and eaten the next day for Christmas dinner.

Our home was down the street from families living in abject poverty. One boy, who often played at our house, brought a present to Juliana on Christmas Day. He gave her some of his little plastic blocks. Even at the age of two, Juliana recognized that the little boy had sacrificed something important to him by kindly sharing his few toys with her.

One night we were walking home after delivering baskets of food to our neighbors; I looked up in the sky directly over our street to see the Southern Cross constellation! This memory will always be a highlight for me!

273

During the three months we lived in the Philippines, Jon and I were asked to lead a Catholic youth group in the barrio.[53]   Many of these teenagers lived in huts on stilts over the garbage dumps near a river. When I went with Jon to meetings, we simply strolled through the streets with one or two young people strumming guitars. Teenagers would pour out into the streets to join us as we passed their homes.

The Catholic Priests accepted us with some reservation, glad for a little help, though we weren't Catholic. Jon was able to share Jesus with the kids, but we only had a few months to help them grow in their faith. God used us while we were there, making the most of the time, though our influence was limited.

One teenager, Joe, grew especially attached to us and liked to visit us in our home. He invited Jon to visit him and his family too. Once, after visiting Joe's family, Jon came down with Dysentery and was so ill for such a long time that he began to resemble a skeleton.

From the beginning, Jon was willing to eat anything. I was fairly adventurous too but drew the line at chicken feet. Another food I avoided was *Balut:* This was the Philippine's national dish. It is a full-grown baby chick in an egg, with feathers, claws, and all. The Balut venders walk the streets each night yelling "Baalllluttt!"

---

53 - Barrio is a Spanish word meaning "neighborhood" denotes
a self-governing community within a rural or an urban area.
Wikipedia.org

Our Filipino Navigator friends were visiting us one night in our home on K-8 Street when one of these venders walked by. They thought it would be funny to watch Jon eat one. They probably would have bought one for me, but I disappeared upstairs to "tend to the baby."

Jon ate one and pronounced it "not bad" to a room full of delighted laughter!

SEARCHING FOR MY TWO DADS

DISASTER AVERTED ON K-8

Two Filipino sisters came in daily to work for us. The older sister, Espy, went to the market every day, and cooked our food, while the younger sister, Esther, washed and ironed our clothes by hand, and scrubbed the floors. They both worked to keep our little four-room house running smoothly.

Esther became attached to baby Catherine. While Juliana spent much of her time with me, Esther carried Catherine around since she was not walking yet.

One night, Jon and I were out at a Bible Study. Esther was staying with the girls. When I returned and went upstairs to check on the sleeping girls, to my horror I discovered a large kitchen knife on the nightstand between their beds.

The next morning, I confronted Esther with my discovery. She assured me that I didn't need to worry and promised she would tell me about it at Christmas. Since Christmas was coming up soon, I trusted her while warning her to never leave a knife near the children again.

She was remorseful and, as promised, on Christmas Day, revealed to me that she had intended to kill herself that night in the girls' room. She had then looked at baby Catherine sleeping peacefully and innocently and realized that the baby was completely dependent on her. She changed her mind because of Catherine. She had been heartbroken over a young man who had rejected her. When we left for Indonesia we entrusted her to friends who led a Bible study.

INDONESIA TANAH AIR [54]

My dream of traveling the United States in a green Volkswagen van to tell people about Jesus did not materialize. We would never own a green VW van; however, we traveled the world doing the most important part; telling people about the Kingdom of God.

Living in Indonesia, the largest Muslim nation in the world, was the hardest thing I have ever done, and one of the most satisfying.

Before we left the United States, Carole Mayhall, an older Navigator staff woman, advised me to be sure to find a good friend in Indonesia whom I could admire. As Carole and I sat on a rock on the shore of a lake at the convention center where she was speaking, she confided to me how this advice had been helpful to her throughout her life.

Our friend Nate Mirza, from Iran, counseled us to keep a sense of humor. A seasoned missionary to Iran, William Miller, from Tenth Presbyterian Church in Philly counseled us to "just love" the Muslims.

On our arrival in Jakarta, when I first stood at the open door of the plane holding our baby Catherine

---

54 - Tanah Air in Indonesian means homeland.
   https://en.m.wiktionary.org

in my arms, the tropical heat of the Indonesia tarmac hit me like a brick wall.

A horrendous thought came to my mind: it was a picture of me shot between the eyes with a bullet.

I would learn that our enemy, Satan, sometimes brings frightening thoughts like this into our minds to terrify or distract us. I had much to learn about rejecting those thoughts in Jesus' Name.

When we had left the States, all the news outlets were buzzing about the Iranian students taking over the US Embassy in Tehran. That's really all I knew about Muslims.

We received no training in what to expect when we encountered the Muslim population in the largest Muslim nation in the world! No doubt this was because The Navigators also didn't know very much about the Muslim world. Fortunately, we were good at learning because we had to learn on our feet.

In most ways it was a good plan, because learning the language on the street was the way to learn how people really spoke and thought.

Juliana at JL Menjangan

I am sure, though, that we offended some people by our ignorance.

Our first home in Bandung, Indonesia was an old Dutch house with a lovely yard on *Jalan Menjangan* (Deer Street).

The first day we arrived, we met our gracious house helpers who had made up the beds and prepared a lovely Indonesian rice meal for us. We ate, nodding our heads in appreciation for the delicious food and then headed to bed, exhausted.

In the middle of the night, which was morning in the USA, we awoke to lights on in the common room, geckos[55] on the ceilings, and locked doors. Our helpers had locked us into our house and returned to their homes. We didn't have a key. Of course, we didn't have any place to go, but Jon and I laughed at the absurdity of our situation.

We ate the food that they had left out for us and again fell into bed with jetlag. The next morning, the helpers returned to open our doors and let us out. For weeks afterwards our communication was primarily through hand signals as we learned language word by word. "Drink, Eat, Go outside."

Soon our toddler, Juliana, knew more words than we did. Gradually as we learned the language, we took walks through the neighborhood. We began to meet students at the local universities, inviting them to our home.

Once when students came to visit us, we asked them if we could "take their jackets." They clearly

---

55 - Geckos are small, harmless lizards, common in houses especially in warm climates. They eat insects. *Wikipedia.org*

misunderstood our intent because they clutched their coats as if we were asking to keep them permanently.

Jon with girls at JL Menjangan

Once, a man came to our house to borrow money. This was a surprise to us, but it became a common request. We were a little afraid that he might rob us if he knew where we kept our money, so we did a silly thing. Jon got up and walked into one room then another pretending to get money. I said to the person in Indonesian, "We don't really even know where our money is."

Imagine the absurd impression that made! As if we had so much money lying around in all our rooms that we didn't know where it all was!

We had a wonderful gardener, Pak Eddy. Two Sundanese[56] women helped us at home for the two years we lived in Bandung, Ibu Eng Kom and Ibu Nani. Eng Kom was my favorite helper of all time. She loved Catherine and cared for her as if she was her own baby.

One day a beautiful stray white dog appeared in our yard. I named her *Malu* (Shy) because she hesitated to approach me. I left food out for her and one day she disappeared. I searched for her and discovered that she had given birth to puppies in a drainpipe near our home. I was worried that the puppies might drown in one of Bandung's heavy downpours, so I took them out of the pipe, put them in a box and brought them to our yard. Malu moved into our yard and for a while, we had a dog with puppies. We even made a doghouse for her. Catherine loved having them. When they were old enough, we gave them away to good homes. Eventually, Malu disappeared.

Catherine first began to walk in our bedroom at Jalan Menjangan. Another day, I noticed she was jabbering away at something in the yard. She had spotted a poisonous banded Krait snake. There she was in her little sun bonnet, talking to a deadly snake. I whisked her away and got our gardner, Pak Eddie, to kill it.

This was one of several times God spared Catherine's life in Indonesia. One night, she tipped backwards off her changing table onto her head on the slate floor. Her little eyes began to roll up in her head and she turned white as a sheet. I felt terrified!

---

56 - Sundanese are a West Javanese Tribal people. *Wikipedia.org*

I held her close to my heart and began pacing and praying, begging God to save her. Juliana paced right behind me. I felt especially terrified because Jon was out of town, and I didn't know how to contact anyone in town. We had no phone, no vehicle. We were isolated with God. Gradually, as I held her close, the color returned to her little face and she began interacting normally.

Juliana on Her Class Trip at the Zoo

Juliana went to Cipiganti Baptis Preschool for three years. It was a wonderful way for her to be with Indonesian children and a perfect opportunity to learn the language. It was a bit risky, sometimes, though. Once we found that the teacher had taken all of her little students on a boat ride without life jackets. Juliana's friends Bryan and Beth Ann Cox were in school with her. Jon and I often took long walks together during the day while the children were in the care of the house helpers or in school.

Our second house in Bandung was on Jalan[57] Tubagus Ismail, a cul-de-sac between a vast

---

57 - Jalan is the Indonesian word for Street. *Wikipedia.org*

rice paddy and a busy marketplace. It was on a floodplain which tended to overflow. Our home flooded one time while we were away in class, and our helpers saved the children and our books, our two most valuable possessions. Juliana has a traumatic memory of something that happened that day, which she related to us years later. She was three years old at the time.

This house had many cockroaches, especially in the kitchen. I flinched every time I opened a cupboard because huge cockroaches lived in them. We set out traps and tried in vain to get rid of them.

Our helper, Pak Eddy came up with a brilliant plan. He spread kerosene over the entire tiled kitchen floor, leaving it overnight. The next morning, we woke up to hundreds of dead cockroaches piled up and laid out like a carpet on the kitchen floor. How he removed them and the smell, I don't know. But the cockroaches didn't reappear for a while.

It was in this house that the front porch was about fifteen feet from the street. The first time the Muslim fasting month of Ramadan came around, we were sadly ignorant about its importance. One afternoon, we sat on our front porch having a tea break with cookies. A group of teenage boys ran past and made rude remarks. Turns out, we were the rude ones to be eating our snacks in front of them.

SEARCHING FOR MY TWO DADS

INDONESIAN CULTURE

Historically, Christians missionaries from the West often went overseas with the idea that they would introduce Western culture along with Christ.

We felt very strongly that this was not what God called us to do. We spent much of our time overseas learning to discern the difference between Western culture and Scriptural teaching. This often meant that we needed to withhold judgment on things that weren't Biblical.

We found many things in Indonesian culture that we loved. The kindness and patience with children was something I found especially admirable. I also learned a lot from having servants. I realized that a really good servant looked first to their employer before setting their own agenda.

It was natural that we felt uncomfortable with cultural values that were different from our western culture. One such thing was the inability to be direct.

One day when Jon and I were out walking we were looking for a bridge to cross a river that ran through the main part of the city. We asked people as we walked along one side, "Is there a bridge?" and everyone answered, *"Barankali"* or perhaps. We thought that was such a strange answer, and we never really understood what they intended, nor did we ever find a bridge. We learned later that it was culturally rude for Indonesians to directly answer, "No." Eventually, we took off our sandals and waded up to our knees across the rapidly flowing river. It was early days, and I did not yet know what things lurked in these riverbeds; besides poisonous snakes and other creatures, also bits of garbage and lots of glass.

We learned that many people dumped their garbage directly into the rivers in Indonesia. The people who lived along the river's edge washed their clothes, bathed in it, and used it as their toilet.

One time, our American friend was riding on the back of his Indonesian friend's motorcycle when the Indonesian guy tossed a candy wrapper into the river. Our friend objected, but the driver simply said, "Why not? It will end up in the river eventually, anyway."

I also hold a value of authenticity. When I discipled women in our Navigator ministry, I was honest about areas where I struggled, especially my anger. One women flatly contradicted me telling me that I didn't have an anger problem. I discovered that in Indonesian culture, it is difficult for people to admit wrong. Apparently, they also didn't like to hear that spiritual leaders did wrong.

Another funny thing, I discovered that Indonesians don't like to compare children to animals. Once when our three kids were all climbing on Jon, I apologized to an Indonesian visitor that our kids were "acting like little monkeys." Our guest became indignant and shocked, telling me clearly that you don't say things like that.

We learned immediately that it is not acceptable to pat children or anyone on the head. Apparently, this is patronizing and something the Dutch did in the Colonial era. Also, standing with our arms akimbo, hands on our waists, was to be avoided. Another sign of Dutch colonialism.

Time was relative. When we planned a meeting, one woman came to my house six hours late. She said that she thought as long as it was the same day it was okay. Indonesian "jam karat" or rubber time is a thing. I never attended a meeting that started on time. Another thing we noticed, when we were rehearsing for any activity, the rehearsals always went badly, but performances went off without a hitch. Indonesians knew how to perform and throw a celebration with flair.

I also learned from Indonesians that any accident to the body requires a good massage in order to heal. Massages in Indonesian cost about one dollar per hour. Most were performed by little old village ladies. Some of these ladies actually sat on top of their client burping out the kinks.

SEARCHING FOR MY TWO DADS

YOGYAKARTA

While we lived in Bandung, West Java, Indonesia, Jon and I were in Indonesian language school (IMLAC) every day. We learned language all morning then went out on the street to practice what we had learned.

As I mentioned, Indonesians considered it impolite to give a direct negative answer. People did consider it perfectly polite to comment on Jon's plentiful arm hair, and to pull on it. They also felt free to ask us how much our cameras cost. A waiter might ask us what type of birth control we used. That was a big topic of conversation. Also acceptable was pointing to their heads and laughing over Jon's lack of hair on his.

Then we moved to Yogyakarta, Central Java the center of Javanese culture. We had learned some Indonesian culture in Bandung, but in Yogya, we became fully immersed in the most polite extremes of all that it meant to be culturally Javanese. There was no pointing, and never showing the soles of our shoes.

When we walked in front of anyone, we practically sank to the floor in order to get beneath the level of their head. We never drank or ate as a guest until the host offered it to us three times. It was rare for women to shake hands with Muslim men, usually they would fold their hands in a sign of prayer or put their hand over their heart.

Romo & Eyang

We lived on Jalan Mawar in a neighborhood of beautiful Dutch houses where Jon and I worked together to encourage Christian couples to grow in the Lord. We both loved living in Yogya, though Jon felt frustrated because we were spending so much time with Christians, and his heart's desire was to get to know more Muslims. We managed to do that with our friend, *Amri's* family from the Kraton, or Royal Palace of Yogya. We spent much of our time there, we even had a Bible study and truly felt like family.

I felt fulfilled in the early days when we were involved in leading our ministry with couples, but as time passed, Jon became more involved in ministry with the arts and less with the couple's ministry.

His arts ministry took precedent over our ministry together. Jon's work in the arts was overwhelming to me and I became increasingly stressed and exhausted as he began to thrive.

Added to this was a problem that I developed from a serious fall that I had one rainy day on our slippery cement back patio in Yogya. I was wearing flip flops as we all did then, and was walking fast, as I did in those days. I hit a slick, wet spot, went down on my right hip, and felt terrible pain. The girls were there, and being little, may not remember it. I limped into the house and got into bed forgetting to put ice on it. I forget if we even had a refrigerator at the time, much less ice. A painful hematoma about the size of a grapefruit developed on my right hip and remained for months. This has had a lasting and painful effect on my life.

In Yogyakarta, we had a sunny house in an ideal location with a yard, near Navigator friends, and we were happy. I had a beautiful green parrot I called Evergreen, and we had lush volcanic garden soil. Once we planted about one hundred tomato seeds and the plants grew to be taller than our heads. We didn't know about pruning, so we simply marveled at them. However, sadly, these giant plants produced one or two tomato flowers at most and no tomatoes.

Our girls went to local schools, and I rode them around town on my little Honda Bebek motor bike. It was a fascinating city filled with music, dance, theater and handcrafts.

We, however, underestimated the spiritual darkness that surrounded us. It was only afterwards that we learned how one of our elderly house helpers was disciplining our little girls to get them to obey her while we were away from home. We learned that they screamed and ran around her in circles whenever she wanted them to eat or sleep or take a bath. To make them obey, she told them that Satan was up on the roof and would come in to get them if they didn't listen to her. Terrified, they screamed louder.

Our Girls in Yoguakarta

CHANGES

In 1980, Jim North, the director of The Indonesian Navigators, asked us to move to Madiun, a difficult place in East Java, Indonesia. I remember feeling mixed about this, partly because we loved Yogyakarta and I had visited Madiun by myself with the two girls. I had not done well in the extreme heat. I had a Migraine every day of our visit.

However, we also wanted to please Jim North and do what we were tasked to do. Jon had originally signed us up to live in Madiun, so it wasn't so difficult for him. Jon was always good at commitment, and once he promised something, he stuck with it. I also knew it was further behind culturally, so it would be a constant reminder of how far we were from modern life. During this time, we were also adopting our baby son.

When we went to Indonesia, I had expected that someone might leave a baby on our doorstep because we were foreigners. I realize now that I still had the vestiges of the "white savior"[58] myth in my mind. That fairy tale didn't happen. Though we applied to an orphanage and prayed fervently, eventually we

---

58 - White Savior is a description of a white person depicted as liberating or rescuing or uplifting non-white people. It describes a white central character rescuing non-whites from unfortunate circumstances. *Wikipedia.org*

began to consider having another baby ourselves.

Our friend, Amri's mom, *Eyang* (Javanese word for Grandmother) was a Princess from the Kraton. She was working as a nurse in a hospital in Yogya. We had become friends with Amri's extended family, including his brother and sister-in-law who were artists. They were living together with an assortment of friends in an art gallery down in the town center. Since Jon was also an artist, we went down all the time to hang out.

During our time in Java, as we developed friendships in the Yogyakarta Royal Palace, we helped one or two members of the family come to know Jesus and grow in their faith. We also met our third child, Adityo. Our girls called the Prince of the Kraton (Palace) *Romo* or *Honorable One* and his wife, Eyang, having a great deal of personal freedom running around in the palace. Occasionally we stayed overnight with them, but it was spooky. It was scary because Eyang warned us that some of the objects in their closets were possessed with the spirits of ancestors. We spent time praying for protection for our family before we went to sleep in some of their rooms where the possessed swords or Kris' were stored.

Their art gallery was a famous one, at the end of the most prominent street in Yogya, Jalan Malioboro. It was on the giant lapangan or field near a large Banyan tree. The entire area was full of mystical significance. *Becaks* (trishaws) parked around the tree, and long into the night at their café, on the lapangan (village square) people sat around drinking coffee, talking, and laughing. We became close friends with *Amri's* family, often going up to the local volcano, Mount Merapi, for hikes.

One of the artists, Pak Budi, loved spending time with our girls. I remember Pak Budi's face lighting up with joy when we arrived. During this time, Pak *Amri's* sister-in-law, *Lia*, became pregnant and had a little girl, *Yuniati*.

She was weak from the time she was born. Though we prayed for her, she grew weaker, eventually ending up in the hospital. The doctors diagnosed her with Eczema. The hospital staff didn't know how to treat her and whatever they gave her to eat made her allergies worse. She was starving to death. Eventually, *Yuniati* died creating a terrible crisis of faith in the family. We spent time with them which we hoped was a comfort.

Jon and I had been going out to lead Bible Studies in homes in the remote villages around Yogya. I enjoyed riding out with him on the motorcycle, even in the rain when we covered over with a rain poncho. We were very busy and spent quite a bit of time away from the girls. Five-year-old Catherine asked if I would stay home more. I was happy to do that.

I already had a ministry to the Navigator wives living in Yogyakarta. I often hosted them in our home for tea. Ants were one of the pests that were always with us. One time I bought donuts as a special treat for the women. After I set the donuts out on the table, I left them for several minutes and returned to find them covered with black ants. The women were due momentarily. What did I do? I dusted off the ants and served them anyway.

SEARCHING FOR MY
TWO DADS

THE BOY WITHOUT A COUNTRY

We had been visiting Eyang's sick little granddaughter, *Yuniati,* in the hospital. Eyang who worked in that same hospital, knew that we wanted to adopt a baby.

One time she brought a little preemie baby boy out into the hallway in the palm of her hand for us to see. She asked, "Do you want to adopt this?" She told us that his unmarried mom had given birth to him there in the hospital and slipped away. We said, "No," immediately, realizing that there were too many illegalities to overcome. His mother had not signed any permission papers for his adoption. However, I often thought of that little premature boy's face and prayed for him.

One year later, we visited an orphanage in Sleman, near Yogyakarta, Central Java, with hopes of finding a baby who might need a home. We saw a little baby boy lying on his back asleep with wrinkled skin and an overly extended belly.

The nurses advised us, "You don't want to adopt him, he's dying of Kwashiocor." This is the worst form of malnutrition. I at once thought, that's right, aside from lingering back pain, I knew I wouldn't have the stamina to restore a dying baby to health, care for two little girls and fulfill our mission work responsibility. It occurred to me then that I am not primarily motivated by the spiritual gifts of mercy and compassion.

We moved on with our lives placing our desire to adopt a child in God's hands. I arrived at a place which has been typical of me, that I trust God until the last minute before God answers prayer and then I cave into unbelief. I had recently suggested to Jon that maybe we should give up on adopting and try for a third pregnancy. A few days later we received a message from Panti Asuhan Sayap Ibu in Sleman. They had a baby for us!

The girls were thrilled that we were going to adopt a little boy. Their only stipulation was that he must be brown.

We drove over to Sleman and walked into the head office. Ibu Utaryo, the director, handed us a newborn baby boy. I looked into his big eyes and to my dismay felt strangely empty of emotion.

However, I trusted that love would develop if he was God's choice for us.

As we were about to sign the papers, Ibu Utaryo gasped, saying, "I've made a mistake! The baby I want for you is the oldest baby in the orphanage. He was a premature baby, had Kwashiokor and liver problems. A team of French Doctors, *MSF Médecins Sans Frontières/Doctors Without Borders* visited the orphanage, planned to operate on him and gave him blood transfusions in preparation. He's now eighteen months old and healthy."

The transfusions had transformed his health.

▲ ▲ ▲

This was our baby! We returned to the main orphanage, and I watched through the windows as the nurses chased a darling little curly haired toddler around the room. He was running across the slate floor carrying a large glass beaker, laughing with glee. I knew he was ours!

Sumijan had been born September 30, 1981. This was the same baby I had been praying for him since I saw him in Eyang's hand soon after his premature birth. We had passed by him dying of Kwashiocor in his crib when he was one year old. God clearly wanted us to have this child.

We signed the papers and before we brought him home with us, we took him to a hospital to have him checked out. We wanted to know what conditions we might be dealing with in his future, and if he had liver damage. Turns out the blood transfusions the *Doctors Without Borders* gave him had miraculously cured his illnesses. But we give credit to God for doing it.

While we were in the hospital, a nice-looking man in scrubs was hanging around watching us. When we went in to get an x-ray, the man was pacing back and forth, attentively watching the procedure. Sumijan was crying, and I was comforting him. The man was watching all this. I hardly paid attention, but afterwards, Eyang asked me if I had noticed this man. She said that it was Sumijan's birth father, that he was an intern, training to be a doctor. He wanted to see his baby one last time.

Sumijan bonded first with me, and because he hadn't seen many men, he cried when he was around Jon. But Jon soon won his heart.

That evening we dressed him in a sweater, which he resisted and then took him to a shoe store where he threw a screaming fit. He had never had shoes on his feet. The shoe store front was wide open to the street, so Indonesians gathered to watch the sight of white people taking care of a little brown boy who was throwing a temper tantrum.

It was so much fun introducing our baby boy to the world! Jon wanted to give him a lofty name and chose Adityo Jonathan. His given name, Sumijan meant "son of a peasant woman" while Adityo Jonathan means "ray of sunshine and God's gift," which Adi certainly was.

There were many adjustments for our little boy. Everything, even his name, was brand new for him, languages, sleeping in his sisters' room, reading books, eating unusual foods. In the orphanage, the nurses gave him cookies when he obeyed them. Or rather, gave him cookies when he stopped being naughty. At our house, we gave him liver to help to rebuild his liver. He hated it and held it in his cheeks like a little bird! I stroked his throat to make sure it went down.

He had never slept all by himself in a room, so at naptime he screamed and cried, when I put him down in his crib. His first language was Javanese, and I spoke only one or two words.

One word which must have alarmed him was "Apik!" I thought it meant "good." So, whenever he stopped crying for even a second, enough time to catch his breath, I rushed into the room saying, "Apik!"

It turns out, that's the Javanese word for "Fire!" It closely resembles the correct word for "good" which is "Api!" But, when I rushed into his room praising him by saying, "Fire," who knows what the poor baby thought.

We often sang to our kids at night. Jon sang the Irish lullaby, "Too-ra-loo-ra-loo-ra."

I sang a traditional lullaby with the words I personalized.

"Lullaby, and goodnight, it's time to start
   dreaming.

Get your dolly and your blanky and
   close your eyes.

Busy day is all done, sleeping time
   came so soon.

God will watch over you and wake
   you tomorrow."

For Adi I substituted, Get your Sandy and your Speak and Spell."

I also sang, "I love you a bushel and a peck and a hug around the neck." A song my mom often sang to me.

▲　▲　▲

The orphanage did home visits before approving us for adoption, after this, we had to go to court. I memorized Psalm 112 in my anxiety, reciting it like a mantra in the days and hours leading up to Adi's adoption.

This was another time of stress and anxiety; we weren't sure we would receive the final approval to adopt our boy. During the process, there were vicious headlines in some Jakarta papers condemning the adoption of Indonesian children by foreigners.

Adi's First Picture

These articles arose out of religious anger by Muslims who didn't like the fact that Christians were adopting Indonesian children. There were very rare cases of the children's Muslim parents abandoning them. Of course this caused shame. In one or two horrible cases foreigners had adopted Javanese children and used them overseas as servants. These cases ruined the legitimate adoption of all the others.

We were very fortunate because Ibu Utaryo, the former Director of Sayap Ibu, Adi's adoption agency in Sleman, had recently been selected as the National Advisor on Adoption. Her position in Jakarta, and her personal knowledge of our case, allowed her to write the laws pertaining to adoption by foreigners around our case.

Still, I had the shakes as we drove into the Kabupaten or District of Yogya courthouse parking lot. We took along two neighbors as witnesses, my friend from across the street and an elderly

Shaman who was also our neighbor. We hoped their presence and possible testimony would give a good impression to a Muslim judge!

I continued meditating on Psalm 112 and when we entered the courtroom, to our surprise, we discovered a Christian judge and Christian court recorder who were favorable to our case.

It's amazing how God works!

On the other hand, when we went to get proper papers for Adi to leave the country for our furlough, the authorities in Jakarta claimed that Adi was no longer a citizen of Indonesia.

Jon & Adi on Our Street

He wasn't a citizen of the United States yet, either. We were at an impasse. Were they being purposely obtuse at losing one of their own? I suspected so. After numerous seventeen-hour trips back and forth on the train from Jakarta to Madiun, Jon finally returned with a stack of permission papers allowing our little boy to leave Indonesia and enter Singapore.

I sometimes joked that Jon had undergone nine months of labor with Adi because of all the trips back and forth to Jakarta. We had been hoping to return to the states for Christmas that year, but no. At one point, Adi asked Jon, "Who is more important, God or Immigration?" We must have given him a mixed message.

We boarded Thai Airlines on Christmas Eve 1984 to fly to Singapore and had the most amazing experience! After years of our choosing to eat simply in our village home in Madiun; small portions of chicken, meager portions of meat or fish aside from the tiny, salted kind, Thai airlines served us all a full chicken leg plus a thigh! Christmas carols were playing over the airplane speakers. I cried! I will never forget that feeling of joy and relief!

Thoughts of returning to the States in 1984 held some anxiety for me. Having listened to occasional taped broadcasts from James Dobson, I began to worry that the USA was becoming so evil, the public schools so degenerate and the cost of living so high, that we would never be able to survive there.

I imagined myself becoming a bag lady with no source of income, dependent on charity. I pictured our family in layers of clothing walking the streets on a cold day without a home. How insulting this was to the true character of our loving God!

I am so thankful for God's Word because at one point He intervened in my thoughts as I read Isaiah 8:11-9:7!

Isaiah 8:11, 12 "The Lord spoke to me with his strong hand upon me, warning me not to follow the way of his people, He said: "do not call conspiracy everything that these people call conspiracy; do not fear what they fear, and do not dread it. The Lord Almighty is the one you are to regard as holy, he is the one you are to fear!"

Returning to the United States always felt like a visit to Disneyland! An airport's first drinking fountain signaled that we were on our way home, whether it was in Singapore, or Los Angeles. We took photos of each of our kids' first drink out of them.

Even though we flew across the strait to Singapore on that first leg of our journey, I felt like I was going to heaven. We had been delayed for over a month because of Adi's adoption paperwork, but it didn't matter! We were in civilization, and we could go to malls and dress as we wanted to with no one staring at us. Adi's visa status turned out to be a blessing because we stayed one more month in Singapore to rest and recuperate.

We were not once able to get home for the Christmas holidays in the thirteen years we lived in Southeast Asia.

I mentioned malls because during that month in Singapore the girls and I spent quite some time in them! We found a Strawberry Shortcake store where they could sit and watch movies. I sat right outside and drank Cappuccino, a new drink for me. It was a grand discovery. We stayed in a vacant Navigator staff's home with a yard, and we watched TV for hours on end.

Once again Jon made frequent trips downtown to the American Embassy seeking permission to take Adi to the USA. At last, we received more papers to add to our stack. We found out that during the delay, the FBI was doing a background check on us to be sure we weren't child traffickers or criminals of any kind!

Enroute, we had a layover to switch planes at the Osaka Airport. We spent several hours looking around when Adi spotted a large Snoopy stuffed animal sitting out in front of a shop. It was nearly as big as he was. We proceeded along about twenty stores to a restroom while Jon was at the airline counter. I was helping the girls when I looked around to find out that Adi had suddenly disappeared! I went up to several Japanese Policemen to tell them I was missing our little boy. But they couldn't understand in English that we had lost our toddler who was brown. At the height of frustration with feelings of crisis building, I looked over at the busy walkway to see our Adi, walking along carrying Snoopy!

He had returned to that store, picked up the Snoopy and brought it back. How he managed to do that at two years old was a mystery to me. But, what a relief!

Because we couldn't get home for the Christmas holidays, we decided to stop in Korea to visit missionaries Young and Mary Lou Son and their kids. We arrived in the dead of winter, wearing summer sandals and thin sweaters, so Young took us down to a huge market in Seoul to outfit us in winter wardrobes, including puffy down coats, boots, wool sweaters, the works. What a gift.

From there, we went over to the UK to visit a pastor and his family in Cambridge, and then to The Netherlands. We wanted to pack in as much as we could before getting home. It didn't occur to us how difficult it must have been for our parents, my mom especially who hadn't seen her grandchildren in four years, to wait in anticipation to see us.

We stayed part-time with my mother and part-time with Jon's parents during our furlough. Adi became a naturalized American citizen at the main courthouse in New York City. The girls both entered grade school in Spartansburg for a time and developed some good friendships.

We also spent time visiting our supporting churches and other friends who prayed for us. Once, at Mount Pleasant Church near Spartansburg, PA, my longtime friend, Ramona, and her husband David, helped us cook an Indonesian dinner for their entire Church. These were fun times but also draining and exhausting.

Mom loved having the kids around to show them off. She took them to visit all the neighbors. But our arguing continued. One time, I suggested to Juliana that she invite her school friend, Jana, over to play. She frankly told me she would feel ashamed if Grandma and I continued to fight like we were doing. She didn't want to invite Jana if we argued like that. She was seven.

SEARCHING FOR MY
TWO DADS

MADIUN, EAST JAVA

After Yogyakarta, we moved to Madiun enthusiastically, eager to begin a new phase of life. We lived for six years on Jalan SasanaSari, a dirt street in the rural suburb of Rejomulyo. For our move, Jon drove in one of three cattle trucks with all our belongings. The kids and I, three cats, and two birds in cages followed on the train.

Our Kids in Pak Slamet's Becak

Moving to Madiun was like going back in history about seventy-five years from the life we lived in Yogya. Our neighbor across the road kept water buffalo in her kitchen which had a dirt floor. She also kept a large heap of *beras*, which was raw unhusked rice, piled to the ceiling in her front room. Farmers surrounded us.

One week we had visitors from Maryland staying in our home. I took them for a walk around the neighborhood and introduced them to an elderly neighbor who planted the field behind our house, digging it up by hand each year with an adze. He was skinny as a rail, all muscle and sweat. He had played an interesting part in the history of Indonesia.

Our guests shook hands with him and we continued on our way. When we returned home, I told our visitors about the part that our elderly neighbor had played in the history of Indonesia.

In the 1965-66 abortive communist coup[59] , which was actually a successful plot by certain elements in Indonesia's military, President Soekarno's government was overthrown. In the aftermath, the Indonesian Army and radical Muslims are estimated to have massacred 500,000 to 1,000,000 + communists and sympathizers. Anyone the new government regarded as a dissident was targeted. In the anti-communist purge, death squads roamed the streets accusing people who were communists but also falsely accusing anyone with whom they had disagreements. Survivors who had ideas outside of the party line were accused of being communists and were not allowed to hold positions of influence.

There was a bit of a gasp when I told our guests that the elderly farmer whose hand they had shaken

---

59 - Indonesian mass killings of 1965-1966. Civil unrest primarily targeting members of the Communist Party . . . sometimes described as a genocide. *Wikipedia.org* Film: *The Year of Living Dangerously*

was the man with a reputation among the death squads in Madiun for slitting the most throats during the communist coup. I admit I enjoyed getting a little shock out of them.

We knew one of the men who had been accused of being a communist. He was fired from his job as a public-school teacher and to preserve his life, hid in a hole in the ground for months to escape execution by the government. He contracted Tuberculosis and other diseases while hiding. He emerged from hiding when the extremist government policy was relaxed. Though he was a free man, he still had to check in with the police for decades, a type of house of arrest, as an assurance that he was complying with government policies. He was never allowed to teach school again. Our friend became a believer in Jesus through his suffering and was one of our closest Navigator friends and prayer partners.

Our Family in Madiun

While we lived in Madiun, during times of unrest, we heard that truckloads of police or soldiers drove through our villages, arriving at the doors of "evil doers" who had slipped through the court system. They knocked on the door of corrupt individuals and "disappeared" them. This was the term that was used when criminals were shot and loaded onto a truck to be tossed anonymously into a soccer field in another town.

In our village meetings we were instructed to tell the truck drivers to move on if we happened to see them come to our street planning to dump any bodies. Once I asked my neighbor if this type of personal vendetta didn't frighten her. "No," she answered in dismay, "they only kill people who are guilty."

We lived in this area near the rice paddies, a goat and bird market. It was rural and close to railroad tracks. Some days, our kids played from morning to night on our front porch teaching the neighborhood children to play the card game Uno and Legos. It was sweet to hear the children shouting, "Wild Card" and "Uno" in their Indonesian voices. They played in the sun, climbing trees and exploring all over the neighborhood barefoot. They tell me that they and their friends grabbed sugar cane from passing trains which were carrying it to markets all over Java.

We had little privacy. Neighborhood children sometimes sat under our table while we ate, though we invited them to sit in chairs and eat with us. If ever we spanked our kids, the neighbor children ran from window to window to get a better view.

We had a group of Batak[60] Navigator students from Institut Teknik Bandung visit us for a training

---

60 - Batak is a collective term used to identify a number of closely related Austronesian ethnic groups predominately found in North Sumatra, Indonesia. *Wikipedia.org*

program during semester break. One night, they sat around on our porch until late at night singing Christian choruses, the beauty of their blended voices wafting over the darkened village. The next day, one of our neighbors who was not a believer commented on how beautiful their singing had been.

When our kids were small, they loved living in this rural area and for that reason I loved it. In fact, as I look back on our years in Rejomulyo, my heart warms with love towards my Javanese friends, Bu Maxum and Ibu Wati especially. I made friends among the women, learned the Indonesian language and Javanese culture very well. Javanese language was more elusive. I attended *Arisan* the local women's organization which was an obligation for all neighborhood women to attend monthly.

We women in the organization had several responsibilities when we joined the group. We had to contribute money each time we met. Money was collected and entered a Rota[61] from which a winner was chosen each month. The winner hosted the Arisan the next month. Hosting involved serving appetizers and tea.

The most comical part of Arisan for me was something that the government took very seriously and caused me to get in trouble. I heard through the grapevine that all women had to join a class in birth control education.

I had ignored the invitations for years until several officials appeared at my door to tell me that I had not yet qualified for my pink birth control

---

61 - Rota is a list showing when each of a number of people has to do a particular job. *Oxford Languages*

card. This card served as proof that Jon and I were using birth control. This was during a time when Indonesia was emphasizing the slogan, Dua Anak Cukup! Two children are enough!

Admittedly, I felt a bit offended. I seldom flouted the rules. I bowed to men, humbled myself to government officials when I sometimes wanted to walk out on them. However, demanding proof of our mode of birth control seemed beyond the pale. I gestured, politely pointing to our three children, answering that it was obvious from the size of our small family that we used birth control.

I added that the idea of birth control had originated in the USA, or so I thought. I wanted to stomp my feet. But the officials insisted nicely that I was required to attend these classes.

So, I did, along with the other women in our neighborhood, several of whom had ten children. I managed with good humor to obtain my pink card.

One of the most frightening things that happened to me was on a day when I had to walk to Arisan in a flood during a lightning storm.

A river had overflowed its banks into our village, and I saw the women heading out to the meeting despite the storm. I, who learned from my mother to be cautious of lightning, waited until the last possible minute to leave. I got my umbrella, took off my sandals, hiked up my skirt and waded out into muddy water up to my knees.

As I joined the group, lightning was cracking, and I was terrified that it would strike me holding my umbrella there in the middle of the flooded street. It did not, and we had a cozy meeting accompanied by cracks of thunder and flashes of lightning.

Jon and I were thankful for the additional help we received from summer trainees, who came to learn about ministry. Through their visits our kids also learned about different ideas and places like Australia and New Zealand. However, we began to realize that neither Jon nor I were adequate for the learning needs of our kids. Much of the time they played freely with little supervision. Both Juliana and Catherine had taken Indonesian dance lessons. They also had tutoring in Indonesian.

One special person, *Peggy*, from the United States, signed on to teach Adi to read English which was difficult for him. He told me when he became an adult that he felt tortured when I read books to him. I'm glad that he let me know though it made me sad. It has something to do with his learning style. However, it is difficult for a reader to understand. He has such wonderful people skills that make up for his lack of interest in reading. When we moved to the USA we tried to get him reading help in elementary school, but he didn't qualify for it.

I've mentioned that when we moved to Madiun we found the city was far from modern. To purchase luxury items like butter and Gouda cheese, we took trips to a neighboring city once a month.

These were our few Western foods. I found Madiun about seventy-five years behind the more modern cities on Java. We added running water and increased the electricity wattage from twenty-five watts in every home we moved to. We never had a telephone and purchased the first refrigerator in our neighborhood.

As the years went on, we found delicious Irish butter packed in foil and learned how to transport it in extreme heat, the four hours back to our house. Then there was Danish LurPak butter! I gained new appreciation for varieties of butter in Indonesia!

It wasn't possible to cash our salary check in Madiun; I don't know if there wasn't adequate cash in the bank there, or what. Which brings me to one emotional Christmas Eve in the mid-eighties.

JELLO PUDDING FOR CHRISTMAS

It was early in the week before Christmas in Madiun, East Java. Jon had left on the train for Yogyakarta four hours away to get our salary check cashed and to purchase gifts for the children. He intended to return a few days before Christmas.

We waited and we didn't hear from him. Quite late on Christmas Eve I put the kids to bed and began to plan Jon's funeral as I sat in our front room rocking, crying, and praying in between the tears. All throughout our marriage I had feared that Jon would die. It was probably related to abandonment issues from my father. I trusted that Jon would never desert me, but abandonment by death, was another matter.

At some point that evening, I went out back to our kitchen to look through the cupboards for something to put into the children's stockings so they would have one gift on Christmas morning.

I found three packages of Jell-O Vanilla pudding which I stuffed down into the toes of each child's stocking.

I sat back down in the rocker and cried a bit more.

Suddenly, around midnight, I heard a motorcycle approaching. Soon, I saw it coming up the dirt path with a passenger on the back. The rider had boxes piled so high I couldn't see his face. To my great relief, it was Jon! Drying my tears, I went out on our porch to greet him!

He told me he had been delayed because our monthly salary check had arrived late. Then the bank had not been able to cash it for a couple of days, it didn't have enough cash, so he wasn't able to buy presents until the day before Christmas.

He arrived by train from Yogya and one lone motorcycle taxi was available at the station to give him a ride out to our home.

The next morning, the kids came out of their bedrooms to presents around the tree and gifts in their stockings. They never knew what I went through the night before. I have forgotten whether they still had the puddings in the toes, though I suspect I took them out replacing them with nice little trinkets and probably an orange bought from the fruit market.

Why didn't I get on a becak and go to town to shop myself in the days before Christmas? Well, for one thing, I had no money. During those Madiun days, we often used up every cent and were dependent on each month's paycheck. We didn't use credit cards yet, and at times we gave away our last few *Rupiah*[62] to beggars.

I also wonder why Jon didn't realize that I'd be worried sick when he didn't arrive home until a few minutes before midnight on Christmas Eve. Why didn't he send me a reassuring telegram? This was before anyone we knew in our area had telephones. I assume that as always, Jon, the optimist, was

---

62 - Indonesian Money

expecting the money to arrive at any minute, so he didn't think it was necessary to let me know. I understand now, years later, this is the way he thinks.

Jon, in his heart, is an idealist, a dreamer of dreams who always expects things to turn out well. He expects the best of everyone and is always surprised if someone feels disappointed in him or doesn't value something he does. I doubt that Jon gave much thought to the idea that I would be frantic with worry over his late arrival. He probably was so happy and excited that he had fulfilled his task and arrived with the presents just in time for Christmas.

SEARCHING FOR MY TWO DADS

TRAUMA

One morning in 1981 in Madiun, I went out for a jog around our local soccer field. I came back, sat down for breakfast and my back muscles went into severe spasms. Since that morning I have had chronic back spasms. I suspect the problem may have come from the fall I had in Yogya in 1980 which caused me to walk with a slight limp, which put a strain on my back muscles.

When I first experienced these paralyzing back spasms I entered Kediri Baptist Hospital in East Java for two weeks.

My doctor was Kathleen Jones, a veteran with the Southern Baptist Mission who had a distinguished history. She had faced everything from dangerous insurgents with the communist coup in the sixties to tropical diseases that were not yet in the books.

I returned home unable to walk more than a couple of feet, and that with help. I mostly lay on a *kapok*[63] mattress on the hard floor. Thus began my decades-long pain journey with back spasms and other back troubles. Eventually, I found a Rheumatologist in Surabaya who gave me Voltaren, a medication which I took for three years. The doctor told me that pain can cause blood pressure to rise which it did.

---

63 - Kapok is a cotton-like plant fiber obtained from the seed pods of trees in tropical forests. It is used for stuffing mattresses and cushions. *Wikipedia.org*

For months I had to lay on that mat on the floor. Traveling in a small van back and forth to Kediri Hospital for checkups was almost unbearably painful. I have never completely recovered or been without pain since that time.

I was fortunate that an American Physical Therapist, Diane Blair, happened to be living in town with her husband. She taught me helpful stretching exercises.

Deborah Hilton from the Australian Navigators was living in our home which was a great help. She had suffered with back problems and introduced me to the McKenzie Method[64], taught by a Physiotherapist from Australia. She knew ways to relieve the pain by rubbing ice cubes directly over the spasmed muscles. During this time, I became very thin, 116 lbs. and fragile looking. I could not do ministry, but I kept a prayer diary, and this was the time in my life when I began to pray for the world in a powerful way.

---

64 - *Treat Your Own Back*, by Robin McKenzie

SPIRITUAL BATTLES

Life in Madiun was difficult for me and I often didn't manage it well. The intense heat and stress wore on my nerves but in the beginning we were unaware of the spiritual oppression in the surrounding area. I felt depleted by the heat, developed horrible migraines, exploded at the children and Jon over small stresses.

We were in constant observation from our neighbors, and I suspect, there were Shamans[65] who tried and possibly succeeded in cursing us. Despite all we know now about removing curses, I have never felt 100% healthy since moving to Madiun in 1981. The air smelled of sugarcane refuse and I had a headache/migraine most every afternoon. Travel made life bearable when we got away to a hotel that had air conditioning. Sometimes I wondered if my migraine was the result of a curse. One time I had taken my pillow apart to wash the feathers and I found a huge needle in it. Had someone been told by a shaman to put it in there to try to induce migraines? Was that possible? In Indonesia, who knew?

---

65 - Shamans are people in the culture who claim to communicate with spirits on behalf of the community, including spirits of the deceased. Their purpose is said to be to alleviate unrest, unsettled issues and to deliver gifts to spirits. *Wikipedia.org*

Our daughters entered the local public schools which taught Islam as a religion. They became proficient in some of the prayers although they had the option to sit outside during instruction.

We had our share of trauma. Juliana suffered with severe allergies and Catherine had nightmares. One time our girls were staying in Madiun with Indonesian friends when Jon and I traveled to the Philippines for a Navigator conference. The girls were walking along a road when they came upon two boys playing with machetes. One of the blades came loose from its handle and flew through the air slicing Juliana's scull. She thought she might have walked into something but wasn't aware of blood running down the back of her head. Poor girl was in shock from the blow.

The boys ran away in a panic and she and her sister continued walking to the home where they were staying to get help. Juliana tells us that her primary concern was her little sister. Their Indonesian care givers took her to the hospital. She remembers this trauma primarily because the people who cared for her said that she didn't get stitches at the hospital. For some reason, they felt they were sparing her by not telling the truth.

When I consider what a terrible tragedy could have happened to our girl, I know our hope is always in the Lord and I am grateful.

A curious thing about Madiun was that most of the foreign missionaries were becoming ill and moving away. I suspected it was because of an evil power over the city. At about the same time, we were reading Frank Peretti's book, *This Present Darkness*. When we shared this with a missionary in another town she felt we were exaggerating, saying we made it sound like Madiun was darkest Africa! Indeed!

Though I persevered through severe back spasms for years, and Juliana eventually grew out of her worst allergies, at times I wondered whether we stayed in Madiun because of sheer stubbornness. The real question was, did God want us to stay? Jon was physically healthy and intended to accomplish the ministry. I wanted this too. We both felt that to leave would be allowing evil to succeed. Having done all we knew to do, we remained.

We didn't understand though that we were experiencing severe burnout. We were not schooled in setting boundaries. We operated on the principle of stretching as far as we could and trusting God to enable us to go until we burned out. It was the philosophy of hundreds of Christian workers in the eras before us.

Jon began to have fainting spells. I, already in extreme pain, blanked out occasionally and disassociated several times. Once or twice, I got into a small bus to travel to a doctor's appointment in another town. I could not remember where I was going, but I remember feeling confident that the driver would deliver me and would let me know when to get out of the bus.

We didn't give much thought to how or when we would recover. We didn't know what to call our problems. When we returned to the States, and learned about burnout, or nervous breakdowns as they used to be called, we learned that it is rare to recover from such severe burnout. In fact, it is rare to reach full capacity again in one's lifetime.

Believe it or not, I look back fondly on those many months I was debilitated with back spasms because I spent the time devoted to prayer. I couldn't go out on ministry, so I sat on our front porch each afternoon drinking tea from my blue cup and saucer, praying for the world. God even led me to pray for Jane Fonda's salvation. I found out years later that she began to follow Jesus during the time I was in prayer for her. I remember hoping that I would give the same amount of time to prayer when I recovered. Unfortunately, I didn't.

Around this time, we had a visitor, a veteran Nav missionary from Mexico, Sam Clark. He helped to open our eyes giving us a crash course in spiritual warfare when he recognized we needed it. He said that unless we were prepared to die, we could not win in a battle against Satan! Wow! Talk about woke! We woke up!

I found the book, *The Adversary* by Mark Bubeck, to be indispensable. It had spiritual warfare prayers for every situation. I prayed those prayers for every issue in our lives. Our daughter Catherine was especially spiritually sensitive and frequently had night terrors. As we prayed, we claimed God's power over Satan to protect her and all of us. Our neighbor, a shaman, gave us a large urn as a gift which Jon kept in the garage. Catherine had a strong negative reaction whenever she saw it and begged us to throw it away. We took it with us to a neighboring city and threw it in a dumpster.

THE MAN WHO TURNED INTO A CAT

This brings me to one of the more shocking events that happened to me in Madiun. I checked it out with our educated Chinese Christian friend from Indonesia, who confirmed that it does indeed happen. So, here goes.

One rainy Sunday night Jon had taken the kids to a church service, and I was at home with Adi, who was still a toddler and asleep in Juliana's bedroom in the back of our house.

As I lay in bed next to him, I heard a shuffling sound in the outdoor kitchen next to the bedroom. I got up and stealthily looked out in the courtyard. Seeing nothing, I crept into the kitchen where I heard shuffling. The sound had come from our student helper's bedroom off to the side of the kitchen.

I was in the kitchen, about to enter the small bedroom when I stopped, suddenly realizing that if someone was in the small room, they might trap me.

I quietly slipped outside into the courtyard, standing against the kitchen wall to wait. Minutes later, a short Indonesian man in black farmer pants, a white shirt and a black *peci*[66] hat crawled out from

---

66 - A cap widely worn among Muslim men in Southeast Asia. It's shaped like a truncated cone, usually made of black or embroidered felt, cotton or velvet. *Wikipedia.org*

under the student's bed and crept out of the kitchen. I yelled, *maling!* or thief! in Indonesian. He jumped, I jumped! We stared at each other as he spun around and took off towards the banana trees in our back yard.

Moments later, a group of neighbor men burst into our yard. They ran up to me, asking, "Is there no **big person** here?" in Indonesian. By that time, I was unruffled by their assumption that the official big person is a man, "No, Jon is not here." I answered them with resignation!

They searched the yard and found no one. I assured them that Jon would return soon so they left. I noticed a strange black and white cat that scampered out on their heels. I didn't recognize the cat because I knew all the animals in our neighborhood by sight.

▲   ▲   ▲

Several nights later, it rained again. Jon and the girls were out. Adi and I were resting in Juliana's back bedroom again when I heard a cat yowling. I grabbed Adi, my flashlight and a big black umbrella and headed out into the dark backyard to search among the banana trees.

What do you know? There was that strange cat sitting on our back wall! I took Adi's hand, walked right up to the cat shining my flashlight into its eyes and said, "In the Name of Jesus get out of my yard and do not come back!" I must have assumed that spirits speak English if they can turn people into cats. The cat fled and I never saw it again.

Was it the same man who was hiding under our student helper's bed? Had he used mystic powers to turn into a cat and run out on our neighbors' heels that night when they came in to search our yard? Did I cast out a man/spirit or feral cat from our yard?

Well, as I mentioned, I asked our Indonesian friend, Ingriani, if she had heard about this happening in Java. She confirmed that she had heard about people who use black magic to turn themselves into animals to evade capture. We never had another visit from him/it.

A different thief stole our children's bikes once but the police caught him and brought him into our yard for us to observe as they beat a confession out of him. We strongly objected to their method.

Another time, thieves broke into our home to steal our electronic devices, our glassware and eyeglasses. We heard that this was the specialty of a particular criminal element under the influence of a spirit who coveted glassware for some reason.

We thanked God that none of us had awakened in the night to be confronted by the thieves possibly carrying machetes. Our children were asleep in the main part of the house where we kept all the electronic equipment that had been stolen. Our neighbors advised us that our sound sleep was the result of a spell that the thieves had put on us.

All the villagers believed that our village was under the control of spirits of some sort. Our close neighbors told us about one spirit whose entire duty in our little village in Salatiga was to keep people in poverty. This demon was alleged to live under a bridge near our home. No one thought to oppose this plot.

Jon's choice to work among artists was difficult for me in part because they were all familiar with using spirits to enhance their creativity. They were also far from disciplined and showed up at our house when we weren't expecting them, at all hours, sometimes, late at night. Many of them also carried spiritual baggage, having been to white or black Dukuns[67] or witch doctors to gain various types of spiritual power. Some had short needles of gold, diamond or crystal implanted in their bodies by shamans to enable them for excellence in dancing, acting, political power, and romantic prowess.

One year, Jon bought a forty-piece set of vintage Gamelan[68] musical instruments in the marketplace in Surakarta. With the help of our friends, Pak Boyati and Pak No No, they worked to restore them to their original condition. These became a source of immense joy and pleasure for Jon. He felt inspired to use them for God's glory following in the steps of some of the Indonesian churches and missionaries in the past. They were not without controversy however because many missionaries believed they carried forces of black magic.[69] It's possible that they did. Jon, however felt complete freedom to sanctify them in prayer for God's use.

The gamelan became a local favorite. As we saw the gamelan used in larger cities in Catholic

---

67 - Dukun is an Indonesian term for shaman. Their role is traditional healer, spirit medium, custom and tradition experts and occasionally sorcerers. *Wikipedia.org*

68 - Gamelan is the traditional Indonesian percussion orchestra consisting of hand forged bronze ornate percussive instruments, typically, xylophones, gongs, metallophones, drums, cymbals, string instruments and bamboo flutes. *https://ich.unesco.org>gamelan*

69 - Black Magic also known as dark magic refers to the use of supernatural powers for evil and selfish purposes. *Wikipedia*

services, Jon adapted the music and began using the instruments in our Madiun house fellowship, PUA[70] as well as in Christmas programs in Madiun and Salatiga. Jon's gifts in music enabled him to learn to play each of the instruments making him somewhat of a local legend.

PUA

Gamelan at Our House

However, storing forty of these instruments in the front and middle rooms of our home overwhelmed me as did hosting gamelan practice in our front room with the neighbors every week. It was a wonderful opportunity for ministry, and I was proud of Jon and his love for Javanese culture. But this was stressful

---

70 - PUA stands for the body of Christ in God, in the Javanese language, Pasamuan Ummat Allah stands for United Fellowship of followers of Allah.

333

for me. While I supported it, the smell of the players' clove cigarette smoke, added to some of the high-pitched notes of the instruments routinely gave me a migraine.

I frequently put the children to bed, reading their stories to the cling clang of the gamelan, some nights with the added splash of heavy rain outside our windows. I admit when recalling it now, a sense of nostalgia and peace settles over me.

Occasionally, Jon convinced me to join in to play one of the instruments. I found playing monotonous, and often became distracted, losing my place. However, I did it to please Jon because he took such great pleasure in hearing the instruments Often, he played gamelan music on a background tape while doing administrative work in his office.

Jon enjoyed the arts of Indonesia, especially the music. He first began learning the zither in Bandung from Pak Nugraha. This talented Muslim man became a close and valued friend. Once he confided to Jon that he wished he could become a Christian because it was so much easier than Islam. According to his understanding, all one had to do to become a Christian was to have faith in Jesus.

We spent many a relaxing day in the Nugraha's home and took day trips with him and his family. Once we went to the Central Java town renown for a unique type of Batik. On these trips we learned that cemeteries are ideal for picnics and mosques are always open for a bathroom stop. From that time on, whenever we drove past a cemetery, our kids shouted, "picnic."

For Jon, developing a Gospel Arts Troop was a highlight of his time in Indonesia. Sometimes during a performance, we served two hundred complete rice meals out of our home. People came from miles around, sat in our living room, our yard, on the porch and in folding chairs set out in the road to watch the shadow puppet plays and to listen into the night to gamelan music that accompanied the shows.

A highlight of my life was raising children with good characters in a developing country. I probably should have aimed for happy children, but that was not yet part of my mentality. It wasn't easy for me, considering the hot weather and stressful living situations.

When Juliana was a pre-teen, she asked me once how I thought she could raise her children so they wouldn't grow up to become "brats." I felt so affirmed by her question because it revealed to me that she thought we had raised our children to be good kids.

Later in her life, she would remember the difficult things, but I held on to her precious words. I don't remember my answer.

After several years in Madiun we realized that our kids needed further schooling beyond what they were receiving at the local Indonesian schools. Juliana continued with added tutoring from her Indonesian teacher until third grade. Catherine until second, Adi through kindergarten.

Both girls were voracious readers and when Juliana learned about the library at the Inter-Mission School in Salatiga, she wanted to go. One day she was on the top bunk of her bed, calling out to me, begging, "Learn me, Mom! Learn me!"

Before this I assumed she could learn from my well-intentioned homeschooling consisting of her own reading and our trips to the local market plus the wonderful experience of travel. However, she wanted and needed so much more than I could offer her.

We packed Juliana's bags and sent her off to Mountain View International School in Salatiga, Central Java, five hours away, which suited her perfectly. We missed her terribly, though. She lived in a dorm with wonderful dorm parents, among them, Jan and Dennis Sheldon and our friends, Al and Elaine Cox. We often brought her home on weekends.

On one of our drives home, Juliana and I stopped in the heat of the day to get a cold drink of Coke from a simple stall set up in the jungle along our route. I foolishly ordered ice. We both got sick with Hepatitis A.

Kediri Hospital told us the best treatment was to rest. We had little appetite and nausea but we ate what we could and waited it out. I could only eat cucumbers with salt and a type of green squash. I was so sensitive to odors that I couldn't open the refrigerator door without becoming nauseous. Juliana and I both turned yellow with jaundice. In time, we recovered completely.

AMONG THE MIRACLES

It was on one of my five-hour weekend drives to pick up Juliana that I had a car accident which could have been a disaster. Debbie Hilton was with me, and as often happened, a large bus was headed toward us on our side of the highway as it was passing a car. It clipped off our car's rear-view mirror just as it barely squeezed back into its proper lane before hitting us head on.

This was horrifying enough but moments later, a Javanese girl with a triangular shaped straw rice hat turned her bike directly into the path of our car. I hit her.

Looking back through the rear-view mirror, all I could see was her hat lying in the middle of the road. My heart dropped. People were smiling and waving at us from the kiosks on the side of the road calling out, "Tidak apa apa!" "It's okay, It's okay!" What had happened?

I pulled off the road and Debbie and I ran back expecting to see the girl lying injured by the side of the road. The girl sat by the side of the road, shaken but unharmed, her bike twisted beyond repair.

We all recognized that a miracle had taken place! We hugged each other, me exclaiming, "Praise Jesus," and her saying, "Allah be Praised." I will never know what happened or how she escaped death other than a miracle from the Lord.

On another one of our commutes through the jungle to Juliana's school, our Toyota began to overheat. We turned off the air conditioning, and the tape player and began to pray. To my great relief, unexpectedly, by the side of that jungle road two uniformed policemen appeared. There were no motorcycles or police cars in sight to explain how they happened to be there in the middle of the jungle. I pulled to the side to ask for their help. They told me they didn't know anything about cars but that they would flag down a passing trucker. They warned us to stay in the car because truck drivers were sometimes unscrupulous.

Before too long, a truck approached. The driver stopped, looked under the hood and determined that our car needed a belt. He thought we could make it to the next town. Off he went, and when I tried to pay the policemen for their help, they surprisingly refused my money. This was very unusual for policemen who were well known to accept bribes, and certainly were not well paid.

We drove on about twenty-five miles to the next town and a garage. When the mechanic looked under the hood, he was amazed, wondering how we had made it so far. He told us it should have been impossible with this type of belt problem. I believe God stationed two Angels dressed in police uniforms by the side of that jungle road!

Juliana had also begun exhibiting symptoms of exhaustion whenever she was very physically active on extremely hot days. It often occurred on track and field days, about every six months. She would suddenly be unable to go to school, just barely able to drag herself out of bed to go to the bathroom. She languished in bed for two weeks, then promptly at the two-week mark, we'd find her up a tree. I researched it when we returned to the states in 1988 and discovered several possibilities. Chronic Fatigue[71] and Guillain Barre' Syndrome[72] were two conditions that seemed to fit, but there was little known about them. She eventually grew out of this syndrome after years of fragility. Looking back, I wonder if stress was a major factor in her illness. At that age, young teenage boys were shouting out to her, asking her to marry them. She tells me that she found reading, and sitting on her swing listening to music was her way of combatting stress. She internalized her feelings.

---

71 - Chronic Fatigue causes extreme fatigue in which symptoms worsen with physical or mental activity but don't fully improve with rest. The cause is unknown. *https://www.mayoclinic.org*

72 - A Condition in which the immune system attacks the nerves. May be triggered by an acute bacterial or viral infection. *Simplyhealth.io*

SEARCHING FOR MY
TWO DADS

AT HOME

IN THE MOUNTAINS OF JAVA

In 1988 we left to go on our second furlough. We stayed with our parents and once again I hoped to resolve things with my mom. Our relationship was difficult, and more so because Mom was becoming more irritable in her older age.

When we returned to Indonesia we still felt exhausted. Our family counselor in The Navigators had urged us to move to a place where we would find more privacy for our family.

It made sense to consider Salatiga. We always enjoyed visiting there, the home of Satya Wacana University, a Christian university.

Though Juliana seemed to thrive in the boarding school in Salatiga, when it came time for Catherine to go, within one term she told us that being away from family gave her stomach aches. The long travel time each weekend was another of our reasons for moving our family to Salatiga.

The kids were already involved there so it was an easy decision for our family to make. It was at a higher elevation and cooler. We found a lovely home on Jalan Banyuputih and added on a pavilion, planting a walled in grassy garden. It was restful, and private. We began a new phase of our ministry there, to university students. We lived in Banyuputih, an impoverished village surrounded by rice paddies and fruit trees at the base of a volcano. The kids rode their bikes to school and explored the jungles, we spent time getting to know our neighbors.

The move to Salatiga was an occasion! Jon and I drove with the children and cats in our Blue Toyota truck which had been converted into a station wagon. We drove from Madiun up the mountain roads to Salatiga. We followed behind three cattle trucks loaded with our household goods. We also rented a huge bus for all our Madiun neighbors who wanted to *antar* us or accompany us from Madiun to Salatiga to see our new home.

We had no idea whether this was customary for anybody else who had ever moved, but we were quite sure that our neighbors had conned us into it. It made us happy that they thought so much of us and they were up for a holiday! We paid for their excursion, providing food and hosting them for a sleepover in our new home.

Our drive up into the fresh, cool mountains was lovely, except that on some of the stretches, the cattle truck got going too fast and a few of our possessions flew off into the rice fields. Imagine my helpless feeling as I watched one of our mattresses fly off into someone's field. I was inclined to stop and pick it up, but we were following behind and no one else seemed of a mind to bother. The trucks were speeding through the mountain passes, and it made sense to follow the convoy.

We all arrived safely, and the Madiun neighbors poured out of the bus into our new house. Of course, they immediately began talking to the new neighbors no doubt sharing all the funny stories about our life in Rejomulyo. Because it was too far for them to return that day, they all stayed the night sleeping on blankets on our tile floor. We realize that they planned to do this ahead of time, because they'd brought blankets, towels, and a change of underwear. Fortunately, we had lined up house helpers on a previous trip because we needed to feed them all, but the bonus was that they helped us unpack our barrels. Help included them examining all our belongings as they lifted them out and unwrapped them from the barrels.

Jon and I had a laugh thinking about how complicated our move had become. At the same time, we felt touched at our Madiun neighbors interest in us.

It is amazing and hard to believe that we lived in Salatiga for three years, because it was such a memorable part of our lives. We added the beautiful private pavilion and bathroom which connected to the house as well as a walled garden because our counselor in the States had advised us that we needed a place to retreat. In Madiun we did not have any privacy, which was a source of stress for me, at least.

The stress there came in all shapes and sizes. At times, people were sitting in our back yard waiting for us when we woke up to go to our outdoor bathroom at five am. We were poor at having boundaries and at the same time, we felt proud that we didn't live within high compound walls with a Jaga, or night guard to keep people out.

▲   ▲   ▲

We loved being near our kids in Salatiga, especially the fact that they could ride their bikes to school every day through the rice paddies and make friends in the villages along the way. One day they came home excited because they rode their bikes over a huge *boa constrictor* snake which was stretched across the road. These are shared memories that they will always treasure. It was nice for me to have Western friends among the staff and other parents living in town also.

Satya Wacana, situated in Salatiga, was one of the few Christian Universities in Indonesia at the time. We hosted students from there for Bible study in our home.

A highlight for me was to welcome foreign students to Salatiga during their school breaks. We hosted them to help develop friendships with local people, also to help the foreign students develop cultural understanding and to help us to gain more contacts.

The visiting students came from Navigator ministries in Australia, New Zealand, and the USA. We supervised them, introduced them to Indonesian culture, found Indonesian families and tutors for them among our Indonesian friends and served as a hospital for them when they were sick.

I loved hosting our summer programs, having an opportunity to serve the students and to translate Indonesian culture for them. It was fun to observe their reactions to culture shock; life in extreme simplicity, bathrooms with squat toilets and no toilet paper, learning to eat huge piles of rice with tiny portions of meat and vegetables, sweeping their beds each morning.

We lined up Muslim homes for most of the students which was a significant help in breaking down barriers for us. Most adjusted well to not having luxuries like screens on their windows and running water, but a few did not.

We enjoyed our own personal ministry among our neighbors and Indonesian students. One highlight for me occurred as I was walking along a rural pathway near our home when I met a woman riding her motor bike. She was clearly in distress, and I stopped to talk with her. In a very clear movement of the Holy Spirit, I shared the gospel with her, and she received Jesus into her life. Afterwards her daughter, also a believer, came to our house to learn how to help her mother grow in Christ. It was a supernatural arrangement and perfect timing.

One time, a young Becak[73] driver turned up at our door late at night asking for refuge. He had run away from his hometown wrongly accused, he said, of murdering his wife. He heard of our home as a safe place for shelter. We prayerfully invited him in to give him dinner and then locked him in the back bedroom where the helpers normally sleep. He went on his way the next day.

Adi raised pigeons in Salatiga, and we always had cats. Our yellow cat, Lisa, died in Salatiga. It had been necessary to leave Becky, her sister, behind in Madiun because she didn't come around the day that we moved. A few years later, I went back to visit

---

73 - A traditional Indonesian cycle used for hire to carry passengers, constructed of three wheels which the driver pedals from the back. *factsofindonesia.com*

Madiun, and asked about her. The neighbors said she had become feral. I went looking for her, calling her name and found her. She came up to me from out of the jungle rubbing my leg, as if she knew me. I know she remembered me. The neighbors were amazed that the feral cat had such a warm response to me. I had to harden my heart in a way to leave Madiun and Becky behind again that day. I prayed for her and asked that the neighbors treat her kindly.

Our children easily adapted to our Salatiga neighborhood as children do and won the hearts of all our neighbors. All we needed to do to find one of them was to send word by way of the neighbors. They might have been in the rice fields, or in the Rambutan forest. Adi got into trouble playing with fire in Salatiga. One of his last spankings involved his smoking a used cigarette butt he picked up from the road when he was four years old. Once he burned down a grove of banana trees next to our house while Jon and I were napping.

Another time, Adi and his friend were riding bikes when Adi's bike went out of control hitting a bridge and hurling him into the riverbed beneath. His friend came carrying our partially conscious Adi home in his arms. The narrow escapes of our children are known to God alone.

We most often found our kids in fruit trees; each child had their favorites, Rambutan and Jambo. How cute they were, climbing up those trees in their bare feet. I admit, I flinched at the heights they could climb, but Jon liked to remind me that they were developing courage. "Better to break an arm and develop courage than to grow up afraid to try things." This was his principle when he'd challenge them to swim long distances across what may have been shark infested waters at Pangandaran (who knew?) and to gallop ponies through the mountain forests of Sarangan. I know the girls were scared, but they bravely followed their dad's lead.

Sadly, the children also learned to mourn in Salatiga when one of their playmates died in an accident involving a minibus. The entire village mourned for days. The sound of nails being pounded as loved ones built a coffin in a neighbor's front yard is a memory I will never forget. It made death more present for us, unlike in the States where death becomes remote, removed to a funeral home. A handmade coffin helped the mourners cope with grief as it took shape right in their front yard.

In rural Indonesia during a funeral, neighbor women come together to cook, and the men and children gather in the home to sit vigil with the family. The mourning goes on for days. Somehow it seems to help process the grief in a more tangible way when it is shared like this.

SEARCHING FOR MY TWO DADS

THE ACCIDENT

It was during our years in Salatiga, that Jon and I had a serious accident on the Northern highway traveling from Jakarta, the capital city, to our home.

We were visiting Brian and Debbie Hilton who had sent us home with bags and boxes of Debbie's clothing for the girls. After stopping for lunch, we set out to drive during the heat of the day on a long stretch of monotonous highway through Central Java.

I laid down in the back and fell asleep. I was jolted awake by a crunching sound as our car lurched to a stop. I had rolled onto the floor of the car in intense pain and Jon was not saying anything. As I struggled to look up over the seat, he was becoming conscious. We had come to a stop practically under the bottom of a semi-trailer truck.

Our car tape deck was playing peaceful classical music and I remember feeling the shocking juxtaposition of the calm music with our dire situation.

At that moment there was another thud, the car shook, and the semi-tractor trailer took off. I began to hear voices coming up to the road from out of the jungle. People were gathering around our station wagon.

I am ashamed to say, I felt quite vulnerable, as I grabbed my purse holding it close to my chest, fearing the villagers might rob us because we were strangers to them, and unfamiliar foreigners.

How vastly different was their compassionate response, as they gathered around, doing everything they could to help. They quickly summoned someone to take us to a nearby clinic. I was in extreme pain from broken ribs and a broken collarbone. Jon had suffered a concussion. Our car had front end damage that looked bad but could be repaired in Indonesia.

I laid in the back seat of the car as a tow truck hitched us up and towed us to the nearby clinic. The local ER physician determined that my shoulder required surgery. We lingered several hours in the hot and humid waiting room until he could contact a surgeon in Solo, a town ten hours away. We then loaded all our possessions into the ambulance, and by nightfall we headed to Solo.

Jon and the ambulance driver loaded me into the austere ambulance, all metal inside with me lying on an unpadded metal cot that jerked and rattled with each bump and turn. I felt every pothole in the bumpy road. All the extra bags and boxes from Debbie plus our suitcases slid noisily back and forth across the floor with each curve.

In the middle of the steamy hot night, the ambulance driver stopped at a hotel for a bathroom break. He and Jon pulled me feet first out of the ambulance, setting me upright and helping me walk into the hotel so I could use the squat pot in the lady's room.

As we walked into the lobby, we must have presented quite a sight, a foreign couple, me with my hair standing straight up and supporting my broken collarbone, unable to manage by myself, with Jon and our hospital ambulance driver supporting me.

However, polite as always, each person who was sitting and smoking in the lobby killing time in the middle of the night, greeted us in the customary way, asking us how we were and where we were from. Of course, in my need to please total strangers, I replied succinctly but politely to them, in the midst of my pain, that we were,

"Fine, thank you, we're from America!"

Our home in Salatiga was on the route through to Solo so we stopped by our home to pick up a change of clothing. As the ambulance stopped in the neighborhood, many of our neighbors came out of their houses and one of my neighbor ladies, whom I didn't know very well, rubbed my cold feet. This was around 5 A.M. I will always remember her kind gesture.

Our kids were staying a few kilometers away in the dorm at their school. We didn't tell them about our accident, though we did tell the dorm parents with whom they were staying. Later when they learned about our accident, Juliana was cross with us because she said she would have preferred to know.

Finally, around eight in the morning we arrived at Surakarta, or Solo, at their finest operating facility which happened to be operated by Muslims.

After waiting for a bit, I was ushered into pre-op where a surgeon leaned over me with a syringe and needle at least seven inches long. Looking into my face he said,

"You're Christian, yes?"

I answered, "Yes."

"I am Muslim," he said with a smile, the whole time holding the huge syringe in front of my face.

"I will pray to Allah," he said. "You pray to your God."

I prayed.

It's ironic that in Indonesia, Christians call God Allah. This is the name written in the Christian Bible and used in our hymns when calling upon the Creator God. Eventually, there was a huge controversy in the United States about whether Allah and God are the same. We've concluded that they are, but both are understood differently. No human being can know God/Allah perfectly.

The surgery consisted of a screw which was inserted to hold my broken collar bone together. It was successful but a few years later the area began to hurt. Once in the USA, an x-ray technician showed me with alarm that I had a screw that appeared to be loosely floating in my shoulder.

I had subsequent surgery to fix the repair and don't recall what happened to it.

All our married life, we have had limited finances. When I say limited, I should also say neither of us have been very focused on finances. When we have money, we are quite generous in giving to others. When we don't have it, I have felt poor and often anxious, though God has always provided for us.

When we lived in Indonesia, our annual salary was around $15,000. This was adequate for our Indonesian life. We were even able to vacation and stay in charming hotels.

Raising finances has been a chore which neither of us liked doing. We would have preferred to pray and have God provide for us as he did for some of the famous missionaries like George Muller.

We have always had enough in the end but sometimes the end came later than we wished it would. God needed to teach us some valuable lessons, one of which was to be more careful in budgeting and rather than giving spontaneously, pray more carefully about where to give our money. Uncertainty is helpful in that regard.

One funny family story we like to tell is about when we lived in New York State and once before pay day, all we had to eat was Caviar and Steak.

Our Ukrainian friends had given us some fancy Caviar and our Mennonite friends had loaded our freezer with steak after butchering their cow. God has a sense of humor.

SEARCHING FOR MY TWO DADS

THE TERRORISTS

In 1986, during the time when the USA was in conflict with Libya, we had a scare when we were staying in a hotel in Surakarta, Indonesia.

President Reagan was on an official visit with President Suharto and members of ASEAN[74] in Bali. While our family lounged and played in the swimming pool, a group of young Arab men noticed us and ambled over to talk. They asked me where we were from and when I told them I was from America, they began discussing Reagan's visit to Bali. They said that their government was against our government, but that it didn't mean they were against Americans. The said, people were different from politics. Then, they proceeded to tell me details about the security in place around the hotel where Reagan planned to stay in Bali.

My anxiety instincts were rising, as I imagined the harm they could do if they decided to hurt our little American family. As soon as I finished talking with them, I quietly urged Jon and the kids to get out of the pool and ushered them back into the safety of our hotel room insisting they stay away from the windows. We didn't see the Libyans again.

---

74 - ASEAN The Association of Southeast Asian Nations
   established on 8 August 1967 in Bangkok, Thailand. *asean.org*

The next day, we heard about foreign terrorists whom the police caught trying to blow up railroad tracks outside the city. I will never know if the friendly Libyan boys were the perpetrators, but instinctively, I felt they were involved in a plot to harm Reagan. Afterwards, I asked my friend in the State Department if I should have notified the American Embassy and she said that it would have been a good thing to do.

FAMILY VACATIONS

Jon's favorite vacation spot as a child was Montauk, NY where his family took him to spend summers at Tick Hall, a beautiful bungalow owned by his father's boss. Mr. Tweed. It was built on the edge of a cliff facing the sea. As a child, Jon explored around Montauk point, once in his bare feet from morning till night.

There are seven Shingle Style cottages in a summer colony in Montauk, historically labeled the Seven Sisters, each designed by the famous architect, Stanford White. Naturally as an architect himself, Jon took great delight in showing them to us.

We were able to vacation in one of these famous cottages, Sharon's Inn, when Juliana was a baby in a carrier. It was a dream come true for Jon to share the experience with me. We hiked Deforest road, the beaches, and picked wild black berries. One highlight was when Jon had the idea to walk up to the front door of Tick Hall and ring the bell asking if we could see it.

Famous talk show host, Dick Cavett and his wife Carrie Nye owned the cottage and were well known celebrities at the time. I thought Jon had a lot of nerve to do that, but celebrity didn't impress him. Sure enough, Dick Cavett opened the door and there we stood, baby Juliana in our front carry pack. Jon explained his history with the house and Dick invited us to come in and look around. He even apologized that he couldn't take us upstairs because his wife was sleeping. Jon was so excited, showing me his childhood memories, and because we have several of his paintings of the house, I recognized them.

Jon was most excited that the architecture had been preserved in its original condition. I was more in awe because we were walking around the house of a famous celebrity. The next day we were walking down the road picking blackberries and Dick drove by. We offered him some of our berries, which he good naturedly refused.

I first heard of ticks at Montauk. Jon warned me to be careful not to get tick bites and I freaked out. Growing up in Pennsylvania I had never seen one and I imagined all sorts of horrific things. I still had never seen any until we found them on our dogs in 1990 in the USA.

The next time we visited Montauk must have been in 1984 when we had all three children. We stayed in Sharon's Inn again, which was lovely. We didn't visit Dick Cavett at Tick Hall, but another of the Seven Sisters Cottages, where a delightful lady, Miss Momeyer, lived. I imagine the owner of Sharon's Inn called and gave us a recommendation because Miss Momeyer opened her home to us and while Jon and she toured the entire cottage, the girls and I were having a spree in her upstairs spare bedroom trying on fox furs and hats.

Mom's and my vacations were tamer. We went on a Pullman train to Washington D.C. once. She wanted me to have an experience sleeping overnight on a train similar to her times with her parents. I remember the awesome feeling of waking up in the morning as we pulled into the station.

As soon as I got my driver's license, we took off on adventures every summer. I drove us to Maine, Quebec, North Carolina, Virginia, Niagara Falls and New Jersey.

SEARCHING FOR MY
TWO DADS

INDONESIAN VACATIONS

Our best holidays in Indonesia were our carefree beach vacations in towns on the Indian Ocean. Our favorite was the quiet beach town of Pangandaran where we stayed in simple cabins and usually gathered with a group of Navigators.

Jon & Me in Pangandaran Cave

We ate at seafood cafes that were a short hike into town, and the children explored monkey jungles while parents sat around talking, often the men played cards. Monkeys hung from the eaves on our cabins looking for food. There were bat caves, gorgeous coral reefs for snorkeling, pontoon boats, and places to swim. Our daughter Catherine used to play with her future husband, Andy, when they were children on these vacations.

Eventually, Jon found other beaches for camping. One was Prigi Beach which is renowned as the most beautiful beach in East Java. It was much more isolated with tall coconut palms and terrifying waves. I remember one shrimp cafe there with huge vats of shrimp. The interior was very dark. We were able to walk in with our towels and take showers there before eating our fill of delicious shrimp and rice.

Once, Jon took the kids on a camping trip near there and pitched their tent under a palm tree that was dropping coconuts. He soon realized his mistake as the wind picked up.

My two further memories of Prigi Beach are of the treacherous giant grey waves breaking far out to sea, and a few years later as it became more developed, when we stayed in a nice cottage. Though it was nice, there was no electricity At night, I got up to go to the bathroom squat pot. As I stepped out of bed in the dark, I stepped on something large and furry. I screamed and jumped, but I never knew what it was. I assumed it was a big spider.

Another beach we all went to was in Java, Parangtritis. There was a modern hotel which was allegedly haunted by the Queen of the South Sea, or Ratu Kidul[75]. The hotel staff maintained a room for her, which we asked permission to visit. We found it beautifully decorated and filled daily with sacrificial gifts of food. There was also a myth about her taking people out to sea who wore green.

---

75 - Ratu Kidul or Nyai Loro Kidul is the mythical spirit queen at Parangtritis, often appearing as a mermaid. Visitors are warned not to wear the color green or they will be enticed into the ocean to drown. Each year the treacherous waters take a few more lives. *Wikipedia.org*

All the Navigators were enjoying a vacation together, lounging around the nice pool, not going into the ocean at all. There were very few Indonesians wading in the ocean, with all their clothes on. I never saw an Indonesian woman wearing a bathing suit in the ocean the entire time I was in Indonesia.

In the year before Adi joined our family, Jon, and I and the two little girls were walking along the beach and Catherine, still a toddler, was wearing a little checkered turquoise blue sunsuit. We let go of her hand for just a second when a huge wave came sweeping up on the shore out of nowhere, lifting her off her feet and throwing her into a pile of rocks at least seventy feet further up on the shore.

We ran to her, terrified, and found her shaken but unharmed. We pondered it because it seemed freakish. Back in the room a few hours later, Catherine went missing and we found her shut in the closet in our room, chewing on a big moth ball cube.

We began praying and I grabbed her and ran into my friend's room next door. I hoped that my friend, Elaine Cox, had Ipecac Syrup to make Catherine vomit. Fortunately, she did, and all was well.

After Catherine had come close to dying twice in several hours, I began to wonder if dark forces were at work. Jon and I prayed for her protection and the rest of the vacation was uneventful.

A few years later, after Adi joined our family, we returned to the same beach and had a wonderful time. After that first experience, I wondered if Satan might have had foresight to know that Catherine had a mission ahead of her in Indonesia that would threaten his work?

We don't know all the struggles that go on in the heavenlies.

Now, in 2023, our daughter, Catherine and her family spend happy vacation days on the South Sea free from fear at this vacation spot and others. God is greater than any curse.

NEW YORK

On our second furlough to the USA in 1988, we decided to settle in Freeville, NY right outside of Ithaca near Cornell University. This was about halfway between Nyack, NY where Jon's family lived, and Spartansburg, PA where Mom lived.

We bought our first house, a small yellow ranch for cash, $70,000 from our savings. We also bought a used Suburban truck/van. We were never again financially flush. We had no credit cards prior to 1984, however we soon learned that we needed one to live and travel in our country. Before that time in our lives, we felt convicted that we should live without debt, so we used up our life's savings to purchase the house. Looking back, we both believe we made a mistake to use all our money. It was a life lesson. We never again had $70,000 savings available in the bank.

Cedar Drive was a quiet little side street where we found good friendships among the neighbors; The Butners, The Almendingers, and the McCarty's. The Butner boys were good friends for our kids, especially Adi and their youngest, Justin.

We decided to send our kids to Academy of Jesus, which was an outgrowth of Faith Colony, a Jesus

People Commune from the sixties. It seemed like a good school, embracing music, good education, dance, drama, and Christian friendships. I reasoned that since our kids were from a Christian school background in Indonesia, it would be easier for them to attend a Christian school in the USA while we were on furlough.

However, there was an ingrown feel to it that we failed to notice in the beginning. Though Academy of Jesus was a blessing to us in 1984 the first time we returned from Indonesia dried out spiritually, in 1988, we realized that not all our children were thriving. Juliana did well and had developed close friendships. Catherine didn't seem to fit in as well. Most concerning for us was that Adi, because of his skin color, faced surprising prejudice from some of the Christians there. This all came out later. It was a cause of great suffering and feelings of rejection for Adı because it came from Christians.

We didn't realize all that our son would encounter because of his brown skin. Of course, God knew. Once, I was traveling alone and sat at an IHOP lunch counter somewhere in the Mid-West. An older African American woman sat down beside me and as we chatted, we discovered our common faith. I told her about Adi's adoption and the trouble he was having.

She spoke a clear word of prophecy[76] for him from Isaiah 54:17; "No weapon that is formed against thee shall prosper; and every tongue that shall rise

---

76 - A prophecy is an inspired utterance by a prophet: the declaration or prediction of divine will, or something to come. A Prophet's role is to make God's Word known. Some believe Prophet's exist today. *Wikipedia.org*

against thee in judgment thou shalt condemn. This is the heritage of the servants of the Lord, and their righteousness is of me, saith the Lord."

There were many good people at Academy of Jesus; The Abbs, Hatterys, Hibberts, and others, I don't want to name them all because I don't know how much they knew about the problems that cropped up later. One dear friend and prayer warrior, Beth North, was a crotchety old soul whom I came to love dearly. She was our faithful house sitter for years. She passed away in 2017.

SHANTUNG COMPOUND

Back in the eighties, while I was in Kediri Hospital with my back spasms, one inspiring book that Dr. Jones loaned to me was about a heroic Englishman in a Japanese internment camp in Shantung, China during World War II. I remembered the story and wanted desperately to find the book when we returned to the States, but before the internet, I had no way to research it.

When we returned to the States permanently, we watched the film *Chariots of Fire*, and it dawned on me that the protagonist I had read about in that book was the same as the hero of that film. How could I find the book when I couldn't remember the author or the correct title? I combed through Ithaca's used bookstores asking the owners if they had ever heard of such a book, no one had.

To my surprise one day, in the tiny DeWitt Mall Used Book Store, I asked the owner about the book. As usual, I hit a dead end. Just as I was walking out the door, I happened to glance down and there it was, *Shantung Compound*, on a bottom shelf! That was the book I had been searching for! On reading it again, I knew in my heart that the author, Langdon Gilkey, had to be writing about Eric Liddell. Though Gilkey was not a believer in Christ, he found no other explanation for the Englishman's unselfish behavior than his love for God. Eric Liddell was the hero of that book, long before he became the hero of the movie, *Chariots of Fire*. Dodi Fayed, the Muslim man who produced the movie died in the car crash with Princess Diana in the tunnel in Paris.

For several years we traveled the eight hours back and forth to Pennsylvania visiting Mom who continued to thrive.

While we were in Indonesia she had been a prolific letter writer and continued sending us positive, upbeat letters with tidbits of hometown news, newspaper clippings and advice. It seemed like her entire personality had transformed while we were overseas.

At least once, and sometimes twice a week, she wrote of her many friends and activities. She told us that she attended church every Sunday, often being "among the last to leave." She treated her many friends at a local restaurant, babysat for the local pastor's children and went to baby showers. She gave devotions at her local Bible Study group and took trips with friends. Each letter included a little bit of cash for the children, stories about her dogs, her beautiful garden and flowers or in winter, her birds.

Never once did she write a word of complaint but thanked God for her good health. She marked the years since her survival from Cancer, until her doctor told her he no longer needed her to return for Cancer checks.

In part, I think it was a perfect situation for her because she was in the spotlight as our mother and grandmother and many people in our small corner of Pennsylvania wanted to hear our news. This gave her a reason to be out and about with people and an opportunity for people to get to know her at her best.

She had been a popular young woman, the president of her high school classes for three years. She was also a beloved elementary school teacher, and with our departure for Indonesia coming soon after her retirement, I think she struggled for an identity. This role as our spokesperson took her out of herself.

But, at one point, we noticed that her health was deteriorating, and her letters were becoming much more concise. When we visited, she was blunt and quickly annoyed. She was losing too much weight, clearly not eating enough.

Eventually . . .

SEARCHING FOR MY
TWODADS

CORNELL UNIVERSITY

1991 -2011

When we decided to return to live permanently in the United States, it was for the most part because of our ailing parents. Jon's father was blind and needed daily care, and my mother's letters were becoming noticeably less conversational. It was a difficult struggle for Jon who felt his work in Indonesia wasn't finished yet. But we agreed that it was important for us to care for our parents, especially for my mom, since she had no other family.

Our years living in Freeville and working with international students at Cornell and Ithaca were very fulfilling for me. I thought that Jon was enjoying the ministry until he began to suffer burn out again, which I will write about later.

Until the 1997 financial crisis in Indonesia, we were involved exclusively with the many Indonesians at Cornell. They were attracted to the University because of its excellent Southeast Asian Program. We were doing weekly Indonesian Bible studies, Jon with a large group of men, I with many of the women. We also had many group activities.

We saw tremendous growth in their spiritual lives as we encouraged them to walk faithfully with God through their time in the States.

Some of them returned to Indonesia where they are serving God in their churches and their careers.

We encouraged the Christians to include the Muslim students whenever they planned fun activities. We felt encouraged that our campus succeeded in maintaining excellent relationships among students from the two religious groups avoiding the polarization which occurred on many other campuses.

We had such wonderful friendships with the Indonesians, which increased when Jon took the position of Archivist at the Southeast Asian Kahin Center. His job was to assist all the students and scholars coming from Southeast Asia. Those were the days of weekly house parties, bake sales, gamelan concerts, hikes, weddings, and baby showers.

At one time several of the Indonesian women and I discussed opening an Indonesian restaurant in Ithaca.

We traveled back and forth to Indonesia during those years, visiting our former students and colleagues. Once we visited a student's brother who was a political prisoner in the notorious Sukamiskin Prison[77] outside of Bandung. This prison houses around two thousand individuals including tax evaders, terrorists, drug dealers and murderers. It turned out that our student friend's wealthy brother was falsely accused of corruption, because his business partners in the national airline company were committing fraud. After several years he proved he was not guilty and was freed.

---

77 - Sukamiskin Prison is a special Indonesian prison for high-ranking officials and businessmen, even popular singers convicted of corruption. *antukorupsi.org*

When we visited, we were surprised by the luxurious flower gardens and the freedom of the prisoners to receive visitors in private cabanas. Each cabana provided refreshments and some even allowed grilling. On the day that we visited our friend, a Tempo Magazine[78] journalist was interviewing him and he was consulting with a human rights advocate. It appeared to us to be a meeting of great minds to which we were permitted to listen. After several years, our friend was vindicated, but as an activist, he made good use of his time in prison. Among other activities, he organized exercise clubs and founded a monthly magazine about corruption within the prison.

After the Indonesian financial crisis of 1997, the flood of Indonesians coming to Cornell slowed to a dribble. The Government resisted funding anyone and few could afford the travel costs themselves. We remain friends with many of our Indonesian students and colleagues and keep in touch through Facebook and WhatsApp.

After 1997, we began to spend more time with students from other parts of the Muslim world. The stories they told caused us to question the way Christians viewed the Israeli/Palestinian conflict and the Arab world in general.

▲　▲　▲

As for me, my sister-in-law, Betty, recommended that I work myself into a job by volunteering at something that I enjoyed doing.

---

78 - Tempo is an Indonesian weekly magazine that covers news and politics. Its first edition was published in 1971. *wikipedia.org*

I began to volunteer at our kid's high school library and discovered how much I loved helping the students to do research. Then I applied to become a teaching assistant and substitute aide in the school district. I was often called to substitute in the elementary grades which I did not like at all. The little kids were too needy and exhausting to me. Eventually, I got a job assisting in the Dryden High School Library and loved it.

I developed close friendships with colleagues and learned that I was good at doing library work. I seldom had the same types of refreshing exchanges with missionaries, though I've had wonderful friendships.

Many of my Christian conversations focused on God's work, and our part in it. I wonder if we subconsciously held one another to such a high standard of excellence that it hindered authenticity. Refraining from idle words required that even our humor had a high standard. I don't mean that I desired to gossip or demean anyone, but there is such freedom in accepting people, as I believe God does, without judgment.

Jon and I both enjoy working with unbelievers because we find them unguarded or restricted by fear of criticism or gossip. Jon considers our comfort with secular friends one of the signs that we are called to minister primarily outside of the church.

I was learning to relax and let conversations go where they needed to go. This was so good for me. It feels stressful and false to try to guide conversations into spiritual topics when my entire world is geared toward Christian ministry.

As it happened, this was also the direction many of our colleagues in ministry were heading.

I had not been outside the Evangelical Christian community in my adult life since working as a young nurse in Erie, Pennsylvania.

I worked in the library while Juliana was in high school. Next, Catherine chose to do a specialized high school nursing program which took her to a local hospital and away from the high school on most days. Because she was seldom at school, I decided to stop working in Dryden and look for a job that put me in closer contact with Cornell students. Adi was less interested in academics and didn't seem to need me around school. We followed his sports and attended every home game and many of his away games.

We joined the Host Family program at Cornell and soon I was coordinating it. Among the first Cornell students we hosted were Oksana and Oleg Biluhka from Ukraine. When they were about to graduate, Oksana recommended me for her job as Family Liaison to International Students at Ithaca High school. I stepped into her job. It was the best job I have ever had!

While doing this job I made many connections with secular friends in the community; I was also busy as a volunteer, coordinating the Cornell Humphrey Fellows Host Family Program.

In this position, I welcomed all the new Humphrey Fellows from around the world connecting them with local families. This position suited me perfectly. I was able to host dinners in our home and naturally share my faith but without the title, missionary. This was so freeing. By this time, our American culture had begun assigning negative connotations to the term, missionary.

Eventually, several of my colleagues and I became involved with The Office of Refugee Resettlement[79] sponsoring Burmese and then Karen refugees.

I naturally involved our church. However, I found the secular community much more available to help than most people in the church. In many cases, I found that church people were already over committed to church activities and home schooling. Eventually, the many volunteer responsibilities began to wear me down and arthritis pain overwhelmed me. It also became a sore point between Jon and me because I wasn't able to assist him very much with the international student ministry. I was asking for his help with the refugees more often than he felt he could do it.

During this time, I was becoming more convinced than ever that we were best at working openly in a secular context using our secular capabilities and spiritual gifting. Jon still identified as a Christian working via The Navigators, while spending much of his time with non-Christians at Cornell and fitting in perfectly. He fit in so well, I was convinced it was because the people he worked with saw him primarily as a colleague and not as a Christian worker / missionary within academia.

We had a dilemma. Jon was hesitant to join the Cornell Religious Counsel. Both of us eventually concluded that the words "missionary," and

---

79 - The Office of Refugee Resettlement (ORR) helps populations who are new to the United States by linking them to critical resources that assist them to integrate into American society. *acf.hhs.gov*

"Christian worker" had many negative connotations and limitations in people's minds. Terms like these erected unnecessary barriers. However, he had no secular identity on Cornell campus with which he felt comfortable. Neither of us wanted to be deceptive.

Jon continued his education at Cornell by getting his Masters in Ethnomusicology, working as the Archivist in charge of the Southeast Asian Program building at Cornell while leading the Navigator International Student Ministry full time. He was an alumnus of Cornell from 1963 when he graduated from the Architecture school. He loved Cornell and organizing the neglected archives at the Kahin Center was the perfect job for him. He eventually joined the Cornell United Religious Counsel and developed great friendships with all the chaplains. He enjoyed studying for and facilitating Bible Studies but we felt the need for a team to do the Navigator work.

SEARCHING FOR MY TWO DADS

GROWING

On returning, from Asia, I got the wonderful job at Ithaca High School where I could take advantage of training at Cornell University's African American Studies Program. I opted to learn about racism and racial reconciliation and determined to talk about it very openly with people of color.

Jon and I attended Obama's first Inauguration in January 2009. The mutual trust and camaraderie among the crowds there that day was contagious. I went from there directly to Dulles Airport to fly to Atlanta for a conference. I spontaneously began telling all the people I met about the Inauguration experience. It was a dazzling moment in my lifetime in which I felt doors opening for instant rapport with strangers, many of whom were Black and culturally unlike me. I didn't feel at the time that I was doing anything inappropriate, sharing the joy of our nation's first Black President. I found everyone eager to share the excitement and not one person responded coldly.

It was a moment in time when Black people felt free to discuss their life experiences with white people like me, a visitor from the north. They were willing to discuss their hopes. A cab driver invited me to his church. It emboldened me to continue dialoging with People of Color.

The following is a snippet of a Facebook conversation with a Black friend.

Teri wrote.:

> *"Wow, what a pivotal moment and what a journey! I think your love for God and knowledge that He IS real and true helped give you the security to be emboldened, but at the same time compassionate. You felt something was wrong here and doesn't quite match up. You could have easily chosen to be dismissive or quiet as so many are. You chose to pursue, and it sounds like it has been impactful to your world. I wish more people were willing to just learn."*

I replied:

> *"Teri, Jon and I have God's grace to stand outside or near the door"*[80] *of the congregation or fellowship. We always look for the outsider, we try to never sit in the same pew in church, we look for the stranger."*

I have seldom found a Person Of Color who hesitates to tell me about their issues. While many white people say they have Black friends who never talk about racial inequalities, I do because I want to learn. We want to intentionally listen when they talk about how a Black American in business must work twice as hard as a white American to prove himself. A Black woman may have to work three or four times as hard."

---

80 - Book by Sam Shoemaker, *"I Stand by the Door"*

Teri:

"Exactly! They are willing to share because they know you intentionally want to listen, and your heart is in the right place. SO true about deaf ears though! Those types of responses immediately alert us that this conversation isn't going to be a safe space to share especially when "Bill" is brought in for back up, LOL. The goal sometimes is just to acknowledge the elephant in the room let alone talk about it . . . I'll share something that MANY take for granted or see as a small thing. HAIR.

SEARCHING FOR MY TWO DADS

THE PERRY HOUSE AT 433

If ever a house became a home, it was the one at 433 on a hill on Ferguson Road in Freeville, New York. Grandpa Perry urged us to sell the little yellow ranch house when we returned to the states. The house on the hill was a gem, and the owner, Mrs. Delahanty sold it to us for an exceptionally low price in 1991, of $112, 000. Grandpa helped us purchase sixty additional acres and through the years we added many trees and burning bushes from his property at Sky Farm in Nyack, NY. It was our paradise from 1990 to 2012.

Our Freeville House

Each year we planted the front meadow with rescued daffodils in honor of my mom's favorite poem by Wadsworth,

A Field of Golden Daffodils. While Grandpa Perry was still living on Mountain View Avenue in Nyack, we dug up enough Burning Bushes from his farm to line our driveway.

We enlisted the help of Juliana and Catherine's current boyfriends to help plant them. The boyfriends helped with several projects; one was to recover heavy rocks from a foundation of a demolished barn on Irish Settlement Road and use them to build raised garden beds. I'm afraid we took advantage of their goodwill.

We had hundreds of picnics and house parties at our home. My international students from Ithaca High School came out on buses for a field trip each year. Christmas was a wonderful time of welcoming students and families. One Thanksgiving, we moved all of our furniture out of the house into friends' vans in the front field. We did this so we could set up tables to host seventy Cornell students from all around the world. Friends from our church helped us and little children dressed up as pilgrims. We even had vegan options for friends from India who were vegetarians. It was such a pleasure and we had fun and energy back then.

Our Kids at Christmas in Freeville

Sometimes I compared our home to a giant ocean-going vessel with Jon as the captain. It felt like we were guiding it through life, maintaining it, and receiving passengers.

There were times when we became too frazzled and exhausted to maintain it well, our bathtub leaked down onto our valuable grand piano and an old painting of my mothers. Neither of us had the strength to do anything about it resulting in thousands of dollars' worth of repairs.

We often had complete strangers stay with us. Once we hosted the family of the famous Chef Boyardee, the pizza icon from my childhood, whose grandson was entering Cornell. Grandpa Perry even helped us build on an addition, amounting to a half a house, enabling us to add bedrooms and a den to handle more people. It was a dream home!

In fact, it was the fulfilment of one of my dreams when I was young. When I was a teenager, I used to pass a home very much like it on the road to Titusville. The main difference from the one I dreamed about when I was growing up was that ours was a brown shingle style not white as my dream house had been. Ours had a Lilac bush in the back and a breezeway between the garage and the main house. It could not have been more perfect! We had so much fun in that house, playing volleyball, capture the flag, water balloon fights! Wow! At one party we hosted for Juliana's friends, a girl told me she never knew you could have so much fun without drinking!

I had the most wonderful kitchen, and energy to use it well! In this home over the years, we had hundreds if not a thousand international students and other friends.

Our students and colleagues from Indonesia gathered around our gamelan to play, talk, and plan the next democratic government of Indonesia. These were the true future policy makers working for changes in Indonesia's future. Sitting around on our floor, eating, laughing, making jokes about Suharto, all the while our kids played in the background. It was a heady time for me. I loved the political discussions realizing that people gathering in our home could make a difference.

We found ourselves in delicate situations as well. One of our international friends wrote asking if I could find a source of flak jackets for her brother fighting a tyrant in her country.

Another of our student's fathers made his considerable fortune as an arms dealer in North Korea. His daughter was a lovely Christian girl and we prayed fervently for her father to come to know Jesus. We shared our lives with these students as they opened up their lives and hearts with us, confident that we would honor their confidentiality.

Similarly, at Ithaca High school, students who were undocumented immigrants came to my office and shared their needs. These students were very careful to obey the law. If they got into any trouble with the police they knew they would be sent back to their home countries.

Our school policy was to not ask about their status, and when they confided in me, I had no need to report them to the authorities.

Another vital aspect of my life came into the forefront during our Ithaca years: the issue of Racism. During our years in Indonesia, talking about politics and even current events had been off limits for us in the ministry. We could have been expelled from the country for mixing in politics. Missionaries in many countries in the past had been accused of being CIA informants, whether truthfully or not.

My freedom to discuss Racism and politics opened a vast new world of interest to me, and it resonated with my heart for justice.

▲   ▲   ▲

We added on the guestroom dedicating it to God so it could be used for travelers. Ironically, the very first person to use it was a man who showed up late at night on the run from the police.

Our friends who ran a halfway house, sent him to us. He had been living illegally in his girlfriend's rented room for several weeks. That evening they had an argument and she had physically defended herself. He had bloody scratches down his cheeks. He told us he was planning to turn himself in to the police the next morning but needed a place to stay that night.

I thought of my pristine guest room sheets but I believed the Lord had sent this fugitive to be our first guest. We invited him in on the pledge that he would go to the police as he promised. The next day he did turn himself in. I checked the pillows and sheets and found no blood. We saw in the paper days later that he had listed our home address as his home.

Jon and I have made a good team throughout our life together. Whether leading Bible studies from our beginnings at Lehigh University in Bethlehem, Pennsylvania, all the way through to leading groups on Faith and Justice at Bethel Grove Bible Church in Ithaca, New York, to Racial Reconciliation groups at Little Fork Episcopal Church here in Virginia.

OUR PARENTS

Jon's mother passed away during our final furlough at the age of eighty-five. Anna Margaret Blauvelt Perry was a graduate of Barnard College and taught Math. She was a patron of the Nyack Historical Society, she died at age 87 on August 28, 1988. Anna was a conservationist and nature student throughout her life. She was the comptroller for the Spellman Fund a Charitable organization and also procurer for the establishment of the Colonial Williamsburg, Virginia restoration and was a member of the Association of Blauvelt Descendants.[81]

Jon's Mom & Dad

We were very thankful that Jon was able to be with her before she died. Jon's mother and I were

---

81 - Association of Blauvelt Descendants *https://blauvelt.org*

not close. In fact, she didn't attend our wedding and never visited our home. She had painful Shingles on her face and head for the entire time we were married. She adored our children.

His father visited us once a year. In his old age he became blind and moved into the Village of Nyack. In Nyack, he lived in a beautiful mansion on Broadway formerly owned by the Perry's friend and his client, Esther Van Slike. Esther was one of the elderly people whose finances and wills Daddy administered right up until three months before he died. After he became blind, he employed Nyack College students to help him continue his legal practice. He worked tirelessly to make sure that his clients had nursing care.

It was convenient for us to live in Ithaca between his father and my mom, which allowed us to visit one of them every other month. In the winters when we visited Mom, we stayed in the Corry Hotel about seven miles from Spartansburg because she had no heat in her upstairs.

The Corry hotel was very nice and it was the only hotel for miles around. One evening while we were eating dinner in the hotel dining room, Juliana left to go to the restroom. A few minutes later we heard men shouting in the lobby. Just as I walked out into the reception area to see what was happening, I saw our little girl standing by the desk as a man with an axe over his head was staggering toward her in a drunken rage. The security guard grabbed him just in time and called the police before he could do any damage. Of all places in the world where we thought Juliana's life would be at risk, the Corry Hotel was the last place we would have considered.

MOM

For several years we traveled the eight hours back and forth to Pennsylvania to visit Mom who had been thriving.

Mom in Her Nursing Home

Eventually, it became unsafe for her to live alone, so we moved her into senior housing two miles from our home in Freeville, New York. We considered having her live with us, but with all of us coming and going much of the day, we realized she needed safer housing.

She lived there quite contentedly for seven years but became increasingly forgetful and unable to cook for herself. I ordered Meals on Wheels for her when she told me didn't like my cooking. However, the food sometimes disagreed with her, and I found that she was hiding it on top of a bookshelf and sometimes forgetting about it. I handled all her bills and medical care for those years. I enjoyed doing it; however, she was difficult, and sometimes I left her apartment crying. It was the old story, I would suggest something, and she would oppose it.

Mom had been a hoarder and was doing well until one day I discovered her wheeling her little grocery cart into the recycling shed and bringing a large pile of newspapers back to her apartment. She intended to read them, but I don't know if she could read anymore.

We put her name on a list for the Groton, NY Nursing home where she settled in and lived happily for the rest of her years surrounded by people she could talk with. We were mostly happy with her care, one time however, when we went to Indonesia for six weeks, she didn't get the physical therapy she required, and her right leg froze up. I was so sad to find when I returned that gangrene had set in. She had to have her shapely right leg amputated shortly afterwards. I never knew how to talk with her about that. Occasionally when she had a lucid moment, she asked me if everything was all right "down there," and I assured her that it was. She trusted me and felt satisfied. As with most everything at that point, I felt reality didn't matter that much anymore.

During her time in the hospital, she once introduced me to her nurse as her mother. The pride on her face showed me that she was in a peaceful place.

I enjoyed this time in my mom's life because she was pleasant and cheerful. Every time I visited, she was in good spirits and always pleased to see me.

I saw glimpses of the young, spunky girl she had been before the melancholy mom had replaced her. That Mom whom I'd known for much of my life. So much of her improvement was due to her having a healthier diet and daily interaction with people.

One time, Jon told her that I was her daughter and she asked, "How did that happen?"

Early in her time there, I asked the nurse if they were giving her medication to make her pleasant and calm and they said, "Oh No, she threw her colostomy bag at one of us." That only happened once. The rest of the time we hear the staff loved her and she was a delightful patient.

That was the Mom I knew.

On some of my frequent visits, I took a pretty teapot and her teacups. She loved shortbread cookies, and we had tea together. Sometimes, I did her nails. I had never seen her wearing nail polish and though her first impulse was to resist; her pretty pink nails made her smile.

Adi's Graduation

Another happy memory for me was watching the Westminster Dog Show together.

Mom settled and became happy, returning to her true, charming nature as she related to people in the nursing home. She began to enjoy eating with companions around the table. Through the years she had several roommates and a special friend, Bertha.

More than once she and Bertha decided to take off to go shopping. After several attempts at escape, the staff put ankle bracelets on them. My mom the escapee.

Several times a week she would pack up her belongings and tell me that her father was coming to pick her up. Each time we visited her, which was usually more than once a week, she would greet us with such joy, we knew she felt she hadn't seen us in a long time.

A remnant of her former trauma was her fear. After a while she didn't enjoy going out to a mall or to a restaurant so I took her out for long walks around the neighborhood in her wheelchair. Sometimes we would sit under the trees or in a sunny garden. There was a bridge and a small stream nearby and whenever we walked over the bridge, she became agitated, fussing, "Don't push me over." Each time I assured her that, of course I wouldn't. I wondered what caused her to fret about that and I always felt sad that she thought I might try to kill her.

Mom, who had been given a death sentence from Cancer, in 1973, was able to see Juliana married to Scott Ruggiero in Sage Chapel at Cornell in July 2002. She was in a wheelchair at this time and Tracy White assisted her during the wedding. We hadn't taken her to Catherine's wedding to Andy Grindheim in January 2000. It was an unusually cold and snowy day, and I hadn't been able to figure out the logistics.

My single prayer for Mom for all those years was that she would not die alone. As she neared her death, she began to sit at mealtimes, and not eat. Then on about the third day she just stayed in bed. She died the next day. The doctor proposed inserting a feeding tube. I remembered from Mom's experience during her surgery long ago that it had been very painful for her. I wanted to be sure what she wanted, though, so I asked her if she wanted one. She was awake but not speaking. Her eyes grew wide, and I could tell that answer was NO to a feeding tube.

Mom in Her Wheelchair

She passed peacefully the next day, March 11, 2005, at age 92, with Jon and me holding her hands. The spiritual director of the nursing home was softly playing old hymns on a little organ she had brought into the room.

We had her burial service several months later in Riceville, PA in a plot next to her mother and father.

I felt happy that she was at rest, finished with her difficult life and reunited with her family that she treasured so much.

Her memorial service was at Mount Pleasant church in western Pennsylvania where her mother had been a member of the Missionary Society. This congregation had prayed for our family during our time overseas. I was so thankful that each of our children and their spouses were able to be there to meet everyone.

Jon's father passed away in 1995 at age 95, having continued to practice law right up until three months before his death. He was the Judge for the Village of Upper Nyack, NY and was a great man, father, and grandfather.

MY FATHER, LYNT

Lynton Azelle Wills was born on February 21, 1908, in Alpharetta, Georgia, the last child of Asberry and Margaret Cogburn Wills. The Wills name became prominent in Alpharetta as it grew, with Asberry's brother eventually becoming mayor. Wills men built the family's church, Midland Methodist, at the intersection near Berry and Maggie's home. It has their greasy fingerprints left behind on the wooden ceiling beams from a chicken dinner they ate while building it.

Berry and Maggie owned a farm and ran a general store. Lynt, must have been a local teenage heartthrob because in every photo I've seen of him he exudes sensuality with his flirtatious grin, and rebellious slouch like James Dean before the *Rebel Without a Cause* actor became popular in the movies.

Lynt fell in love as a teenager with a petite, brown-eyed girl named Behre Susie Hawkins. When he was nineteen and she was seventeen they ran off to Heflin, in Cleburne County Alabama where they got married in 1927. I've learned that Behre had dark hair and big round eyeglasses. She eventually became a principal in a Fulton County School.

Lynt joined the Army in wartime around 1941 and went to Camp Reynolds[82], a military training camp in Greenville, Pennsylvania. He met my mother in Pennsylvania in a local park one afternoon while he was on leave. They seemed to fall madly in love, with him sweeping her off her feet. Mom was traveling with her girlfriend down to Duke University where they were enrolled in a free summer school program for teachers. She had spent seven summers there.

Mom and Lynt were married on August 20, 1943, in a civil ceremony in Greenville. There were no witnesses listed and I haven't found any marriage licenses registered. I discovered that Behre and Lynt were divorced in January 1944. It appears that my father married Mom before he was officially divorced.

My Father in England

From the time they married until they divorced after I was born, my father was in and out of Mom's life, visiting her off and on and then disappearing for months at a time. When he went to war in Europe, he stayed away for years, not returning home until several years after the war ended. Mom received occasional letters postmarked from Prague, Paris, and even Egypt. She never knew what he did on these trips. His first letters assured Mom that he loved her, but he was too busy to return home. His commanding officer sent several letters in response to Mom's inquiries assuring her that he was a good soldier and would return home soon. She learned somehow that he had been selling stockings and cigarettes as a side business on the black market. Maybe he told her about this when he came home in 1947 for a short visit. Mom's friend Harriott told me that he returned home again when I was a small baby. He held me in his arms and told her he really didn't want children. He said he would come back when I grew up! She told him to forget that.

When I went south to meet his family in the autumn of 1993, I was in my mid-forties. After I had completed my telephone search for him and narrowed it down to the town of Alpharetta, Georgia, I still didn't know if he was alive. It happened that there was a Larry Crabb Inside Out Conference occurring in a suburb Northeast of Atlanta during a week when I was available, so I took that week to fly down to search for my father.

The Christian Counselor Larry Crabb had authored a book with the title *Inside Out*. The book and the conference theme were about learning how God meets all the needs that our family of origin can never meet. It is natural to try to get our needs met by our parents, but they will always fail us. I had been reading this book and now, the father who had truly failed to meet my need as a parent might be nearby. I thought it was the perfect opportunity to search for him. I also felt a great need to forgive him.

My plan was to attend the Conference mornings and evenings and to search from my Red Roof Inn hotel room during the day. I also hoped that if I needed to debrief with a counselor one might be available at the conference. This turned out to be achingly disappointing. I wonder if the counselors at this conference were unprepared to counsel someone like me, who was daily confronting such an immediate crisis in life. I scheduled times with them, but their counseling seemed shallow. Not one of them seemed to hear me. Looking back, I realize they were prepared to give me spiritual answers but appeared to be unprepared to give me the substantial emotional support I needed at that time.

SEARCHING FOR MY FATHER

My first step in the search when I arrived in Georgia was to call all the people in the phone book, named Wills. Previously, whenever I visited a city or town in the United States, I always looked up the name Wills in the phone book and speculated if this person might be my father or one of my family members. I've read that children of broken families tend to do this. Now, for the first time ever, I was able to call people named Wills in Alpharetta who might actually be my family members.

One woman I called sounded elderly. Sarah Wills, said in a deep southern accent, "I don't want anything to do with it," as she slammed the receiver down. I was intrigued! She lived in Alpharetta. I drove there each day walking the streets, popping into stores to ask about the Wills family. Most shopkeepers told me they didn't know anyone named Wills, though the town park was named Wills Park and there were streets named Wills.

Finally, I discovered the Alpharetta Historical Society and hit the jackpot! An elderly lady named Nellie Rodgers was the curator of Mansell House[83]

---

83 - A Queen Anne-Style Victorian home constructed in 1912. Mansell House is Located in Wills Park Recreation Center. *Mansell House website*

where the Milton County Historical society was located. She immediately took to my cause; possibly because I told her that we had been missionaries, and she was a devout believer. She told me she would do some digging and be in touch with me. In the meantime, I returned to Atlanta and the conference. This was in the days prior to the internet, so I had no way of knowing that the woman I had disturbed, Sarah Wills, had been the wife of Alpharetta's former mayor. Who knew what scandal she thought I was digging up?

However, I remembered a story my mom had told me about my father's brother, and I wondered if this was him. Once, in the early 1940's, Mom had traveled down to Alpharetta by train to look for her husband. Sadly, and ironically, the same search that I was on. I often thought of her on my journey and felt so sad for her. If I had to look for my husband as I was looking for my father, I would have been devastated. I wonder if she had some of the same feelings when looking for my father as I had when I went down to Georgia to find him?

Mom told me the story about sitting in Sarah's kitchen when my father Lynton and Sarah's husband came in carrying a rope with news that a white woman had been assaulted by a Black man and they were going out to look for him. I imagined Mom's stunned response as she sat there in that Alpharetta kitchen.

Several days later, Nellie Rodgers called to tell me that she had contacted the Wills family and they were willing to meet me at the Historical Society. I was elated! She arranged a meeting.

When I arrived, I could see they were skeptical. One of the family members, a woman, looked me up and down disapprovingly. Another man looked at my hands and concluded I could not be related to Lynt because my little fingers didn't bend outwards like his did. They seemed determined to refute my claim that Lynton was my father.

This didn't bother me too much but when they told me that he always claimed that he didn't have any children it offended me on behalf of my mother. His denial clearly implied that Mom had been unfaithful. I kept calm and humorously said, "I'm not here for his money." At which point they all chimed in, "Oh, he doesn't have any money!"

I don't like to give into intimidation or shame. I do try to gain a person's confidence by getting to know them, and above all, letting them know who I am. If they were determined to reject me, I wanted them to at least reject the real me. At one point in the conversation, one of the relatives mentioned getting a DNA sample and I jumped at the opportunity. I called a local hospital but I found out that it cost several hundred dollars. As I returned to the group, I probably looked as dejected as I felt, when I told them that I couldn't afford to take a DNA test.

I was ready to give up when an elderly relative, Nathan Bagwell, my father's nephew, told me "You know, your mother sent a photo of you to my mother (Effie, Lynton's sister), and he kept it on his dresser for years. I think he's been lying to us all this time."

A glimmer of hope appeared!

He asked me if he could call Lynton and ask if he'd like to meet me. My answer was of course, "YES!"

▲ ▲ ▲

We arranged to drive four hours south to the border of Georgia and Florida where my father lived with his third wife, Louise Snow. I called Jon to tell him that I would be driving to, "I didn't know where with a couple I didn't know, to meet my father." I had a momentary thought that they might dump me somewhere to get me out of their lives, so I wanted Jon to know about the trip. I let my instincts about these people being good and my confidence in God's protection overrule my lively imagination.

Nathan and his wife Lou invited me to stay with them in Winston, Georgia the night before the trip. I met their daughter, Vicki Huston, my cousin, who was a Baptist minister's wife. She was so welcoming and thrilled that I was the one Wills relative she knew who followed Jesus.

▲ ▲ ▲

We took off the next morning for Quitman, Georgia, and when we arrived at the small home, I walked in to find my father, an elderly gentleman with slicked back white hair, sitting at his kitchen table. My feeling at that exact moment was, "Gotcha." I felt as if I was playing a board game and my token had landed on my father. I don't remember hugging him. I may have shaken his hand.

His wife, Louise, invited me into their sunny living room. My father walked in and sat in his recliner. His back was bent over like Mom's as he walked, his legs must have been weak because his recliner was the first of its kind I had seen which raised up electronically to push him into a standing position.

Meeting My Father

He sat down and I sat on a little stool at his knee and began to cry. I cried for two hours. I felt broken. As my tears poured out, I realized that I must have spent a lifetime holding in my grief and emptiness at being abandoned, blocking the hole in my life where I was missing my father. To my surprise, the emotional barrier opened and years of sorrow poured out in tears.

How I longed for someone to touch me, to comfort me at that moment. But all I felt was distance, despite the smiles, caring from people in the room, maybe embarrassment from my father. How wonderful it would have been had he been able to take me in his arms and say the words I will never hear, "I'm sorry."

In between quiet sobs, I asked him questions. The first one I asked, "I understand you are telling people that I'm not your child?" I pursued my quest through tears with a breaking heart.

"Oh, your mother was never unfaithful to me," was his answer.

He didn't ask me any questions about myself or about my mom.

I looked across the room at a beaming Lou and Nathan. On our trip down to Quitman, we had bonded, and they were genuinely happy to have me in their family.

I looked around the room to see spiritual books and Bibles. I mentioned this and asked my father if he had an interest in spiritual things. He answered in his deep Georgian drawl, "I figure all the years that you spend hunt'in and fish'in the Lord doesn't hold against you."

I was speechless and left there feeling sorry I couldn't minister to him spiritually, but I wanted more than anything to forgive this man who had abandoned me and my mom so long ago.

I asked him what a highlight of his life had been, and he said, "Well, there was this Can-can dancer in Paris."

I thought of Mom and me scraping by while he traveled the world. It was hard. How nice it would have been to have someone touch me, to let me know I wasn't all alone in my emotion. Instead, he told me that he had thought about me but he "Never did anything about it." I wondered if he had been the man on the phone that time at EMC, but I didn't ask.

His plump, pretty wife, Louise, seemed slightly defensive, but pleasant. I did everything I could to put her at ease. My father's infidelity was not her fault. She showed me the needlepoint kits featuring colorful birds that Lynton had done. I would have loved for her to have offered me one of the small, framed pieces. I wish I had asked her for one. Even after he passed away, and I went to visit her I saw them again but I didn't feel I had the right to ask for one.

Louise took me outdoors to see the pet songbirds that my father doted on. I went back in and told him that I also like birds and we had kept caged tropical birds in Indonesia.

He still didn't ask me any questions, but I told him about his grandchildren. Nathan and Lou had warned me not to tell him about adopting a brown child, though. Apparently, he spent time hunting and fishing with men of color but having a grandson of color crossed the line.

Two hours after our visit, we took off with a wave and I never saw him again. He called me once around Valentine's Day of that year. I could hear Louise in the background urging him to stay on the phone while he clearly wanted to get off. I was also prolonging the phone call by bringing each of his grandchildren to the phone to hear their grandfather's voice.

The first and last time they ever would. I also sent him a York Mint Candy for Valentine's Day telling him I wanted him to know the type of candy that I liked.

He died one month later on March 2, 1994, at age eighty-six. I planned to go to his funeral, but it coincided with the worst snowstorm of the century in Tompkins County, NY. The airport closed; our driveway piled with three feet of snow. Cars were ordered to stay off the highways. For a reason, God alone knows, I wasn't allowed to go.

I visited Louise twice more when she took me to Lynton's grave and introduced me to her relatives, even Butch Snow, her son by another man.

She seemed proud of me. She was, however, a diehard southerner. I asked her about the Confederate flags flying in the area and she blurted out, "Sherman never should have burned Atlanta."

I visited Lou and Nathan's daughter, my cousin Vicki, several more times, once with Jon and once with our daughter Catherine on a visit to Flagler College in St. Augustine, Florida. During these visits, I was introduced to several other members of my /Lynton's family. They told me that he was the type of man who showed up at their doors unexpectedly, and then disappeared without notice throughout the years

They never knew where he was or where he went. This was his pattern throughout his adult life until he married Louise in his eighties. One relative suggested that after living together with her unmarried for thirty-plus years, he married Louise because she then had to take care of him in his old age.

Louise told me something that did hurt my feelings. She said, "Your father couldn't have been better to my son, Butch, if he had been his own child." I stood there aghast, my father's own rejected broken-hearted child.

Each time I visited Georgia, despite Louise's welcoming me, I felt like an intruder. I was reminded in a way of the feeling I had when I lived with the Robbies as a little child. No one ever implied it especially after my father agreed I was his child. But I felt the repercussions from all those years that he had refused to admit I was his.

To meet a man who was a serial adulterer, and for that man to be my father was a shock to me. I have wondered what flaw caused him to become the way he was. Did I inherit my unbalanced temper and combative nature from him?

SEARCHING FOR MY
TWODADS

DEPRESSION

When I returned from Georgia, I told Mom that I had met my father. She said she thought that I might have. She didn't ask me any questions about him, just as he had not asked any questions about her.

When I settled back home I began to sink into a deep depression. Winters in New York were dark and cold and possibly the fact that our children were beginning to leave home triggered it. I was anticipating an uncertain future.

A friend and fellow Navigator who is a therapist, Shelly Ishii, suggested that I find a psychiatrist to ask for help. She thought that I needed medication and counseling. Sure enough, I found a Catholic Psychiatrist in Syracuse who diagnosed me with Mild Anxiety Disorder, Mild OCD, and Dysthymia which is a mild, chronic depression. At last, I began to discover the answer to my persistent question, "What is wrong with me?" I had been asking this for much of my life.

I began taking medication which I have used now for thirty years. I thank God for meds, and counseling for success in the remainder of my years in Ithaca and beyond. With meds I am able to think clearly before overreacting and also to gain focus in my spiritual life.

I notice that I tend to want to take care of my feelings within myself, that is I don't know how to name them very well. I also find that I don't explain myself very well. Possibly that's why my mom didn't teach me household chores like baking bread. It was easier to do these things herself than to explain complicated steps.

When I came home after meeting my father, It was difficult for me to talk to explain to Jon the depths of my hurt.

SEARCHING FOR MY
TWODADS
PART TWO

SEARCHING FOR MY TWO DADS

THE WEST BANK AWAKENING

2010

During my years of attending Evangelical churches and Philadelphia College of the Bible (now Cairn University), Israel was always the undisputed noble hero in military contests in the Middle East.

It never occurred to me that there was a problem with that. There was no question in my mind that they always did right because God blessed them. They were His favored nation. How could they be at fault for any troubles?

My first inkling that there might be another side to this was early in 1979 when a young Muslim friend in Bandung asked us, "Why does the USA always favor Israel?"

The answer seemed obvious to me. Because they are God's chosen people.

However, the question lingered in my mind and, as we continued into service to Muslim people around the world it remained. When Jon and I returned to the USA in 1991 we attended numerous Common Ground Conferences which helped us learn better ways to communicate with Muslims about faith. At these conferences people who loved Muslims taught us about the Biblical history of God's love for Hagar and Ishmael.

417

All of these stories were clear in Scripture, but we had failed to learn lessons from them. We learned in the book of Revelation that nations from the Muslim world will be gathered around God's throne. How did we miss this?

I struggled. I prayed and asked God to direct my thoughts because I had been raised to believe that the Jews were God's chosen people and Israel was always in the right. Palestinians were the terrorists, right? I wanted to talk to Christians and Muslims from the West Bank to find out whether what I was learning about Israel mistreating the Palestinians was true.

I learned that I firmly held ideas based on western cultural viewpoints that were not based on Scripture. I needed a break to consider what God thought about the world in general and the Muslim world in particular. I look back in sorrow that I had a difficult time believing such a simple truth, that God so loved the entire world, including the Muslim world. I prayerfully took a break from reading the English translations of the Bible for a bit to untangle my mind from its cultural bias. When I began to reread the Scriptures, it was with a fresh understanding that God's love extended to all people in the world, including Muslims.

In 2010, I read in *Sojourners Magazine* about a conference, Christ at the Checkpoint[84] occurring in Bethlehem, Palestine. This was to be a gathering

---

84 - A Biennial conference hosted by Bethlehem Bible College. Its mission is to help Christians understand the theological, social and political realities through the Palestinian Christian perspective and to motivate participants to become advocates of peace in the context of the Holy Land. *christatthecheckpoint.bethbc.edu*

of Christians from around the world dedicated to learning about the Israeli/Palestinian conflict. It was hosted by Bethlehem Bible College, an Evangelical college in the West Bank.

I knew I had to attend this conference! It was eye opening for me as I listened to scholars from around the world with years of experience present facts about how Israel had illegally occupied the West Bank. We heard firsthand testimonies from godly Palestinian Christians whose families had been badly impacted for generations at the hands of the Israeli Defense Forces, check point guards and even Israeli settlers. I attended this conference twice.

This first time, I went to Palestine alone and walked among armed soldiers from the IDF and the PLO with no problem. I even purposely took a little side trip to purchase toothpaste in a store owned by Hamas[85] "to see," as my mom might say, "how bad they were." I was invited to join a small tour with a group of believers from several churches in the USA. We were able to see sights most westerners people never see. We visited Hebron and ghost towns made so by the 1948 Nakba[86].

We were also invited to a Jewish settlement where the mayor of the town was from New York City. It was a once in a lifetime opportunity. I also learned a regrettable lesson about abuse.

---

85 - Hamas is a Palestinian Sunni-Islamic fundamentalist militant, nationalist organization operating in opposition to Israel. It is the de facto governing body in the Gaza Strip since 2007. They are present in the West Bank. *Wikipedia.org*

86 - The Nakba refers to the violent expulsion of approximately three quarters of all Palestinians from their homes by Zionist militias and the new Israeli army during the state of Israel's establishment (1947-1948) *IMEU.ORG*

"Hurt people, hurt people." When people have been abused, they sometimes abuse others. This is not always the case, and never an excuse. I witnessed this and heard many accounts of Israeli Army training which taught cruelty in defense of Israel. The Jews had been hurt by the Nazis and felt they had to train their soldiers to hurt their so-called enemies or they might be hurt again.

▲   ▲   ▲

From the year 2000, I was the Host Family Coordinator for Cornell Humphrey Fellows. When I returned from Christ at the Checkpoint, we had an opportunity to become host family to *Moh Amsal* from the West Bank. We jumped at the chance to learn firsthand from his experience. We also wanted to share Christian hospitality with him and treat him justly. We were somewhat concerned that other Americans might have negative preconceived ideas about Palestinians.

We learned that Mohammed came from an aristocratic Palestinian family living in Tubas, in the Jordan Valley. Moh eventually began working with OXFAM and lived in Ramallah. He invited us to come to visit him and his family.

Jon and I decided to visit him when we attended the next Christ at the Checkpoint in 2012. This began many years and hopefully a lifelong friendship with Moh's family, the Amsal's. We visited Mohammed Amsal, and his family twice.

One of my personal highlights was a time when I was reading in the Bible in the book of the Prophet Ezekiel 47:21 on the veranda of the Amsal's home in Tubas, under the shadow of their neighborhood Mosque. Grandad *Amsal* asked me if the Qur'an was in the Bible. I said no but let me tell you what I'm reading. It happened to be about God telling the Israelites to treat the aliens in the land of Israel as if they were natural born.

Grandpa Amsal said, "I don't think the Jews have ever read that!"

The Amsals are a highly respected Palestinian family with a prestigious history. Their daughter is married into the family of one of the founders of the PLO. A truly delightful man.

Another highlight for me was when I shared with *Nur*, Mohammed Amsal's beautiful wife, the story of Hagar. Nur cried when she told me that a Jewish woman told her that Palestinian Muslims were intended to be servants. Her tears dried as I told her the Bible story about how God had "seen" Hagar. Genesis 16:13

Christ at the Checkpoint Conferences were instrumental in our better understanding of the Israeli/Palestinian conflict. Previously, as typical Evangelicals, we only heard the viewpoint of Israel. We had never met a Palestinian who was a Christian, nor did we know they existed.

Highlights of my visits to Palestine for me, were touring the areas where Jesus lived and preached: Capernaum, Peter's house, the Mount of Olives. Shepherds field where we had communion and sang, and the simple garden tomb located outside the city walls of Jerusalem. These will always be memories that are dear to my heart.

At one of our last international Christmas parties in our home in Freeville in 2010, we read the story of Jesus' birth in the Qur'an and the Bible with our Muslim guests. They were from Pakistan, Afghanistan, and other Middle Eastern and East Asian countries. It was a beautiful moment. When I consider that I used to assume that Muslims were only terrorists and enemies of God, it breaks my heart.

The Book of Revelation verse 7:9 says,

> *"After this I looked and there before me was a great multitude that no one could count, from every nation, tribe, people, and language, standing before the throne and in front of the lamb."*

I have no doubt that our friends from the Arab world who know Jesus will stand before the throne of God.

The natural result of all we were learning resulted in Jon and me offering a Sunday school course, Faith and Justice, at our Church, Bethel Grove in Ithaca. Many were interested and came to hear the speakers we enlisted. We covered issues that we had never heard discussed in our Evangelical church before. Issues of racial equity and social justice that we believed Jesus cared about. Many affirmed us for our courage. A few did not.

RACISM COMES HOME

In Indonesia, becak drivers and other street people often pointed at our son Adi and in jest, demanded an explanation for why he was different from the rest of our family. I joked with them and told them that when I was pregnant with the girls, I ate potatoes, but when I was pregnant with Adi, I ate rice.

They laughed it off and walked away.

When we moved to our small Central New York town permanently in 1991, racism was not on our minds at all. It never occurred to us that our beautiful brown skinned son might encounter it in his Christian school. To our sorrow, one of his Christian teachers had been teaching in his classes that the Old Testament curse of Noah's son Ham[87] was still upon people of color.

Boys in the school were telling other children not to play with Adi, because he was Black. One day he came home to me and asked me if he was Black. "Of course, not," I answered indignantly, later realizing how loaded that question was and how my answer betrayed my ignorance. For several

---

87 - In the Book of Genesis, the curse of Ham is described as a curse which was imposed upon Ham's son Canaan by the Patriarch Noah. Because he "saw the nakedness of his father." *En.m.wikipeia.org*

years, Adi suffered from insults coming from certain of his classmates. I regret that I wasn't aware of his suffering, and after I became aware, I didn't take action to confront the teacher or the parents. I was in inertia due to my depression, and I deeply regret it.

Our Kids Grown Up

He was an ace soccer player, and I suspect some of his teammates were jealous of him. They told him that he would never get a girlfriend because he was Black. Ironically, he always had a girlfriend. Even in elementary school, little girls were holding his hand. He was a natural comic and people were drawn to his gregarious personality. He had loyal friends, but he was unhappy much of the time during his high school years. He told me once he was only going to high school so he could get done with it once and for all.

In the years between 1974 and 2000, I had only worked in Christian ministry. Though I had traveled widely, my vocabulary and gifting experiences were limited largely to Christian activities.

In 2000, when I got the job of my dreams in Ithaca High School as a Family Liaison, I began to better understand what some of my strengths were and to use them fully. I began to practice using my voice and to realize it was useful for more than what might be labeled as spiritual things.

While working at Ithaca High School, I had an opportunity to learn about our country's historical treatment of Black people and I connected again with that spark that had touched me long ago at Urbana when Tom Skinner spoke about systemic racism in our country. I took courses at Cornell's African American Center and learned facts about racial inequality in our nation.

Possibly because of what I learned about my southern father, the desire to fight racial injustice took root in me and I longed to be part of a change. I began networking, talking, writing and growing. As Congressman John Lewis has said, "Make good trouble." Facebook became a platform for my activism.

I will move on to a conversation I had on Monday November 25, 2019, over Facebook when I posted that I had seen the film, Harriet with the grandkids.

My Facebook friend, LSK, who is the daughter of Tom Skinner, became my Facebook friend. She wrote the following:

> *"Mary, we may not be friends in the spend time with each other definition, but I want you to know how deeply I value your words of wisdom in my life FRIEND!!*
>
> *Thank you for encouraging open discussion that will enable the children in your influence to determine how the history will be written during their lifetime. Giving THANKS for you!!" LSK*

Here is my response:

Thank you, LSK. I feel the same way, and maybe someday we will meet on earth? As I have mentioned, your father's message was pivotal in my life's direction back in 1970, and to be in friendship with you is a special treasure.

Next writer was Teri whom I met at a Via Affirmativa (Christians in the Arts) Conference many years ago.

"Hi Mary! I almost saw this movie on my birthday. I had read reviews from some moviegoers that shared how they were disappointed with the inaccuracy and portrayal of some characters, so I opted for something lighter that time around. This article and your open discussion make me reconsider seeing it, though! I have to say that I have never heard frank open discussion with such honesty and awareness of various perspectives and critique on our US society as a whole today. I have ONE Caucasian friend that I can think of (born and raised in this country) who has openly shared on this subject without prompting and shown a genuine interest AND who allows/wants/seeks answers that aren't sugarcoated or truncated. Most that I'm around don't openly acknowledge (racism, its effects or blindness to it) & tell me that it's in the past and they don't see it anymore. So, thanks to you and Summer for this post and commentary.

Maybe it's the part of the country I am in? May I ask how did you get to this level of sensitivity and awareness? Is it because you are educators? How is it that your children WANT

426

*to learn more? How old are they? I apologize for
the twenty questions, LOL.*

Our journey continues, and I am so thankful that
Jon shares my heart to make right the inequities of
our nations' past.

SEARCHING FOR MY TWODADS

TRAGEDY

Little could we have known that our quiet little town and school of Dryden, NY would become a center of horrendous tragedies with our children's friends front and center.

Close to home was the shooting murder of Dryden's beloved football coach in 1994.

What had begun as a casual dating situation had ended in obsession and stalking of the coach's beautiful high school daughter, a friend of our girls.

Eventually, the family took out a restraining order on the young man.

Many of us in the area followed the tragic situation over the police dispatch that day shortly after Christmas when the obsessed ex-boyfriend was on the hunt for the coach's daughter, his ex-girlfriend. We feared he might come to her friends' homes in his search for her.

Tragically, he broke into their home shooting her father the high school coach who stood in front of the shot gun, defending his daughter.

Over the years there were more Dryden high school teenagers killed in tragic deaths. These were so traumatic to all our kids in Dryden High School. They will never forget.

On the evening of October 4, 1996, two cheerleaders, friends of our daughter, Catherine, failed to show up for a football game. Catherine called to ask me to pray. My first thought was that they probably decided to skip the game. But our daughter assured me they would never do that. For several days kids gathered in one another's homes for prayer and comfort . The school was on lockdown.

Days later, as I was working in the high school library, we could hear the kids cries rising from the other end of the school. At that moment we received a phone call telling us that the girls had been murdered with their remains found in several counties. Because my library colleagues knew the girls very well, none of them felt capable of announcing it to the students, but the cries in the hallway were nearing us by the second.

Knowing the kids would hear the cries, I stepped up to tell the kids who were in our charge. I told them as much as they needed to know, "The girls have been found, they are dead." The gruesome details were to be on every newscast and everyone's lips for weeks and months afterwards.

In a few days, their next-door neighbor was arrested with irrefutable evidence of the brutal crime. He hanged himself in his jail cell.

For about ten years afterwards whenever I called our daughter Catherine, her first question was, "Did someone die?"

COPING WITH TRAGEDY, OUR PETS

Everyone in our town had their own way of coping with the tragedies. High school students gathered in prayer meetings to talk and seek God. We encouraged our kids to talk and pray. Once again, I was face to face with the question of whether God was good. Could I trust Him for the lives of our children? Did I believe that "our days were numbered and in his book of life"? Psalm 90:12. I did.

After the murders I opted to get another dog, Madison, or Maddie, our part German Shepherd, who became my favorite dog of all time. Our home had many entrance doors and I felt better knowing that our dogs would sense an intruder entering before I did. We already had an older dog, Roxie, whom we had adopted from an ad in the newspaper. She was our first family dog in the USA.

Roxie was the dog who marked our Christmas holidays with crises. One Christmas she was hit by a car. We were walking to the neighbors for Christmas dinner when she followed us. The car hit her sending her fifteen feet in the air, we were sure she was dead. She was in shock for at least an hour, I sent Mom and the kids ahead while Jon and I called our friend, a vet. Jon sat and held her, his very precious girl, in his arms.

At last, she came around with no broken bones.

Another Christmas, Roxie got a small animal scull lodged in the roof of her mouth. She was choking, and gagging and could neither eat, nor close her mouth. We took her to the emergency vet, and the vet removed it.

I had been looking for the ideal dog, visiting the SPCA frequently. One day, I saw a little part German Shepherd puppy sitting all alone in her cage. Her paws were big. I knew she would grow into a beautiful, large dog.

The head of the SPCA said to her as he brought her out of the cage to me, "I told you this was your lucky day." I learned that she was the last of a litter and all her litter mates had already been adopted.

She became my dog soul mate, following me everywhere, a comfort when I needed her. I loved to walk her on the old railroad bed around Dryden Lake. She and our older dog Roxie were best mates. Both lived to around the age of thirteen, and gradually wore out. I never cried over a dog as I did over Maddie's death.

After Roxie died, we found a beautiful curly-haired apricot colored Cocka-poo male dog at the SPCA. His name was Biscuit, and he and Maddie made a fantastic pair. As they played in the yard, Maddie, who was so much larger than he, would throw him up in the air and he would be right back for more rough housing. He and Maddie loved their walks, which were always really runs. We invested in an electric underground fence for those two.

One time after we boarded Maddie for one week at our vet's, she became very lethargic and went downhill immediately afterwards. We don't know what happened, but she never fully recovered. We suspect that the cage in the kennel was too small, and she injured herself. When she returned home, she laid about on the floor never wanting to play. It was so sad to see her like that.

As was our custom, as soon as Maddie died, we looked for another dog. We found an advertisement in the local newspaper offering a six-month-old Miniature Schnauzer for sale. The ad said she was too active for her elderly owner. When we drove up to the house, the little pup was looking out the window from a bed and began barking. When we entered the house, after a moment or two of shyness, she began running from Jon and me jumping into our chairs. Biscuit was sitting with me and was quite startled to have this little shrimp jumping around, so he edged behind me for protection. This was our introduction to Jon's absolute favorite dog, Maximillia Lisbet, or Mila, a perfect silver Miniature Schnauzer. She had papers that proved her pedigree.

When Mila came to live with us, Jon felt our little Biscuit should now have a grown-up name, being a big brother, so, he gave him the manly name, Bismarck.

Mila's father was Maximillian; hence we named her Mila. She was intrepid, as Miniature Schnauzers are and seldom has stopped running in her excitement, even now at the age of fourteen. Early in her time with us, I noticed her dragging something huge across our back yard. It was a hawk, much larger than she. Our housemate at the time, Mifta Syed, went out to examine it and found that it had little teeth marks in its neck. Apparently,

Mila had killed it. I speculated that it had seen our little puppy in the yard, swooped down to grab her and been surprised by Mila's response. Had she turned around and bit it in the neck? Mifta, our student boarder from Kashmir, buried it in our woods because we learned that it was illegal to kill this type of hawk.

Mila and Bismarck traveled with us to Broadkill Beach in Delaware. It was such a pleasure to watch them running along the water's edge. One day, Mila, however, got stuck in the brambles and Jon had to find her and bring her home. Several times, Jon has had to rescue our dogs from shallow ponds, and wells. It endears them to us.

Both dogs were excellent travelers as they rode with us to Colorado Springs and back and lived there for six months. Bismarck always ran with his "joy toy" in and out of the house when we returned home from a shopping trip. Mila simply stands up to kiss Jon and talks to him. Both Mila and Bismarck moved with us to Virginia, but Bismarck stayed in our first yard as he passed away and is buried in Saddle Run.

Mila has never wanted to be cuddled or picked up, and immediately squeals and reaches around to bite the person who tries. I've wondered if this is her reflex from the trauma of being attacked by the hawk, or did her reflex simply save her from being carried off that day?

Mila is very much like a little child. One time, we were staying in a hotel with Mila and LiLing, our newest dog, a Shih-Tzu/Poodle mix. When we walked across the street to eat dinner, we locked our dogs safely in the hotel room. Later, we returned to our locked room to find Mila missing. In a panic, primarily because we missed our dog, but also because someone entered our room and may have taken her, we went out to the lobby asking what happened. Someone in the lobby said that there was a dog out in the parking lot. We went out to find our Mila, standing faithfully beside our van.

We had several cats, the most memorable being Abu, the gray and white kitty who could say, "I love you." Alternately, it could sound like the Muslim call to prayer[88]. He sometimes said it in the middle of the night, sitting outside a guest's door.

---

88 - Adhan is the first call summoning Muslims to enter the mosque for obligatory prayer (salah) five times a day. *Wikipedia.org*

SEARCHING FOR MY TWO DADS

WHEN THE WORLD CHANGED

SEPTEMBER 11, 2001

September 11, 2001, affected the United States and New York State in particular. It felt like it was in our front yard. It brought our ministry to the Muslim world into focus as never before. We volunteered to walk alongside our Muslim Cornell students when they told us about the mistreatment they had encountered. One of my Muslim friends had a taco thrown at her as she walked down the street.

We immediately became useful consultants because we had close friends who were Muslims and knew how to talk with non-Muslims about them. We also knew how to keep communications flowing with our Muslim friends, One of my high school students from Bosnia told me, "Now, Americans will understand how we feel."

The week of 9/11, I had been reading the Bible in the book of Habakkuk and Chapter 2: 6-12, reminded me of what I had been learning about our nation's past.

> *"Will not all of them taunt him with ridicule and scorn, saying, 'Woe to him who piles up stolen goods and makes himself wealthy by extortion! How long must this go on? 7, Will they not wake up and make you tremble? Then*

you will become their victim. 8, Because you have plundered many nations, the peoples who are left will plunder you. For you have shed man's blood; you have destroyed lands and cities and everyone in them. 9, Woe to him who builds his realm by unjust gain to set his nest on high to escape the clutches of ruin! 10, You have plotted the ruin of many peoples, shaming your own house and forfeiting your life. 11, The stones of the wall will cry out, and the beams of the woodwork will echo it. 12, Woe to him who builds a city with bloodshed and establishes a town by crime."

When we attended church the following Sunday, our Pastor, Chuck Tompkins, preached from the same Bible passage. I was astonished. I wondered how many people would take this scripture to heart and repent of our part in provoking the Muslim world to such hatred?

BREAKDOWN

2011

I began to feel worn out by the Refugee Resettlement work and I often asked Jon's help with the Faith and Justice Class at church. That, on top of the Navigator ministry became too much for him. At one point, I asked him to make a phone call to contact a speaker for the Faith and Justice class. It was too much. We argued and he told me that I was "giving him a nervous breakdown." I was on my way out the door to the grocery store and by the time I returned he told me that he needed a Sabbatical! I was so grateful for Jon's growing self-awareness! I relished what he probably considered a low point. He was still at the point that if I had suggested it, he probably would have rejected it.

We consulted with The Navigators and since we had not had a Sabbatical in thirty years, they were eager for us to get away.

Jon and I chose to rent a bungalow on Broadkill Beach near Lewes, Delaware and we spent the winter there. Jon sketched and painted and I created a blog on Faith and Justice which eventually reached around the world to over 10,000 subscribers.

Then we moved out to Colorado for the second half of our Sabbatical to take personal assessment tests and for counseling by The Navigators. The counseling was a revelation for Jon especially, who, with Navigator's help, began to understand that he had been operating outside his gifts for the entire time he had served with The Navigators, almost fifty years. His counselors urged him to return to his first love, the arts.

Many years ago, a Navigator leader had led him to believe that architecture and his creative gifts were less important than working full time in the ministry reaching men with the Gospel. He was convinced that this should be his priority, setting his education and career aside. The thinking had changed over the years, but Jon, whose value was loyalty and consistency, never wavered from his commitment to the traditional ministry of the Gospel.

I had been observing Jon's struggle with various aspects of ministry for years. He loved research, and teaching, had grown in people skills, but checking in with people wasn't a part of his make-up. He believed the best about people, and this included assuming everything was going well in their lives. It was against his nature to ask probing questions.

Professional counselors in the Navigators helped him to reevaluate his calling. His greatest strengths were creativity and mercy, service and teaching. His lowest value was leadership. I was so relieved when they helped him clarify this. It changed the dynamics of our lives overnight!

He no longer felt pressured to be the "Boss" in our relationship, which is the way it seemed he had been interpreting, "Leadership." He was freed to accept my initiative, and my ideas without feeling that I was trying to control him. He began to understand that for me, respect meant that I shared my ideas without fearing he would feel threatened.

The assessment tests also confirmed what I knew about myself, influencing others is important to me. I am strong in leadership, exhortation and discernment, but low in mercy. As Jon says, "You can imagine how these differences worked out in our marriage."

The counseling helped me to learn how to assert my strong ideas in ways that were less offensive to Jon. I learned to say, "I wonder," rather than to blurt out, "Do this." It was my greatest take away and I use that phrase all the time now.

We both had strengths in giving and generosity. Hospitality was also a strength for both of us which we had proven over our lifetime together.

SEARCHING FOR MY
TWODADS

VIRGINIA

2012 - 2023

We didn't see any way that Jon could stay in the Ithaca area, remain full-time Navigator staff and also pursue art. I resigned from my job at Ithaca High School and stepped away from all my duties at the Humphrey Program and Refugee Resettlement. This wasn't as difficult as it might have seemed for me because I had been eager to move to a warmer climate and I wanted Jon to be freed from constant stress.

We prayed and thought about where we wanted to move. We considered moving to one of our favorite states, Colorado, and began looking at homes in the mountains there. However, when our daughter, Juliana in Virginia, told us she was pregnant with her fourth child, we realized that it could be difficult for their growing family to travel to see us in Colorado. If we wanted to see our grandchildren very often, we needed to live closer to them. We especially felt that as grandparents, God wanted us to be an influence in their lives.

As I write, I realize one reason the move south has been difficult for me. We decided to move to Virginia to be closer to our daughter and the grandchildren. We hoped this would be our opportunity to have an influence in their lives. I had hoped that we might be helpful to their parents. I was giving up everything that gave meaning in my life besides my family to move to a place where I didn't know anyone except family.

In talking with our daughter, I realize that I was unrealistic about this. None of us could have known what our move would look like. We had all been functioning well independently and I expected we would suddenly be able to easily fit into our daughter's family's life. Long ago in Indonesia, I remember a Navigator speaker, Jean Boardman, spoke to our staff on the subject of family. She said, "Either you tear up your expectations for your family, or you will tear up your family."

It's been a struggle to keep this in mind.

Jon and I never completely recovered from our episodes of burnout[89] that we experienced throughout our years of living in Madiun and beyond. Sometimes it was difficult for us to spend time around four normal, noisy grandchildren, though we loved them so much.

After our move in September of 2012, we immediately found a small Episcopal church. Jon had been a lifelong Episcopalian and had prayed for years that he might be able to minister within the Episcopal church again. We began developing valuable friendships. Jon began leading a men's Bible study group at our church which encouraged

---

89 - Burnout is a form of exhaustion caused by constantly feeling swamped, overwhelmed, emotionally drained and unable to keep up with life's incessant demands. It's a result of excessive and prolonged emotional, physical and mental stress.
https://www.webmd.com/burnout

the men in the congregation to grow spiritually! They were reading the Bible and applying it to their daily lives! I also started a women's Bible study group. Bible study groups continue to this day personally and over ZOOM.

Jon had chosen our homes in Indonesia, so I chose our first house in Virginia, a cute little Federal style with a yard full of bountiful fruit trees and a lovely front porch. Our children had urged us to "downsize," which I felt we had done. I loved the name of our development: Saddle Run!

Jon began to thrive here in Virginia as never before. He returned to painting, joined a group of dedicated artists, Firnew Farms Artist's Circle, and began showing and selling his art! Jon also began meeting to mentor and share time with several men in the artist's group. God was using him here.

Our home soon became too small for all of Jon's paintings and because there was no room for a studio, we moved to a larger home, a log cabin.

Our Log Cabin

Our log cabin's location in a rural Black neighborhood made the move very appealing to us.

Intentionality seems to be the clue to developing interracial relationships. I have been doing this by opting to prioritize non-white businesses and choosing non-white physicians and specialists.

We became involved with our neighborhood church, Beulah Baptist and hosted meetings for racial understanding between our Episcopal church and theirs. I spoke at Beulah's missionary conference one year. As with all relationships, time was the key to building trust.

After building friendships in New York State for twenty years I missed my friends, but I was making new ones.

However, I missed a sense of personal calling. We became involved in local activities. Jon and I enrolled in a fitness program. I met women at water exercise and yoga classes for years before Covid. I was driving one hour south to Fredericksburg once a week to tutor Afghan women in ESOL. This meant a lot to me and I was excited when one of my Afghan friends passed her citizenship exam.

There was stress involved in living in rural Virginia, however. I didn't anticipate that we would have to deal with "critters." I learned that three-foot-long Black snakes were "friendly" because they ate mice and rats, though I didn't enjoy having one coiled up in our kitchen. Both of our dogs at the time sat on either side of the snake when Jon walked into the kitchen. He grabbed it as it slithered away, and before he could throw it out the door, it bit him. Fortunately, we learned that these snakes aren't poisonous.

I learned to deal with a constant barrage of Stink bugs after finding them in my bed, but it took me a long time to recover from finding a small striped, green lizard or "skink" on my pillow one night before I went to bed.

By far the most traumatic infestation we experienced was the rabid Bats! We learned that log cabins are the "Hilton hotels" for the bat populations. With their vaulted ceilings, and numerous small vents and gables, log cabins provide easy entry for bats. We discovered after we moved in that we had over sixty bats living within our house. This didn't count the ones living under our eaves.

This became an imminent danger when one dead bat fell beside me as I sat in a chair in our living room. We took it to the Health Department to be tested and it had Rabies. That signaled our Insurance Company to begin exclusion procedures which took one month during which time we couldn't enter our home. The company paid for our hotel room and meals. The Virginia Health Department gave us ten Rabies shots each (no longer in the stomach). Bats have a powerful homing instinct and after the exclusion process, poor mother bats return to our cabin every year trying to gain entry. Since they can't get inside, they give birth in mid-air dropping their poor babies on our back deck to die.

SEARCHING FOR MY TWO DADS

FULL CIRCLE WITH THE CIVIL WAR

Living in the south has rekindled our love of history. We've grown to understand why the Civil War still matters in the South. As Northerners we had not learned nearly enough about its current importance.

We're reading about the war and Culpeper's central place in it. My favorite book so far is written by Virginia Beard Morton, a local historian. Her novel, *Marching Through Culpeper*, is well researched and tells the stories of Northern and Southern soldiers, slaves and Culpeper families.

The book affected me so much that for a while when I went downtown, I imagined men and horses lying dead on the streets.

Civil War hero, Major John Pelham from Alabama is featured in Mrs. Morton's book. He was shot and killed on March 17th, 1863, at Kelly's Ford near our home, as he crossed the Rappahannock River. He had a sweetheart living in Culpeper whom he had visited the previous day.

Until this year, 2023, Culpeper honored his memory by our local Lake Pelham. It was recently renamed Lake Culpeper. In reading history, we've learned that Major Pelham was a much more honorable character than Lord Thomas Culpeper who was Colonial Governor of Virginia 1677-1683. Our town and now the lake are named for him.

Several miles from our house, a two-story frame structure located beside the railroad tracks is believed to have been a hospital used by Confederate soldiers following the Battle of Brandy Station, the largest cavalry battle of the Civil War on June 9, 1863.

Many Civil War soldiers died in the nearby Graffiti House, which is now an obscure tourist attraction. Soldiers from both North and South scribbled notes on its walls. It's heartbreaking to see their writings, for many, their dying words scribbled close to the floor as they lay there near death. Some of those soldiers may have been my father's relatives.

Southern soldiers gave their lives for a cause they believed in and fought for, which they claim was about preserving their land and income as well as slavery. Many lost their plantations because they could not operate without slaves.

There is currently a great deal of controversy over monuments dedicated to Southern soldiers. Robert E Lee's statue in Richmond was recently taken down and is in storage. Just last month, the remains of Culpeper's Civil War hero, A.P Hill were reinterred in our local cemetery with a thousand people in attendance, including Civil War reenactors whooping the rebel yell[90], the war cry of Confederate soldiers.

I try to be sensitive to the feelings of my Black friends and agree with them that these statues

---

90 - The rebel yell was a battle cry used by Confederate soldiers during the American Civil War to intimidate the enemy and boost their own morale. *Wikipedi.org*

should not be in prominent public places. I believe the valor of the men who fought for what they believed, was misguided. The "Stars and Bars" or Confederate flag has become an enduring symbol of racism. In my opinion, the Confederate statues and even the flag might more appropriately be on display in parks that tell the history of the Civil War.

There were men like William Frawley, who was a scout for J.E.B. Stewart. He died a few yards from where these flags fly in Culpeper's Lenn Park. General Custer fought here too, for the North. Devotion to the Civil War is not without controversy, however. Recently, both the American Flag and the Confederate Flag were torn down by protesters. I've learned that there are as many thoughts and feelings about slavery and the history of the south as there are individuals living here. Most important to me are the stories told by Black people who lived in segregation here in Virginia schools until 1965.

SEARCHING FOR MY TWODADS

MUSLIMS IN CULPEPER

To our delight, God brought us together with Muslim families in Culpeper. We were able to advocate and support them when they petitioned to build an Islamic Center in Culpeper in 2017. Many of the more conservative church congregations were praying against them in public meetings. Our understanding of Islam was in vast contrast to most of the Christians in this Southern town.

When we moved here to Culpeper/Rixeyville, we had not known there were any Muslims here. One day I was shopping in Kohls Department Store when a woman walked past fully covered in a black Abaya. I greeted her, "Assalamualaikum" which is translated, "Peace be with you." She, rather startled, answered me, "Walaikumassalam, are you a Muslim?" I answered her, "No, but I'm a Christian and I love Muslims." *Khalida* is a Palestinian, and a local public-school teacher. We've became friends.

Khalida once invited me to a party at her home. There were about twenty lovely Palestinian women sitting around the room. Our conversation turned to divorce, and I mentioned that I was from a divorced home and how my experience had driven me to find God as my perfect father. I hope this encouraged the women to see God as Father.

We have found that friendships with all people groups are dependent on seeing them as loved and valued by God. We all have our unique problems and our wonderful qualities. When we focus on the things we have in common, instead of the things that separate us, friendships are possible.

In 2022, we invited a large and diverse group of friends to Jon's eightieth birthday party. One Afghan friend, a leader from the local Mosque told us that he would slaughter a lamb and barbecue it for us.

Sure enough, he brought his homemade barbecue grill and the most delicious lamb kebabs to grill and serve our guests. His wife brought Afghan Pilaf and a delicious dessert. Afterwards, he put his hand over his heart and told me that Jon is like his brother.

I wonder if I will look back at this party as a highlight of our time living here in Virginia. It reminded me of our times in New York. Friends from every part of our lives came, from all our Bible Studies, Church, even a few from Cornell and Freeville days. Ten different nationalities sang Happy Birthday to Jon in their languages. Our entire family was able to be here, which I've yearned for much of our ministry life, that is, to have our adult children and their families meet people we minister to and vice versa.

The highlight of my career was working in Ithaca with internationals, but those years were a very difficult season for Jon. Now, Jon is reenergized at age eighty-one. I am very thankful for his health. At the same time, when I compare his activity with my immobility, I feel dismayed.

AGING

A series of physical setbacks related to aging began placing speed bumps[91] in my path a few years after we settled in Virginia. I had several minor car accidents and I began falling flat on my knees and sometimes on my face. Stiffness and discomfort from a total knee replacement in 2018 prevented me from taking long leisurely walks.

As I think about my issues, I'm reminded of the "falling hand syndrome" which was facetiously, and I think, unkindly referred to by a Christian radio preacher many years ago.

He was referring to women's health ailments as they (we) age. It's no wonder I have a dread of growing older because, indeed, I can point to various ailments beginning from my head down to my feet which cause difficulties with age.

Though I had years of full activity in Virginia, I found I was not handling this phase of aging at all well. I loved when our kids told us that we didn't seem "old." They had not mentioned this in quite a while. I looked in the mirror and saw my elderly mom but with worse skin. I wasn't prepared to be old and infirmed.

---

91 - Speed bumps are little bumps on the road meant to slow you down and take extra care. *informedinfrastructure.com*

I understand now that God wanted me to work out heart issues that I'd been avoiding. These issues were related to growing old and losing my independence. I realized that I was vain and took inordinate pride in holding on to my youth. Pain and grief over losing agility was difficult to cover up with a charming smile.

Added to that was a feeling of obscurity. Few people knew my name here in Culpeper, Virginia, and I hadn't felt physically able to begin doing meaningful activities. For the first time in many decades, I felt like I wasn't doing anything significant to influence my world. I see now how very much my identity depended on this. Jon urged me to find my passion here in Virginia. I spent time in prayer and landed on writing this book.

▲　▲　▲

So, now at the far end of my life, I find myself again in the shadow of the Blue Ridge Mountains of Virginia contemplating my future as I did back in 1968 at EMU. I've concluded this is my time to face the lessons I've avoided. To face my dread of growing old.

The most difficult next step for me in being faithful to my calling to grow old, is to see the goodness of God in old age.

Reading the book of Job has been helpful.

Like Job, God is my best friend and creator and I believe He has created me uniquely for His purposes. There is no comparing my slight suffering and dread of infirmity in old age, with the suffering of others. I know that my pain is mild in contrast to

456

many other issues that people suffer. We each have our own suffering to handle.

I've never been mad at God. I would not know how to do it. He is the only one who has been with me from the beginning. Is my pain God's fault? He could remove it. What is the benefit of pain?

Shall I curse God and die as Job's wife suggested? NO! Job didn't! Job never charged God with doing wrong and neither shall I.

My years of back pain have been stressful and limiting for me and Jon. But God knew and allowed this to be our life's course. What are God's purposes and what caused all of my ill health? There are recently some good studies that point to Complex Trauma in the womb and in childhood as the reason for ill health, auto immune disease, depression and other conditions. I wouldn't be surprised about this.

Job cursed the day he was born, but I've always considered my birth a miracle. I still do. Unlike Job, I don't rue my birth. But, when I am in pain, I sometimes have trouble remembering the good.

Job is reported as saying, "Though He slay me, yet will I hope in Him," Job 13: 15. I still hope in God.

I have a merry heart for the most part, and this has often been a comfort, but in pain it's hard to pull it up. Sometimes I can't smile. When my body is in anguish, old age feels disappointing.

Job was blameless and shunned evil. When I asked God to show me my offense, I was reminded that I struggle with envy at others who are enjoying good health and active lives in old age. Sometimes I resent people who take life for granted due to financial security and good health. I looked to God and He answered!

> *"Resentment kills a fool; envy*
> *slays the simple."*

Job 5:2

Covid suited me in my decline, it was the perfect storm, and possibly my inactivity caused some of my symptoms to exacerbate.

How do I return to civilization now after five years of living in relative isolation? I never dreamt that I would ever doubt God's interest in me. Maybe that is the last temptation we humans face? The apparent apathy of God towards us, as we wonder if he created this world and left it to its own devices.

I grieve, but not without hope.

AFTERWARDS

I am so grateful that Mom didn't put me up for adoption to another family. They might not have taught me about God. In spite of some of the difficulties, how pointless my life would have been had I not been assured that God was good.

God has been a sheltering presence in my life, the perfect Father.

Reading to Luki & Niko

I'm thankful that God kept Jon Perry single for me to marry. He is the best man I could ever have made up even in my dreams. We are only seven years apart in age, but in some things, such as sharing our emotions, we sometimes seem generations apart.

I am at peace that there are some things that we will never understand about each other, and even about ourselves. I can't imagine any other man who would have loved me so patiently as I grew to become the person I am now.

Jon has been a steady presence in our lives, always hopeful and optimistic, sometimes with little encouragement. I love all the ways he is faithful and loving to me, even in small things like immediately writing both of our names into a new book when he buys one.

I realize that my nature is to pursue an objective like a hunting dog on a fox hunt. I've learned how to tame my bark by God's grace, but the instinct is still there. This can drive my family crazy. I am, however, encouraged as I see my "heart of stone being transformed into flesh" (compassion.) Ezekiel 36:26

May it be so until the end.

The Whole Family, Summer of 2021

SCRIPTURAL REFERENCES

BIBLIOGRAPHY

Fletcher, Tim, Founder and President of RE/ACT (Recovery Education for Addictions and Complex Trauma) "Complex Trauma." *YouTube* https://youtu.be/6IxEwPMqB-c uploaded June 21, 2023.

Henry, Marguerite, *Misty of Chincoteague*, Simon & Schuster, 1947.

Moody, Jane, *Breastfeeding Your Baby*, Da Capo Lifelong Books, 1997.

Quoist, Michael, *Prayers*, Sheed &Ward; Originally, 1954; Revised ed. (September 1, 1985).

Chambers, Oswald, *The Love of God: An Intimate Look at the Father Heart of God*, Discovery House Publishers, 1988.

Cowper, William, *God Moves in a Mysterious Way*, Public Domain, use: Scripture Songs, 1773, England.

Beam, Joe, Founder and Chair of *Marriage Helper Workshops* Nashville, Tennessee.

Sinclair, Upton, *The Jungle*, Doubleday, Page & Co. 1906.

Richter, Conrad, *The Awakening Land*, Alfred A. Knopf, 1966.

Gilkey, Langdon, *Shantung Compound*, Harper One, 1975.

McKenzie, Robin, *Treat Your Own Back*, Spinal Publications New Zealand Ltd. 1980.

Peretti, Frank, *This Present Darkness*, Howard Books, 2012.

Bubeck, Mark, *The Adversary*, Moody Publishers, 1999.

Bessel Van Der Kolk, M.D., *The Body Keeps the Score*, Viking Penguin, 2014

Brown, Brene', *Atlas of the Heart*, Random House, 2021

ACKNOWLEDGEMENTS

I am very grateful to **Tim Gilman** for encouraging me to write and publish my work. Meeting you in Bethlehem, Palestine at Christ at the Checkpoint many years ago was one of those God encounters that occasionally happens to change our lives.

My husband **Jon** has also been my constant encourager and patient beyond what I could have dreamed.

Our Children and many of my friends have told me they would read my book. Most of all, I thank my **Mom**, who gave me her favorite book, *The Rolling Years*, by Agnes Sligh Turnbull, many years ago. It told the story about a mother and daughter and became my inspiration for writing this book.

Thank You one and All!

ABOUT THE AUTHOR

Mary Wills Perry has been avidly studying the Bible and sharing Jesus' Good News as a way of life for over fifty years. Mary worked as an LPN and graduated in Bible and Social Work from Cairn University (formerly Philadelphia College of Bible) in 1973. She married Jon Perry who was with The Navigators, an interdenominational Christian organization, in 1975.

They moved to Southeast Asia with The Navigators in 1978 and returned to the States in 1991 to lead The Navigators' International Student Fellowship at Cornell University. Mary coordinated the Host Family Program for Cornell Humphrey Fellows and held the position as Family Liaison at Ithaca High School for five years.

During this time, Jon and Mary helped to sponsor and resettle more than sixty Burmese refugees. They moved to Virginia in 2012 to be closer to two of their married children and five of their grandchildren. One of their daughters is married and living in Indonesia with two sons. The Perrys now share a log cabin next to a forest with their two dogs.